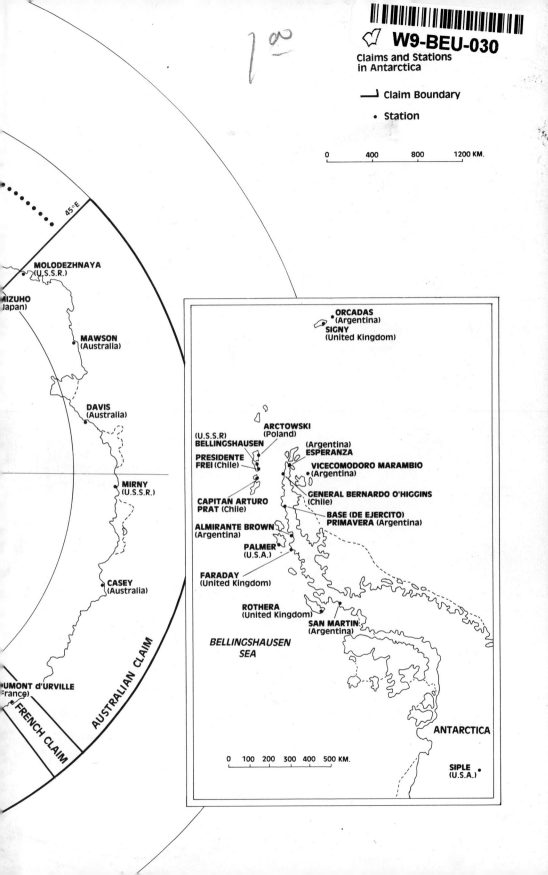

W9-BEU-030

**Claims and Stations
in Antarctica**

⌐ Claim Boundary

• Station

0   400   800   1200 KM.

45°E

MOLODEZHNAYA
(U.S.S.R.)

MIZUHO
(Japan)

MAWSON
(Australia)

DAVIS
(Australia)

MIRNY
(U.S.S.R.)

CASEY
(Australia)

DUMONT d'URVILLE
(France)

FRENCH CLAIM

AUSTRALIAN CLAIM

ORCADAS
(Argentina)
SIGNY
(United Kingdom)

ARCTOWSKI
(Poland)

(U.S.S.R)
BELLINGSHAUSEN

(Argentina)
ESPERANZA

PRESIDENTE
FREI (Chile)

VICECOMODORO MARAMBIO
(Argentina)

GENERAL BERNARDO O'HIGGINS
(Chile)

CAPITAN ARTURO
PRAT (Chile)

BASE (DE EJERCITO)
PRIMAVERA (Argentina)

ALMIRANTE BROWN
(Argentina)

PALMER
(U.S.A.)

FARADAY
(United Kingdom)

ROTHERA
(United Kingdom)

SAN MARTIN
(Argentina)

*BELLINGSHAUSEN
SEA*

ANTARCTICA

0 100 200 300 400 500 KM.

SIPLE
(U.S.A.)

BEYOND
THE
FROZEN SEA

BEYOND
THE
FROZEN SEA
VISIONS OF ANTARCTICA

Edwin Mickleburgh

THE BODLEY HEAD
LONDON

British Library Cataloguing
in Publication Data
Mickleburgh, Edwin
Beyond the frozen sea.
1. Antarctic regions
I. Title
998'.9   G860

ISBN 0-370-31027-6

© Edwin Mickleburgh 1987
Printed in Great Britain for
The Bodley Head Ltd
32 Bedford Square, London WCIB 3EL
by Butler & Tanner Ltd,
Frome and London
Set in Linotron 202 Times by
Rowland Phototypesetting Ltd
Bury St Edmunds, Suffolk
First published 1987

To the memory of my father who opened my eyes
to the profound beauty of the natural world,
and for the gift of wilderness
of which I went in search.

CONTENTS

PART IV THE FOURTH WAVE

ILLUSTRATIONS

MAPS AND GRAPHS

ACKNOWLEDGEMENTS

Many people have contributed to the evolution and eventual writing of this book. They are too numerous to name individually and I hope they will forgive me for not doing so here. Anonymous and unaware as they may be of the part they have played in the pages that follow, I am deeply conscious of their varied contributions – for lines of thought not previously followed, for words of encouragement and criticism, for generosity of spirit, for the sharing of knowledge and imagination. I have been fortunate indeed to know their company and to have received their friendship.

My expression of this encompassing appreciation would remain singularly incomplete, however, without particular mention of the following; the staff and personnel of the British Antarctic Survey; the captains, officers and crew of the Royal Research ships *Bransfield*, *John Biscoe* and *Shackleton*; Sir Vivian Fuchs and Dr Richard M. Laws, distinguished former Directors of BAS; David MacTaggart, Roger Wilson and Peter Wilkinson of Greenpeace International and lastly, Eric Salmon, whose friendship in moments of despair provided a lifeline back into the world of action. Without the support of these people I could not have gone to Antarctica and for this privilege I owe them a lasting debt of gratitude.

I also wish to thank the following for their help in the preparation of the manuscript; Mr R. K. Headland and Mr H. G. R. King (Scott Polar Research Institute); Dr David Drewry, Dr Charles Swithinbank, Mr Geoffrey Renner and Miss Anne Todd (British Antarctic Survey); Roger Wilson (Greenpeace International); Julie Williams, Lizzie Mickleburgh and Margaret Oswald; University Library Aberdeen; my publishers The Bodley Head, particularly Chris Holifield, Sara Kerruish and Ian Craig.

The author and publishers gratefully acknowledge the following for permission to use material from their archives and collections: Scott Polar Research Institute, Cambridge for the black and white photographs; National Portrait Gallery, London for the portrait of Samuel Taylor Coleridge by P. Vandyke; National Maritime Museum, Greenwich for the portrait of Captain James Cook by N. Dance; Ardea London Ltd.

INTRODUCTION

The first accounts to enlighten us about the Antarctic regions appeared in the eighteenth and nineteenth centuries. They were written by the great maritime explorers and by a small, determined band of merchant adventurers. The books are masterpieces in the voluminous detail of their enquiry into everything they saw and which so astonished them, and their narratives sing with high adventure, endeavour and the excitement of crossing successive horizons into an unknown world, of pushing back frontiers of geographical and scientific knowledge. This was the age of enlightenment, confident in itself and in the future, the confidence rising from every page with startling freshness. The darker aspect of their quest, the terrible slaughter of innocent wildlife that they discovered, is treated with remarkable frankness. The impending upheaval of the industrial revolution is somehow removed from sight. Barely concealed beneath the surface of scholarship, one senses a belief in the unchecked progress of mankind towards the Utopian dream.

With the position of islands and continent defined from seaward there came the explorers whose object was the land, whose prize the Pole itself. This was 'the heroic age' of polar exploration. It lasted barely twenty years, an immense push of science and geographical exploration during the first two decades of our own century. The intensity of feelings and the sense of purpose which these expeditions generated gave rise to a unique literature, the 'polar classics'. These books contain all the familiar excitement of crossing new frontiers, the astonishment at a world utterly unlike anything experienced before, and again the narratives are alive with the action of being first on the scene. But there is something more which is contained in the heightened awareness of men stretching themselves beyond the imaginable limits of physical and mental endurance. A new note begins to sound in the indefinable association of man with this overpowering environment that finds him also humbled before it. We begin to sense, as they speak to us of this most terrible and beautiful place, that they represent the end of something ancient, something that is passing away with them for ever. To them the planet is giving up the last of its great secrets. It is the end of exploration in the true sense, that of self-reliant expeditions, totally cut off from the world left behind, unaided by the psychological bolt-hole of rescue in the event of disaster or failure. Their endeavours, their unshakable idealism produce such extraordinary adventures that they move before us like twentieth-century versions of the Greek myths. There is a simplicity, a purity here that casts a spell on the divide between their world and ours leaving something that we cannot grasp because it exists no more. After them comes, by comparison, only a game of exploration in a known world where the wild places recede before the human horde and we are left most often to search for them in vain.

In recent years it has become fashionable to belittle the achievements of these men. Captain Scott in particular, as one of their more questionable leaders, has been set upon by certain critics with a vengeance that borders on abuse. He and they have suffered from the fate of being created 'heroes' for reasons which appear to us both bogus and distasteful, and in an age of imperialism which we now deplore. Unfortunately this has only served to obscure the true nature of their achievements which were not won without great hardship and remarkable personal courage and sacrifice. Fortunately, the legacy of these achievements and the qualities of character which went into their making remain in so much of what makes Antarctica unique in the human experience today.

Finally we come to the modern age in Antarctica where the virtues of international scientific co-operation are extolled together with the benefits accruing to mankind of nearly thirty years of research under a unique international treaty. The debt to the past of polar science is acknowledged and the future is viewed and seen to work if the present system is allowed to evolve undisturbed. But this assumes a reasonableness, an acquiescence on the international scene which does not exist in reality. It assumes that Antarctica's isolation from the rest of the world will continue indefinitely, a situation which contemporary developments call seriously into question. How long before we betray the peaceful dream and Antarctica becomes a scene of conflict? How long before we blast away the ice, mine the rocks, drill the ocean floor and turn this last great wilderness into a wasteland, a monument to a civilization whose ultimate bankruptcy is concealed from us only by the power and violence of its technology?

When I look back upon these three distinct periods of Antarctic history, it is the speed with which events have unfolded to their present point in time which strikes me most forcibly. To the protagonists in this polar drama who unveiled the continent, it must have seemed a painfully slow business. But placed against 4000 years of man's exploration of his planet, the exploration of Antarctica becomes only a brief moment. It is still within living memory when man first stepped ashore on the continent. To us, who have watched men walk upon the moon, this 'quantum leap' performed within a single lifetime is both astonishing and traumatic. It challenges the very fabric of our existence. Less than a hundred years ago Antarctica still awaited the sound of a human voice, the imprint of a human boot. Two hundred years ago and no human eye had looked upon it. Antarctica was the object only of speculation which had absorbed philosophers and geographers alike since Aristotle first postulated the existence of a southern continent.

And yet there is a theme, a thread linking past with present, uniting the first explorers sailing into the unknown south with the scientists now working in Antarctica. From the beginning men have revered this place, acknowledging the power of its elements to humble even the most determined amongst them. Few places remain today to exert this influence over man—the highest mountains, the most remote deserts, what is left of the untouched jungle, the least frequented stretches of the ocean, but each is diminished daily by the actions of man until its eventual disappearance for ever is assured. The scale of wilderness in Antarctica is of a different order. Here man is still face to face with the world as it has evolved without him. Even his recent intrusion has so far scarcely ruffled the surface. It is interesting that in Antarctica, despite his sophisticated technology, man has never quite lost the feeling that he is an intruder. As a result a unique relationship developed in which he was forced to adapt to an environment which yielded nothing, and which extracted a heavy price if taken for granted. Surviving in such extreme conditions harboured the beginnings of a new approach, changing the way man saw himself within the intricate structures that determine the natural environment and thus his own well-being. There is a glimpse of a possible re-orientation of values that has its genesis in Antarctica, a way in

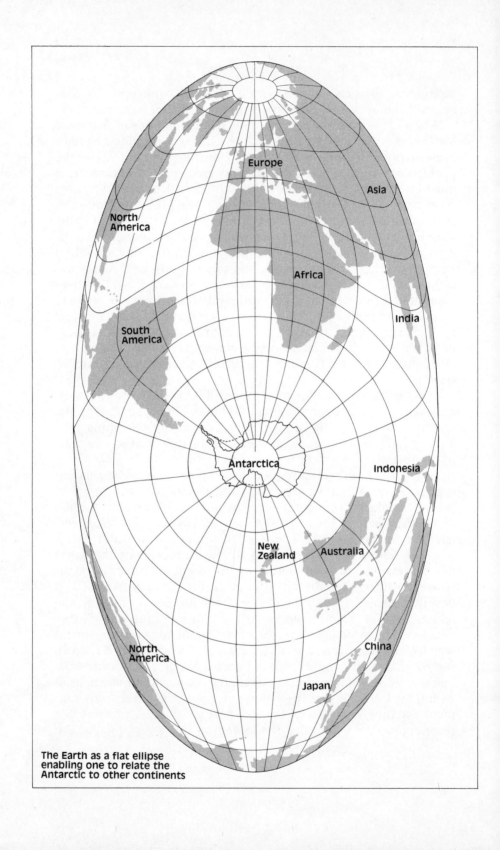

The Earth as a flat ellipse
enabling one to relate the
Antarctic to other continents

which man might come to regard the earth as a whole, politically, economically and environmentally.

The continent has become a symbol of our time. The test of man's willingness to pull back from the destruction of the Antarctic wilderness is the test also of his willingness to avert destruction globally. If he cannot succeed in Antarctica he has little chance of success elsewhere. Antarctica is the point at which the poetry of the earth transcends the science with which man attempts to explain all things. Since the industrial revolution we have lived increasingly with only one aspect of the truth, the great obsession with which we have all but blinded ourselves to the nature of existence. Science, and the technology which has arisen from it, is only a means towards an end, not an end in itself.

There are few who return from Antarctica unmoved by what they have seen, unchanged by what they have thought and felt and been. The greatest difficulty is in sharing this experience with those who have not seen this great wilderness and to explain why Antarctica has a fundamental importance which its isolation would appear to contradict. If this book provides a small stepping stone in that direction, it will have achieved more than I dare hope for.

PRELUDE

For six days we had been lying in our tent waiting for the blizzard to blow itself out. With each gust the wind punched the canvas at our ears like a mad drummer and the roar of the primus between us was a lost note in the storm. Conversation was shouting until our voices became hoarse and we lapsed into long silences. We read and ate and slept until we could sleep no more, then we would eat again and read what we had read before. Our watches became reminders of the kind of time that had ceased to matter. Food became the focus of our attention, the subject of lengthening preparation, the limitation of the sledging ration a challenge to our ingenuity and our stomachs.

And when we had exhausted our capacity for social relations in such close confinement we withdrew into our private worlds where daydreams could absorb the hours unnoticed. Human beings I think can exist happily in this state almost indefinitely providing the cares of the world cannot intrude. Lying back we stared into the apex of the tent with its cargo of windproofs, socks, mitts, mukluks, hanging there like some disordered chandelier, quivering with each unruly gust.

Outside in the storm, the dogs lay curled up beneath the snow, nine slumbering hummocks in a sea of drift beyond which rested the upturned sledge, like a ship dismasted and foundering on a reef. Twice a day at the height of the blizzard, one of us struggled outside to dig out the dogs and free their traces, although usually they would raise themselves and shake off the accumulating snow. We roped ourselves together remembering how death once came out of the whirling drift and took two men unroped. The man on the doglines froze to death unable to find his way back, his companion died in the mouth of the tent where he had remained shouting for his friend until the blizzard claimed him too. This is an unforgiving climate.

On the morning of the tenth day the dogs began to howl. They scented a change in the weather, heralded by a series of enormous gusts and equally disturbing lulls. At last the long mesmeric chorus of the storm was broken. Ten days had not really been so long. Twenty, thirty and even forty days of 'lie-up' have been experienced.

By the middle of the day the storm had died away completely, leaving only a void into which our conversation now fell in whispers. The human voice sounded strange and out of place when all around lay only total uncomprehending emptiness. We heard only the stillness of eternity echoing in the soundless landscape of an unbroken ice-age.

The vast stillness of the polar wilderness, the plateau of lifelessness where men come and go like passing shadows and some are gone for ever, entombed in the white shroud; this is a place of the most terrible beauty, of the white night and darkness at noon. This is Antarctica. And out of her unearthly silence there came back to us only the answer of gently rattling dog chains, like laughter in a hushed cathedral, defying our seriousness, and questioning our presence there at all. We hardly spoke, but when we did our voices sounded far away as if they did not belong to us any more. Slowly we put on our windproofs, our mitts and socks, laced up our mukluks and prepared to go outside.

Only now as memory, with all its imperfections, passes along the shores of the past do I begin to understand something of the meaning in that silence, the moment in the tent between the passing storm and the unseen landscape of the new day. There is a conspiracy of eye and mind and soul that breaks the divide between imagination and reality affording us a brief glimpse of true horizons somewhere on an unmapped journey. The clouds part for an instant and then roll back again as if the view had never been. All this was conveyed only as if it were a slight shiver catching me unawares—the flicker of a compass needle.

Daylight almost blinded me with its intensity as I pushed out of the tent. The sight which met my eyes and seemed to stare back at me made me feel somehow awkward and very small. We had travelled to this place in poor weather seeing little of our surroundings so that we were quite unprepared for them now that we stood face to face. A map may tell you all these things and the inner eye may respond to contours, peaks and valleys, but this is still not to see them.

At three thousand feet we were camped on an extensive ice piedmont, suspended, or so it seemed, between polished surfaces of glittering ice and the clear blue sky. Slightly to our east the piedmont rose a little higher to the foot of mountains that almost touched the sky. Southward, there extended towards a finely etched horizon of white summits a view surreal within a clarity of atmosphere that I had never seen before. Two hundred miles away and more, it was surely quite impossible to see such detail, to see at all? The map dispelled the doubts. And to the west lay the ocean, stretching from an ice-locked unapproachable coast to a berg-scattered place where it met the open sea. Finally we looked out over a great bay where the winter sea ice had been broken up by the storm. It formed a white mosaic on the dark sea, a constantly changing pattern where secret currents shipped in procession marbled icebergs to an unknown destination. And out of the north came clouds trailing their sleeping shadows towards the setting moon, its mirage on the curve of the earth.

Antarctica was spreading away from us in giant white waves, waves without beginning, without ending, spreading far away across all her countless horizons. This white continent surrounded by the ice-filled ocean daunted the imagination and called for a new form of language, a sharpening of perception. And so we might expect to discover, in those rare moments where poetry and science meet, the most profound symbolism. On the threshold of man's explorations in Antarctica such a moment occurs. As he breaks into this ice-locked place, poetry and science speak briefly with a single voice.

PART I
THE FIRST WAVE

A reproduction from the original series of engravings by the great French illustrator, Gustave Doré, for Coleridge's 'The Rime of the Ancient Mariner', depicting the ship entering the icy seas surrounding the South Pole accompanied by the Albatross.

1

COOK AND COLERIDGE
A Universal Theme

It is an Ancient Mariner,
And he stoppeth one of three.
'By thy long grey beard and glittering eye,
Now wherefore stopp'st thou me?'

So begins one of the greatest allegorical poems in the English language, Samuel Taylor Coleridge's *The Rime of the Ancient Mariner*. Coleridge began work on it in 1797, aware that he was writing at a time when the mystic importance of the poet in society was being steadily eroded by the ascendency of scientific attitudes. Romance was giving way to a new form of rationalism, intuitive wisdom was increasingly subjected to a new and powerful logic emanating from the dominance of mathematical thinking. A revolution was under way which would eventually touch upon every aspect of as person's life, reaching into the most inaccessible corners of the world. It was sparked by European man's emerging technical inventiveness and nothing would ever be the same again. In future the measure of a society's success would be based upon its technological achievement, a practical reflection of the belief in the supremacy of science. Hand in hand with this was the increasing desire for dominance over the natural world, to invent means powerful enough to remould the earth in man's image and to control ultimately the apparent waywardness of nature. And so the trickle of inventions that became the flood of the industrial revolution can be seen as the first fateful step in this direction.

Welcomed as the great liberator of mankind, the industrial revolution carried within it the seeds of a bondage far greater than man had ever known. He would become wedded to a creed which preached strength and freedom through the power of the machine, unleashing forces out of which would one day emerge the grim spectre of global destruction. There are few in any age who look beyond the immediate horizon of apparent benefit and fewer still who can foresee consequences other than the ones intended.

Writing on the eve of the industrial revolution, Coleridge sensed that all might not be well. He saw a rift opening up between man and nature and he dreaded the consequences. In this, of course, he was not alone amongst the poets of his age. Blake and Wordsworth were of similar mind. But it is Coleridge, with his holistic approach to the events of his time, who seems most easily to grasp the drift in philosophy, politics and science. Combining this with his knowledge of the great voyages of exploration and the age of discovery into which he had been born, the ferment of his imagination, the anguish of his thoughts begin to touch us; and looming out of the mists comes the archetypal figure of the Ancient Mariner, who,

> with his cruel bow he laid full low
> The harmless Albatross.

And suddenly there is this magnificent bird, wanderer of the southern ocean soaring as a messenger from an undefiled world, lying dead on a heaving deck. In every one of us stands the mariner at that moment of execution. The Albatross becomes the symbol of man's guilt and Coleridge uses the shooting of this bird as an example of all the offences against life whereby men divorce themselves from the natural world and the central harmony of creation.

Soaring to the sunlit crests and gliding down into the black troughs of an endless succession of waves, the Wandering Albatross is a constant companion to any ship on passage in these wide and stormy waters, its great wings enabling it to circle the world with an effortless grace unmatched by any other species. For weeks it will keep faithful watch, describing in the perfection of its flight the winds which once invisibly shaped the course of those who first came here under sail, men in small wooden ships pressing southward in search of that elusive landfall 'Terra Australis Incognita', the unknown continent, and perhaps secretly also seeking

> the spirit who bideth by himself
> in the land of mist and snow,

the spirit that

> loved the bird that loved the man
> Who shot him with his bow.

Until the eighteenth century man's impact upon the natural world was one of minimal interference. It was in many respects still the world into which man had emerged and evolved. The forces which had shaped it were those of climate in all its extremes, fire, the forces within the earth itself and the gradual movement of entire landmasses. For all of his existence man had walked precariously but successfully in the shadow of these great natural forces. He respected them and incorporated them most sensibly into the fabric of his life and the pattern of his development. He recognized his dependence upon the gifts which flowed from them in the form of food, water, timber and stone, the winds which blew, the air he breathed and above all the sunlight which quickened the pulse of life in himself and the amazing array of creatures with whom he shared the earth. And there was no harm in gently tapping these resources. This was the pre-industrial world and if we consider man's evolution as one hour within the year of earth's own evolution, then he has evolved in balance with nature for all but the last few seconds of his existence. That other world in which man lived is so recent in our past, yet already so remote as to be unimaginable to us who preside over the tattered remnants of this once prolific wilderness.

Into this arcadian world sailed the European explorers and, at this critical time in the second half of the eighteenth century, the greatest among them, Captain James Cook. It was Cook who established the process whereby Europe would come to dominate the rest of the world, politically, economically and culturally. Apart from their intrinsic geographical and scientific achievements Cook's voyages are a graphic record of the peacefully sleeping earth before its awakening to the chaos which merchant, missionary, politician and soldier were to bring from the complex societies of the old world. And it was the fate of Cook, once described as 'the most moderate, humane and gentle circumnavigator who

ever went upon discoveries', to be the man who would open the
way for this onslaught. He was one of the last to see the world in
a state of natural balance.

Explorer, scientist and leader, Cook was an extraordinarily
gifted man. His concern for those who sailed with him was virtually
unheard of at that time. His fellow officers, the scientists who
accompanied him on these long voyages, and not least his crew,
all were constantly the object of his attention. Such an attitude
no doubt helped towards the success of his ventures and did much
to enhance his outstanding contribution to our knowledge of the
world. It was a time when men were flogged, starved, hanged
and killed in action across the oceans of the world in numbers
unrecorded and anonymous. Disease and particularly scurvy
added to the death toll and misery. The conditions of life at
sea were so appalling that, for those who had most often been
press-ganged into service, death at an early age was the most
likely outcome. It is a measure of Cook's stature that, against this
terrible background, both officers and seamen volunteered to sail
with him again and again. The arduous length and the dangers
which naturally attended such voyages in the unknown were no
deterrent when men could be assured of a fair hearing and just
treatment in the small self-contained world of their ship.

So this was the man who only a year after returning from his
first voyage around the world, during which he had crossed the
central Pacific, charted the eastern coastline of New Zealand and
sailed on to discover the east coast of Australia, set out again on
an even more unpredictable and hazardous voyage.

Cook sailed in search of Antarctica in July 1772. Samuel Taylor
Coleridge, for whom this voyage was to assume such importance
in the years to come, was born just three months later in the
village of Ottery St Mary in the county of Devon, England.

Cook was to sail as far south as he could and, in the words of his
instructions from the Lords of the British Admiralty, 'prosecuting
your discoveries as near to the South Pole as possible'. The voyage
lasted three years. With the approach of each summer Cook
pushed south in search of 'Terra Incognita'. He failed to find the
continent, but in his pursuance of that objective he made a
remarkable circumnavigation of the southern ocean in high latitudes, thus reducing dramatically the extent of any landmass,
which many had believed would be discovered not far south of
Australia, South Africa or Tierra del Fuego.

On 17 January 1773, Cook's ship, the *Resolution*, crossed the
Antarctic Circle. His were the first men to do so and later that
day Cook wrote, 'an immense Feild composed of different kinds
of Ice such as High Hills or Islands, smaller pieces packed close
together and what Greenland Men properly call feild ice, a piece
of this kind of such extend that I could see no end to it, lay to the
south east of us.' The Antarctic Coastline, since named Enderby
Land, lay in the same latitude 300 miles to the east of his position.
It is an irony of this dramatic voyage that wherever Cook was able
to push south through the ice, there also the continent itself
receded away, denying them any sight of land, difficult enough in
any case in the confusion between pack-ice, icebergs, and the ice
cliffs which for the most part define the edge of the continent.

In the following December Cook again crossed the Antarctic
Circle and on 30 January 1774 he reached latitude 71° 10' south.
He was now on the opposite side of the continent, although he
did not of course know if the continent was there, in an area now
called the Amundsen Sea. Here the *Resolution* was halted by an
impenetrable field of pack-ice. It is incredible that Cook should
have reached so far south with the limited means at his disposal.
'I will not say it was impossible anywhere to get farther to the
south, but the attempting it would have been a dangerous and
rash enterprise, and what I believe no man in my situation would
have thought of. It was indeed my opinion, as well as the opinion
of most onboard, that this ice extended quite to the Pole or
perhaps joins some land to which it has been fixed from creation
. . . I, who had ambition not only to go farther than anyone had
done before, but as far as it was possible for man to go, was not
sorry at meeting this interruption.'

Cook's ship, the *Resolution*, was a mere 460 tons of timber in
imminent danger of being trapped by an incalculable weight of
ice. The *Resolution* had been parted from her sister ship, the
Adventure, in a storm off New Zealand during the previous
November. To be utterly alone in this small vessel in ice-choked
seas at the unknown ends of the earth must undoubtedly have
been a terrifying predicament. Having come full circle in his
search for the continent Cook turned north. It would be almost
half a century before anyone claimed sight of land or exceeded
his record latitude. With this voyage man's history and exploration
in Antarctica properly begins.

Cook shattered for ever the dreams men had entertained for

centuries of 'Terra Australis Incognita'. Even as he was doing so
men clung to the belief that Cook would find something as
promising as those strange and newly discovered lands in the
Americas. Dr Alexander Dalrymple, who has been described as
'an obdurate, cantankerous Scot, of some ability, much self-
conceit, and no sense of proportion', was one of those who
proclaimed most loudly in favour of the unknown continent.
Dalrymple declared that Cook would find an El Dorado inhabited
by 'hospitable, ingenious and civil peoples'. 'The scraps from this
table,' he extravagantly declared, 'would be sufficient to maintain
the power, domination and sovereignty of Britain.'

Tractless, ice-infested ocean; remote, desolate and glacier en-
cumbered islands were, in the event, all Cook had to offer on his
return to England, and it came as a shock to much established
thinking. However, he had seen enough to suspect that, somewhere beyond its battlements of ice, a continent did exist, but he
concluded, 'should anyone possess the resolution and fortitude to
elucidate this point by pushing yet further south than I have done,
I shall not envy him the fame of his discovery, but I make bold
to declare that the world will derive no benefit from it.'

Although Cook had turned north into the Pacific the voyage
lasted for another eighteen months and, true to type, he decided
to incorporate into his homeward course one final sweep through
the southern ocean from New Zealand past Cape Horn and on
into the South Atlantic. It was an afterthought, and from all
accounts not a particularly popular move amongst his loyal but
tired crew who were more than ready for home. And yet here, as
he entered the South Atlantic and in only 54° south, he made a
spectacular landfall and a discovery which altered the whole
outcome of the voyage and was to have profound consequences
for the future of Antarctica.

On 14 January 1775 Cook came within sight of the island of
South Georgia. The island had been discovered a hundred years
earlier by Antoine de la Roche, who had been blown off course
in a storm rounding the Horn, a common enough experience in
the days of sail. However the accounts of the island were vague
to the extent that Cook believed he might at last have discovered
the continent. In what must have been an atmosphere of intense
excitement and speculation, Cook spent over a week charting the
deeply fjorded and dangerous coastline on the north-east side of
the island. During the course of this week he went ashore and

1 Samuel Taylor Coleridge (1772-1834), poet and visionary – author of 'The Rime of the Ancient Mariner'. (From a portrait by P. Vandyke – courtesy National Portrait Gallery)

2 Captain James Cook (1728-1779), greatest of the maritime explorers, precursor of the Antarctic age. (Portrait by N. Dance, courtesy National Maritime Museum)

3 The Ice Islands – an engraving by William Hodges, the artist on Cook's myth-shattering voyage into the Southern Ocean 1772-75.

4 Admiral Baron Thadeus von Bellingshausen (1778-1852) of the Imperial Russian Navy. Credited with first sighting the Antarctic Continent in 1819.

5 Captain Sir James Clark Ross (1800-1862), who found the gateway to the Antarctic Continent.

6 Ross's ships *Erebus* and *Terror*, whose names he gave to twin-peaked Ross Island with its active volcano which he discovered in 1841.

7 Carsten E. Borchgrevink (1864-1934), a Norwegian emigrant to Australia who may have been the first man to step ashore on mainland Antarctica in 1895 and who led the first expedition to over-winter on the continent at the turn of the century.

8 Borchgrevink's base, 'Camp Ridley' at Robertson Bay, Cape Adare, Victoria Land.

9 & 10 (9 top) Bowers, Wilson and Cherry-Garrard before setting out on the winter journey to Cape Crozier on Scott's Last Expedition in 1911. (10 bottom) photographed on their return 5 weeks later after surviving 'The Worst Journey in the World'.

formally took possession of the land 'in his majesty's name under a discharge of small arms'. He describes the spot as being 'terminated by a huge Mass of Snow and ice of vast extent . . . the inner parts of the Country was not less savage and horrible: the Wild rocks raised their lofty summits till they were lost in the clouds and the Vallies laid buried in everlasting snow. Not a tree or a shrub was to be seen, no not even big enough to make a tooth-pick.'

A few days later on 20 January Cook's hopes were dashed as he rounded the southern extremity of the land. With appropriate finality he named the mountainous promontory 'Cape Disappointment', writing that it 'proved to a demonstration that this land which we had taken to be a part of the great continent was no more than an Island of 70 leagues in Circuit'. 'A country doomed by nature', he called it, 'never once to feel the warmth of the sun's rays, but to lie buried under everlasting snow and ice, whose horrible and savage aspect I have not words to describe'.

Such a judgement from a man of Cook's reputation might have consigned South Georgia back into the frigid oblivion from which it had emerged so briefly. That it did not was due to the timing of the voyage which required him to arrive in these waters in the height of the summer and therefore in the middle of the breeding season. In contrast to the lifeless land, the seas surrounding the island supported huge concentrations of wildlife, one of the most spectacular examples of an abundance common around the whole of the southern ocean, and Cook and the naturalists aboard the *Resolution* had marvelled at this fact throughout their voyage. By comparison with temperate and tropical latitudes, species diversification in the cold Antarctic waters is limited, but the numbers for any given species are frequently immense and never more amazing than when the animals and birds come ashore to breed during the short season available to them.

Great whales like the Blue, the Fin and the Humpback abounded, blowing impressively around the ship and gently nudging the wave-worn timbers of the vessel in their innocent curiosity. Their haunting sounds, songs from the deep ocean, assailed the crew below decks giving rise to the strange myths, monsters and superstitions of the sea. Inshore and along the beaches of South Georgia, the sight which greeted Cook was equally remarkable; Macaroni, Gentoo and King penguins played in the waves around their ship and the air was filled with the tumultuous sounds of the

fur seal colonies at their most active. Cook writes that 'the shores
swarmed with young cubs' and that it was impossible for a man
to get ashore amongst them. And high above them, whirling like
snowflakes in the shifting winds, huge colonies of seabirds thronged
to their nesting sites on the precipitous cliffs and along tussock-
covered slopes. Among them they could see once more that fabu-
lous and mysterious bird, their constant companion throughout
these years, the Wandering Albatross. Such a wealth of wildlife in
these inhospitable surroundings was a most unexpected and extraordinary sight. It was a fitting climax to a momentous voyage.

Cook reached England a few months later in July 1775. Before
long his discoveries came to the attention of the merchant adventurers, the sealers who were already working on the coast of
Patagonia and in the Falkland Islands. From the Bering Strait to
Cape Horn the sealers had wiped out virtually every colony of fur
seals they had come across. It was a greedy, selfish, ruthless
industry and the need to search out new hunting grounds drove
the sealers on into ever more distant waters. It was only a matter
of time before they arrived at South Georgia.

Cook did not live to see the carnage that followed upon his
discoveries in the Southern Ocean, as he did not live to witness
the disease and destruction of the Pacific Island communities or
that which eventually attended practically every part of the world
which he had discovered and brought to the notice of Europe.

And it is here that we may pull gently at that thread which links
the past and the present, drawing together a more tenuous pattern
of events. We may choose to call it coincidence, but it is perhaps
the guiding hand in a dimension fleetingly revealed and which we
do not understand at all.

Among the scientists who disembarked from the *Resolution* was
the ship's astronomer William Wales. Wales later took up a
teaching post as Master of Mathematics at Christ's Hospital in
London where, in the early 1780s, Coleridge arrived as a young
pupil. During the next few years it seems inconceivable that Wales
would not have related the details of his voyage to the wide-eyed
boys. Coleridge especially must have been spellbound by the
images which this man conjured before him. Unknowingly Wales
was sowing the seeds of the great allegory, and imparting the
description of the Albatross, here making its first appearance
over the turbulent horizons of the emerging poet's mind. Wales'
journal, overshadowed by those of his more illustrious com-

panions on the *Resolution* but still in existence, in the possession of the Mitchell Library in Sydney, contains a number of passages that bear more than passing resemblance to the words and images evoked by the Ancient Mariner. Later Coleridge became well acquainted with Cook's account of the voyage and, bearing in mind what we have read of Cook's reaction to the Antarctic, Coleridge's symbolism came to rest firmly on the ground of the explorer's experiences:

> And now there came both mist and snow,
> And it grew wondrous cold:
> And ice, mast-high came floating by,
> As green as emerald.
>
> And through the drifts the snowy clifts
> Did send a dismal sheen:
> Nor shapes of men nor beasts we ken—
> The ice was all between.

At the age of fifty-one Cook was killed at Hawaii on his third voyage into the Pacific. It was 1779 and Coleridge was just seven years old. Although neither ever met and the years which separate their lives only marginally overlap, they are held together in an indissoluble relationship which the passage of time has not diminished. Different in temperament and separated by profession, the poet and the scientist were nevertheless joined by a shared vision of the world. It is a vision obscured only when we isolate ourselves from the reality of the events which inspired it.

Despite his enormous success, perhaps even in some way because of it, Cook was well aware of the dangers facing the world he was opening up. He knew it could not withstand the unleashing of the powerful forces that were stirring in Europe and that would follow in his wake. Cook the determined explorer of the physical, external world had pushed back its frontiers to the very edge of the impenetrable pack-ice. It was from here that Coleridge, the inspired explorer of the human inscape, went on, warning through the hypnotic figure of the Ancient Mariner with his 'glittering eye' that man's ascendency over the natural world, unchecked by any sense of responsibility towards it, must end in disaster. In this he echoed Cook's fears and through the power of his imagination we continue to catch that echo.

As Coleridge worked on the poem and the old century gave way to the new, the sealers were already established on South Georgia. In 1800 there were seventeen ships around the island, mainly British and American. Between them in less than four months they slaughtered 122,000 animals. One vessel alone, the *Aspasia* under the command of Edmund Fanning, secured in its hold over 57,000 pelts. By the time *The Rime of the Ancient Mariner* was published it was all over. James Weddell, visiting the island in 1822, estimated that 'not less than 1 million 200 thousand seals' had been taken from South Georgia during the preceding years, concluding bluntly, 'these animals are now almost extinct.' South Georgia had formed the catalyst of a disaster which eventually engulfed the entire southern ocean. One by one the sealers discovered other remote islands and to each in turn befell the same fate. It was an immense and shocking slaughter in which the vision shared by two men had already begun to turn into a terrifying reality. But the killing grounds were far removed from places where simple necessity, fashion, vanity and outright greed dictated such things. It did not touch the conscience of those pleased to call themselves 'civilized' and nor would it for a very long time to come.

2

DISCOVERY AND DEATH
Sighting Land, Killing Seals

Cape Horn thrust a last defiant wedge of rock against the dark waters of the Drake Passage. I had watched it surfacing at dawn like a great whale, a shadowed blue back of land, and as mysteriously slipping away again in the gathering daylight, evaporating between sky and sea, leaving me to contemplate the sudden and peculiar emptiness of the surrounding ocean. This must have been the moment the early mariners felt fear creeping in their flesh, as they sailed on into the unknown, some convinced they must surely drift on towards the precipice of a flat earth where they would fall for ever into an endless void. Certainly there is, even today, a finality about entering this stretch of water, and when you are there it is easy to understand the terror it once evoked in men. Its raging hurricanes force the waves into mobile mountains with toppling crests two miles apart and troughs between them like the valley of the shadow of death. And yet these 600 miles from Cape Horn to the South Shetland Islands you can cross with scarcely a breath of wind to ripple the sea, with only the long rolling swell to unsteady the reflections of the huge changing skies.

In such weather we sunbathed on the ship's hatches or in sheltered corners amongst the deck cargo, lying beside drums of aviation fuel lashed to the foredeck in rows ten deep. Their black surfaces absorbed the sun's heat turning them into giant radiators; next to them we could sleep or read, chatter idly to each other or merely sit and watch the patterns of the sea and sky, lost in thoughts and subject to the kind of time that only exists on a ship in the wide open spaces of the ocean. Petrels and Albatross followed in our wake, gliding in dream-like flight between mast-top and tilting horizon, their wings following each nuance of the breeze. The nights were filled with stars and then the moon rising before us found the ship pitching gently along a silver causeway. On the third night the first ice appeared. These were small pieces at first, 'growlers', no larger than boulders in a river. They moved along the dip in the swell under the cover of each passing wave, stalking us like cats their prey.

We had by now crossed the Antarctic Convergence and the air was chilled in a raw grey mist. Snow flurries danced on the wave tops and the darkened seas broke half-frozen across our bows.

The Antarctic Convergence is the Southern Ocean's natural boundary. The upwelling warmer waters to the north finally meet the deep cold waters flowing outwards from the Antarctic Continent. The Convergence is found between latitude 49° and 61° south and it is distinguished by a marked drop in sea surface temperatures occurring within the distance of a few miles. Initially the temperature drops by several degrees to around plus 6°C, whereafter it continues to fall the further south you go. Eventually it falls below zero, but the sea being salt water will not begin to freeze until the temperature is close to minus 2°C. Such a startling change produces responses both above and below the water. The air becomes progressively colder and the wind has a keen edge. The Convergence is a major biogeographical division. There is a distinct change in the flora and fauna from the sub-Antarctic species to those truly Antarctic in character.

As the ship continues on its southward course, the officer of the watch plots its progress, updating its position every twenty minutes; the state of the weather and sea are recorded every three hours and the ship's performance noted with a regularity in keeping with the rhythm of the engines themselves. The strength and power of modern ships operating in Antarctic waters, together with the navigational aids available to the contemporary seafarer, bear little comparison with the vulnerability of the old sailing vessels. Radar, echo sounders and satellite communication reduce a whole sea of storms and ice to a constant sequence of detailed images whose all encompassing dimension and predictive ability now guide the mariner with margins of safety undreamt of by his predecessors. Ships are constructed of steel and mathematically designed to an ideal strength and proportion for maintaining course against wind and current while breaking and manoeuvring through pack-ice and for giving speed in open water. There are

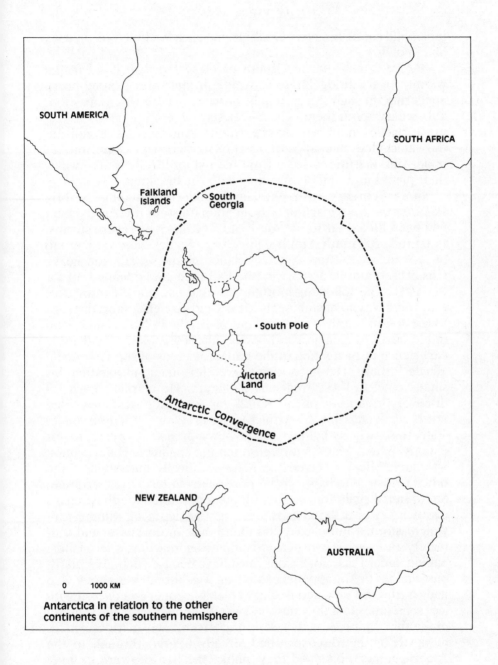

SOUTH AMERICA

SOUTH AFRICA

Falkland
Islands

South
Georgia

• South Pole

Victoria
Land

Antarctic Convergence

NEW ZEALAND

AUSTRALIA

0   1000 KM

Antarctica in relation to the other
continents of the southern hemisphere

tables and charts for every coastline and each landfall is recognized and known.

On the fourth morning south of Cape Horn, I stood in the warmth of the bridgehouse watching distant snow-capped peaks appearing through the grey light of dawn. There was a questionable reality about them, a pale hyalescence resembling the softest brush-strokes in a Chinese watercolour. And this was, I realized, the same view that appeared to those men who came this far under sail, the first to see it from their ships leaning to the wind, their planks and timbers straining with the breaking seas.

On 18 February 1819, William Smith, commanding the brig *Williams* carrying machinery from Valparaiso to the River Plate, had been forced far to the south of Cape Horn by severe storms. In latitude 62° south, Smith sighted what he believed was a group of mountainous, snow-covered islands. Snow squalls and heavy seas caused him to doubt what he had seen, so he hauled off for the night. The following morning dawned fine and clear and this time there was no mistaking the peaks and glaciers a short distance to the south. Smith was a pilot out of Blythe in Northumberland in the north of England and he had already gained considerable experience of navigating in the dangerous seas of the Greenland Whale Fishery. His skills now proved invaluable in handling his small vessel in these treacherous waters. He marked down his discovery in latitude 62° 40' south, 60° longitude west and sailed north, delivered his cargo in the River Plate and returned to Valparaiso where he broke the news of his discovery to his employer John Miers, an English mining engineer. His reception was cool. Miers received the news sceptically and none of the other British merchants in the port believed him at all. In June, Smith sailed again for the River Plate determined to follow up his discovery with a landing. But it was the depth of winter, with violent storms, bitter cold and long hours of darkness, and ultimately the pack-ice prevented him from reaching the islands. Sailing under these conditions must have been alarmingly hazardous, and no doubt appalling suffering was borne by his crew who had to trim the sails and maintain tackle frequently covered with ice, sometimes to a thickness and weight endangering the stability of the ship. Smith turned back for the River Plate. In Montevideo, news of Smith's discovery had already filtered through to the American merchants and they, unlike the British, were inclined to believe him. Smith records some lengthy interrogation by them, but he resisted their bribes to divulge the whereabouts of his landfall, prefering to heed the patriotic impulse—the honour of his country.

So for the third time that year Smith sailed south from Montevideo and on 15 October he finally reached the islands he had first seen eight months before. The ice was open, the weather fair, ideal conditions for a landing. On 18 October he sent a boat ashore with the first mate, who planted the Union Jack and claimed the land for the King, naming it 'New South Britain'. Smith later renamed the islands 'New South Shetland' describing them as 'barren and covered with snow, with seals in abundance'. Once again it was the mention of seals which caught the attention of others and thus condemned the islands to what was becoming an all too familiar fate.

Smith sailed for Valparaiso to take the news of his discoveries straight to John Miers. This time Miers listened. He was a cultured man with interests ranging beyond the immediate concerns of his business. Although quick to appreciate what Smith's discoveries would mean for the sealing industry he was more excited by the prospect of further exploration and of making his own contribution in the field of natural history and geography.

Miers set about equipping the *Williams* for an extended voyage of exploration and in doing so met Captain William Shirreff, at that time British Naval representative in Valparaiso. Shirreff and Miers were two of a kind and their meeting was to have far-reaching consequences. Shirreff, a man of considerable influence, soon persuaded Miers to take on Edward Bransfield, the master of his own ship the *Andromache,* as commander of the expedition with Smith as master and pilot of the vessel. Preparations were rapidly completed and, a few days before Christmas 1819, the two men sailed for 'New South Shetland' with orders to survey the coasts and 'to observe, collect and preserve every object of natural science' that they encountered.

From mid-January 1820, through February and well into March, Bransfield and Smith sailed the uncharted coastline making a detailed survey as they went. Towards the end of January, landing on the largest island of the group they named it 'King George IV Island'. For the next few days they sailed south-west past many rocks and islands with precipitous slopes and cliffs alternating with glacier outfalls. On the 30th the weather deteriorated and they were forced to sail a course almost due south. It was thick weather and they believed they were heading away from land. Around the middle of the afternoon the weather cleared and there to the south-west they were astonished to see an extensive coastline. Within an hour they were sailing among a long chain of islands. 'The whole of these', according to the midshipman's log, 'formed a prospect the most gloomy that can be imagined, and the only cheer the sight afforded was that this might be the long sought southern continent as land was undoubtedly seen in latitude 64°S and trending to the eastward. In this bay or gulph there was a multitude of whales, and a quantity of seaweed, apparently fresh from the rocks. A round island was called "Tower Island", latitude 63° 29', longitude 60° 34', and the land "Trinity Land" in compliment to the Trinity Board'.

Miers' enthusiasm and Shirreff's persuasiveness a few months earlier had led Bransfield and Smith into making a totally unexpected discovery. The land in 64° south was the northernmost projection of the spine-like peninsula that runs northwards for almost 1000 miles from the main body of the Antarctic Continent. This was indeed 'Terra Australis Incognita', the object of men's dreams for over 2000 years.

But were Smith and Bransfield really the first to sight the continent? Subsequent events throw doubt and not a little confusion on their claim. That Bransfield recorded so carefully what they had discovered and, more importantly, ventured to suggest that this was in fact the continent, brings to his claim an enterprising sharpness lacking in other more cautious contenders.

Unknown to Bransfield and Smith, a Russian explorer, Captain Baron Thaddeus von Bellingshausen of the Imperial Russian Navy, was, at that very moment, engaged in a circumnavigation of the continent. It was a journey in many ways as remarkable as that of James Cook, whom Bellingshausen greatly admired and upon whose work he had based his own voyage. On 28 January, only two days prior to Bransfield's discovery, Bellingshausen recorded in latitude 69° 21' south, nearly 2000 miles to the southeast of Bransfield's position, 'a solid stretch of ice running from east through south to west'. On account of poor weather Bellingshausen had soon to turn north for the safety of his ships *Mirnyi* and *Vostok*. But early in February he again made several sightings, clearly recording the ice cliffs so characteristic of Antarctica's continental coastline. On 19 February, continuing eastwards, he saw a range of ice-covered mountains, possibly miraged, along the southern horizon far beyond the uninterrupted profile of the ice cliffs. Yet curiously Bellingshausen seems quite unaware of what he was looking at. Nowhere does he, nor any of his officers or crew, make any reference to having sighted the continent. This is extraordinary when one considers the nationalistic mood of the times, when those engaged in voyaging around the world would lay claim to anything that looked remotely promising, sometimes to the point of imagining land where there was none. Bellingshausen was not the sort of man to make such claims lightly and his serious nature may explain what otherwise seems an incredible omission. The closeness in time of Bellingshausen's discovery to that of Bransfield's remains however and the story unfolds with yet a further coincidence.

One problem confronting explorers well into the beginning of the twentieth century was lack of communication. There was no wireless telegraphy until near the end of this period and then it was useless over the enormous distances involved in the Antarctic, and there was certainly no radio. Once embarked on a long voyage the explorers could neither contact each other nor their home country. The only way a message could be sent home was by ship—lengthy, unreliable and open to misinterpretation. This led to claims, counter-claims and disputes of all kinds. An explorer could not communicate his own discovery immediately, and neither could he know if someone else had been in the same place a few days, a few months or even a year or two previously. The remoteness of Antarctica made it ideal territory for such confusions.

While Bransfield and Smith were sailing off the coast of Trinity Land and Bellingshausen was sighting the ice cliffs of Antarctica, an American sealer, Nathanial Palmer, mate of the sloop *Hero*, was leaving his home port of Stonnington in New England. News of Smith's discoveries in the previous season and his reports of seals had spread rapidly through the seafaring communities of North America and Europe. Palmer, in company with a fleet of five vessels under the command of Benjamin Pendleton, set a course for New South Shetland. They arrived in early November and, on the 16th of that month, Palmer's log records 'at 4 a.m., made sail inshore and discovered a strait—trending SSW and NNE—it was literally filled with ice and the shore inaccessible— we thought it not prudent to venture into the ice.' The latitude of this strait he records as 63° 45' south.

The South Shetlands lie about sixty-five miles north of the

Antarctic Peninsula. If on a clear day you climb a few hundred feet on the islands, you can see to the south a wonderful range of mountains. This, apparently, is just what Palmer did and, reporting what he had seen to Pendleton, the Commander sent him off to make a more thorough search. This resulted in Palmer discovering 'an extensive mountain country'. Returning across the strait he ran into thick fog and, because of the danger of icebergs and submerged reefs, he hove-to.

Imagine Palmer's astonishment when, as the fog lifted, he found his small vessel lying between two much larger ships. They were the *Mirnyi* and the *Vostok* and Captain Bellingshausen was equally astonished to find himself in the company of the little sloop. The coincidence of this meeting is remarkable. Palmer told Bellingshausen that the islands they could see ahead were the New South Shetland group, recently discovered by Bransfield and Smith. Being already familiar with the islands prior to the fog, Bellingshausen was somewhat taken aback for he had assumed them to be his own discovery. All this is recorded second-hand as an account of a conversation between Palmer and Bellingshausen reported by Edmund Fanning, the same Fanning who had been so successful in the South Georgia seal slaughter twenty years earlier. Fanning, whose account we should regard with some scepticism, says that Bellingshausen further conceded to Palmer the discovery of the Antarctic mainland, although Palmer himself never claimed that this was the Continent.

What does become clear in all this is that neither Palmer nor Bellingshausen were aware of Bransfield's activities the previous season. Thus, three nations, Russia, Britain and America, all claimed to be the discoverers of Antarctica. It has remained a controversial issue amongst polar historians to this day. Of course it does not arouse the passions it once did and it is generally accepted that Bellingshausen was the first to sight the Continent of Antarctica, while the Peninsula is no longer referred to as either Trinity or Palmer Land but neutrally as the Antarctic Peninsula. Yet even in this attempt to tidy up the loose ends there remains an area of doubt.

When Smith returned with Bransfield to New South Shetland in the New Year of 1820, the sealers had already arrived. It seems reasonable to suppose that any one of the hundreds of sealers who visited the islands that first season would have looked to the south in much the same manner as Palmer, and seeing on the horizon the mountains of the mainland turned away again to the slaughter in hand, giving his glance not a second thought. In recent years, as the logs and journals of the many vessels which sailed to the Antarctic sealing grounds have come to light, the list of contenders with a claim to first sighting Antarctica grows. The true identity and nationality of the first man to do so will almost certainly remain a mystery, for whoever he was took with him his casual observation anonymously to his grave. The idea is to me an attractive one, befitting contemporary thinking which contends that Antarctica is no nation's single possession but the common heritage of everyman.

New South Shetland proved to be the last refuge of the fur seal and along the island's shores the bloody trail reached its climax. Smith, who so resolutely opens this new chapter in Antarctic exploration, now closes it with equal but inglorious determination. By the beginning of April 1820 he is reported to have taken some 60,000 skins, thus contributing largely to the total of 80,000 seals slaughtered in that season. Within three years the seal population of the islands had been effectively wiped out. During the same period further island discoveries were being made, notably the South Orkneys in 1821 by Captain George Powell, accompanied again by Palmer, but here they found only a small population of seals. Between the sealers, rivalry became intense and voyages were carried out under the utmost secrecy. Log books and records were often burnt to prevent them from falling into the hands of an opponent; sometimes no records were kept at all and ships sailed 'blind'. What had happened at South Georgia had been repeated but this time there was nowhere left for the sealers to go.

The idea of a finite world with limited resources was not yet part of the European way of thinking. How could it be when that same world they were discovering seemed so huge and limitless in what it had to offer those with the enterprise and daring to take it? Nevertheless, then as now, there were always one or two individuals with a deeper awareness than their fellows, whose observations led them to conclusions out of tune with the thinking of the time. Captain James Weddell was such a man. He was the captain of a sealer but possessed of an uncommon interest in natural history coupled with an enquiring scientific frame of mind. Weddell came from a poor family and was almost entirely self-educated, and may well have been inspired by Captain Cook who rose from similar humble beginnings. He was employed by the firm of Samuel Enderby and Sons, whose London based sealing company contributed so much to early Antarctic discoveries. Charles Enderby, who initially employed Weddell, was a founder member of the Royal Geographical Society, and ploughed back a large proportion of the sealing profits to equip his vessels for voyages of exploration which were incorporated into the company's sealing activities. The Antarctic coasts of Enderby Land, Kemp Land, Graham Land and the Balleny Islands were all to be discovered as a result of the Enderbys' larger scientific interests. This policy encouraged Weddell to make a remarkable voyage into the sea which now bears his name, when he set a new record in 74° 15' south, more than three degrees further south than Cook's attainment. In *A voyage towards the South Pole* Weddell later recorded his visit to the South Shetlands at the end of 1823.

'The quantity of seals taken off these islands, by vessels from different parts, during the years 1821 and 1822, may be concluded at 320,000, and the quantity of sea-elephant oil at 940 tons. This valuable animal, the fur seal, might, by law similar to that which restrains fishermen in the size of the mesh of their net, have been spared to render annually 100,000 furs for many years to come. This would have followed from not killing the mothers till the young were able to take to the water: and even then, only those which appeared to be old, together with a proportion of the males, thereby diminishing their total numbers, but in slow progression. This system is practised at the River Plate. The island of Lobos, in the mouth of that river, contains a quantity of seals, and is farmed by the Governor of Monte Video, under certain restrictions, that the hunters shall not take them, but at stated periods, in order to prevent the animals from being exterminated. The system of extermination was practised at Shetland; for whenever a seal reached the beach, of whatever denomination, he was immediately killed, and his skin taken; and by this means, at the end of the second year, the animals became nearly extinct; the young having lost their mothers when only three or four days old, of course all died which, at the lowest calculation, exceeded 100,000.'

Weddell's statement, horrifying though it is in its implication of thoughtless carnage, foreshadows, albeit in simplistic form, some of the ethics of modern conservation, although another century would pass before such things were seriously considered.

Just ten years after William Smith had sighted New South Shetland, W. H. B. Webster, surgeon on board HMS *Chanticleer*, visited the islands in 1829. 'The harvest of the seas has been so effectually reaped,' he wrote, 'that not a single fur seal was seen by us during our visit to the South Shetland group; and although it is but a few years back since countless multitudes covered the shores, the ruthless spirit of barbarism slaughtered young and old alike, so as to destroy the race.' It was clear that not everyone at that time viewed with equanimity the results of the sealing industry.

The slaughter of the fur seals was so great that it has tended to overshadow the fate which befell, as a result, many of the other principal species inhabiting the remote sub-Antarctic islands.

As the fur seals declined, man turned upon the wallowing herds of elephant seals, killing them in huge numbers, so that by the end of the nineteenth century these creatures likewise had been reduced to a pitiful remnant of their former population. The elephant seals were killed for their oil. This had to be extracted from the blubber by rendering it down in huge iron 'trypots' set over fires which were kept burning day and night. For fuel the sealers used penguins; the oil and feathers from the unfortunate birds produced a highly combustible material. For this reason whole rookeries were wiped out within a few seasons. On South Georgia, King penguins, one of the largest and most beautiful of the penguin species, were also decimated for the oil which they could provide—about one pint per bird. In common with all Antarctic creatures they had little or no fear of man and it was therefore a simple business for the sealers to drive them into pens where they were clubbed and flung into the bubbling pots. It is recorded that some birds, in the interests of faster production, were driven down crudely constructed gangways directly into the pots where they boiled alive. It is difficult to conceive of a more callous way of treating one's prey, even among such hardened men as these sealers undoubtedly were. Whether it was fur seals, elephant seals or penguins, the sealers killed them all with the same indiscriminate abandon. The result, as Weddell and Webster graphically recounted, was the death from exposure and starvation of all the young animals that were not themselves killed in the general carnage.

As if all this was not enough, the sealers left one final legacy of their trade which is with us to this day—the introduction of rats onto a number of the sub-Antarctic islands. The sealing vessels were infested with them and, once ashore, they multiplied rapidly. As a consequence, on islands like South Georgia, the damage to bird colonies has been permanent. Fortunately the rats did not reach the smaller off-lying islands where some of the largest colonies are situated. The sealers also collected birds' eggs to supplement their miserable and inadequate rations. Albatross eggs were a favourite and those of the Wandering Albatross were also used for decorative engravings, now much prized collectors' items.

The age of the sealers leaves only an image of nightmare clarity where dark smoke drifts along the tragic shores, smudging the leaden skies where the air is fouled with the stench of burning flesh. The tides are thick with blood and the beaches littered with dismembered creatures, the echo of doom-laden surf broken only by the bleating of so many lost and dying pups.

For more than a century the fur seal was thought to be extinct. Then in 1936 a small group of scientists from the *Discovery II* found a remnant colony in a secluded bay on Bird Island off the north coast of South Georgia. They counted thirty-six animals including several pups. It seemed quite remarkable to these men who watched the seals playing in the rock pools, the pups bleating constantly under their mothers' watchful eyes. It was the survival of a species against overwhelming odds. These few animals formed the nucleus of what was to become a repopulation of South Georgia.

With enlightened conservation measures currently upheld in Antarctica under the terms of the treaty and its conventions, and effective protection provided on those sub-Antarctic islands like South Georgia that lie outside the immediate treaty area, there are some grounds for hoping such destruction may never happen again. The hope we cherish for the survival of the natural world, symbolized here by this small miracle of the returning seals, has its beginning in these waters, on the desolate islands and upon the Continent itself. The paradox is clear and we should not forget those species that have perished due to human thoughtlessness.

There are now around three-quarters of a million fur seals breeding on South Georgia. At the height of summer the beaches are again filled with the shapes and sounds of this beautiful, ebullient creature. To watch them, to listen and to know their

11 Captain Robert Falcon Scott (1868-1912), whose name has become synonymous with Antarctica and the triumphs and tragedies of the 'heroic age'.

12 Scott's ship the *Terra Nova* at Cape Evans, Ross Island, Jan 1911.

13 Scott's Last Expedition celebrating Mid-winter's Day at Cape Evans, 22 June 1911.

14 Amundsen with his three companions at the South Pole, 16 Dec 1911.

15 Scott with his party at the Pole a month later, 17 Jan 1912.

16 Roald Amundsen (1872-1928), possibly the greatest polar explorer of all time – the complete professional who left nothing to chance.

17 Ernest Henry Shackleton (1874-1922), a born leader and natural survivor of whom Amundsen said 'his name will be written in letters of fire'.

18 Shackleton's ill-fated ship the *Endurance* beset in the pack-ice of the Weddell Sea in 1915.

19 Launching the *James Caird* from Elephant Island at the start of Shackleton's
incredible 800 mile boat journey to South Georgia.

20 The end of the 'heroic age' – Shackleton's men gathered around his grave at
Grytviken, South Georgia, 1922.

past is also to sense the profound disunity that exists between us.
Again the Ancient Mariner whispers in the ear:

> Like one that on a lonesome road
> Doth walk in fear and dread,
> And having once turned round walks on,
> And turns no more his head;
> Because he knows, a frightful fiend
> Doth close behind him tread.

3

A TIMELESS JOURNEY
Ice and the Continent

What was the nature of the Continent the explorers were about to enter and what forces had contributed to the shaping of Antarctica and created its unique environment? As the dream of El Dorado receded these questions began to assume importance and we can detect the hint of a change in man's attitude towards Antarctica. Knowledge for its own sake begins to be sufficient justification as the scientific institutions show a willingness in backing several Antarctic expeditions. Of these nineteenth-century expeditions the British Royal Navy Expedition 1839–43 under the command of Sir James Clark Ross was by far the most successful. It revealed dramatically what awaited man in this last great continent.

On 28 January 1841, Ross describes man's first view of Antarctica's great ice barrier, named by Ross the Victoria Ice Barrier, but known today as the Ross Ice Shelf.

'As we approached the land under all studding-sails, we perceived a low white line extending from its eastern extreme point as far as the eye could discern to the eastward. It presented an extraordinary appearance, gradually increasing in height, as we got nearer to it, and proving at length to be a perpendicular cliff of ice, between one hundred and fifty and two hundred feet above the level of the sea, perfectly flat and level at the top, and without any fissures or promontories on its even seaward face. What was beyond it we could not imagine; for being much higher than our masthead, we could not see anything except the summit of a lofty range of mountains extending to the southward as far as the seventy-ninth degree of latitude.'

Ross was no stranger to polar waters having already spent seventeen years in the Arctic, but clearly nothing in his previous experience had prepared him for the sight which now confronted him. He and his crew looked in awe at one of the wonders of the natural world. To this day people are still spellbound by their first sight of this imposing ice cliff.

'It was however an obstruction of such a character,' Ross continued, 'as to leave no doubt upon my mind as to our future proceedings, for we might with equal chance of success try to sail through the Cliffs of Dover, as penetrate such a mass.'

Ross's remarkable pioneering voyage through the sea which today bears his name was the key that unlocked the gateway to Antarctica. And what a spectacular gateway it proved to be as he sailed southwards along the Victoria Land coastline, with its glacier-filled fjords, headlands of wind-scoured rocks and cliffs rising vertically out of the sea to almost 5000 feet. The entire coastline was backed by a lofty mountain range, whose peaks Ross named after Lords of the Admiralty, his associates, and those aboard the expedition's ships *Erebus* and *Terror*. These two names he gave to the mighty volcanic summits, one active, the other dormant, on Ross Island that lay at the western end of the ice barrier. From this point it seemed the only way forward would be overland, or more correctly, over the ice. However Ross had found the weak spot in Antarctica's defences, for the western Ross Sea, unlike the Weddell Sea and almost any other approach to the Continent, clears substantially of ice during most summers and the remaining pack-ice tends to be lighter and less obstructive than elsewhere around the Continent. Sixty years later, the first land-based explorers benefited directly from Ross's experience.

Sailing to the east Ross coasted along the edge of the ice shelf for over 200 miles. The *Erebus* and the *Terror* were designed specifically for polar work—double-decked, double-hulled and strengthened throughout with massive timbers. But despite all these precautions they were still vulnerable. On several occasions they came near to disaster when drifting belts of pack-ice bore down on them almost driving the ships against the ice cliffs. By 15 February they had reached their furthest point along the edge of the ice cliff. Here they were forced to turn back by the worsening conditions due to the rapidly advancing winter. Ross could only guess at the extent of the ice cliff, its white face receding away into the distance, a thin chalked line fading into the indigo silence of the gathering winter darkness.

The ice cliff actually continues for almost another 300 miles. From Ross Island, dominated by Mount Erebus with its smoking, 13,000 foot volcanic cone, to King Edward VII Land almost 500 miles to the east, the ice cliff runs without an interruption of land at any point. For the greater part of its length, rising vertically from the sea, it stands over 150 feet above it, below the surface extending to an average depth of 850 feet. It looks as solid as the land itself and yet the whole cliff is afloat. It is one of the earth's most extraordinary natural structures. Beyond the ice cliff, stretching more than 500 miles towards the Pole is the largest of all the world's ice shelves, even in Antarctica a floating giant among giants, so extensive it would cover an area almost equivalent to the entire Iberian Peninsula of Western Europe.

The ice shelf is a region of unearthly desolation, a place of strange forebodings stirred by the loss of horizons into an endless encirclement of ice invading the explorer's mind. Man travels here on a surface of white silences, punctuated only by the whispering drift. Such an environment created a new type of explorer, forcing upon him a sterner discipline than anything his discoveries had previously demanded. Antarctica was to prove the most alien of all environments, ice the most intractable of man's opponents.

Ice has been a major controlling influence in man's world. His evolution, his rise towards civilization, his culture and recorded history, the very fibre of his being and the nature of his mind have been fashioned by ice. When natural catastrophe strikes we think only of earthquakes, fire and flood, of tornadoes and hurricanes, those forces whose speed of destruction is the essence of their drama and terror. By contrast ice moves with deliberation, its progress measured not by seconds or minutes but by decades and by centuries. We pay little attention to the ice that hides beyond the horizons of our lives and we are lulled into a sense of false security. In the northern hemisphere, where the greater proportion of the world's population is concentrated, we forget that many of the river basins where we have created our cities, and the broad plains beyond which supply us with the bulk of our food, once supported an ice sheet as lifeless and hostile as that which covers Antarctica today. We forget that less than 8000 years ago this ice was still retreating and that the evolution of our civilization has only been possible since then. Still less do we care to dwell on the minor aberrations of climate that could herald the advance of the ice once more, while the interventions of man himself can no longer be ignored as we contemplate the horror of the nuclear winter.

Ice is a most ancient music playing over the surface of the earth, its themes transcribed into the rocks and the progression of the geological ages, its rhythm that of the pulsating sun and the slow heartbeat of the universe. The shivering consciousness of man comes late in such an orchestration and it came last of all to the ice age that remains in Antarctica.

Life on earth has existed for at least three thousand million years. Seen against this perspective, the evolution of man remains an unresolved blemish within the mirage of time. Less than two million years separate modern man, homo sapiens, from his immediate predecessor, *australopithecus*, the dark little creature who walked upright from the edge of the dwindling forests onto the open savannah that was spreading like a golden sea across the sun-baked plains of East Africa.

Australopithecus was not only the forerunner of modern man, he was also the prototype of man the explorer. That initial move from forest to savannah was a critical response to a climate altering from downpour to drought, a small portent of the massive changes in world climate that were to follow, profoundly affecting man's evolution.

His response in East Africa was only the first of many successful adaptations to a constantly changing world that marked the beginning of a spectacular migration, carrying him and his descendants across the face of the earth. A million years ago he was in North Africa. 700 thousand years ago he had reached Java and South East Asia. Four hundred thousand years ago he settled in China and had arrived in Europe. Here the pace of his migration faltered, coming finally to a halt before suffering a series of reverses, produced by a wholly unexpected development.

In Africa just as the changing climate first prompted man to move off, so imperceptibly but relentlessly it continued to alter as he advanced northwards. For at least 200 million years before the appearance of the first man-apes, the northern hemisphere seems to have enjoyed a relatively stable climate of unprecedented warmth. Lush vegetation and abundant animal life evolved and flourished and it was into this world that man emerged. Wild game and fruits surrounded him, and the hunter-gathering groups could always rely on a plentiful source of food. Then, almost coincidentally with man's appearance in northern latitudes, the climate began to turn colder. A permanent ice cap developed over the North Pole gradually extending southwards. Man must have shivered in the icy winds blowing off the advancing ice sheet, uneasily watching the animals departing, the birds migrating from unending winter. He must have seen the trees die and the grass wither and felt the ground iron-hard beneath his feet.

Eventually ice and man would have met. The impact of that moment must have been overwhelming. He would surely have experienced fear, surprise, shock, sensing his vulnerability in the shrinking habitable world. This was the beginning of a series of four ice ages starting around 500,000 years ago, advancing and retreating across the lands and oceans of the northern hemisphere. The effects were global—even where there was no ice the climate was adversely affected. With each advance and retreat the land was reshaped and the oceans fell several hundred feet then rose again. The ice ages brought about a profound change in man. On the edge of the ice sheets he adapted to the rigorous sub-arctic conditions, retreating into the shelter of caves, where he discovered how to make fire. Animals were scarce, life hard, but he developed tools and artefacts, communicating through time his life in the remarkable paintings with which he adorned his underground sanctuaries. Surviving the ice ages, man was inevitably toughened by the experience, but I believe also it has left its mark in the form of some indefinable fear that resides deep in the collective unconscious of his species. Climatic improvement came only about 10,000 years ago; not until then could man embark upon the creation of the civilizations associated with recorded history.

There were few places in the world that man had not already reached even before the last ice age, and descendants of our nomadic ancestors still survive in the earth's more remote and inhospitable regions. If man could find his way across the world adapting himself to each environment, despite ice ages, the evaporation and inundation of oceans, and massive geological disturbances, why could he not reach in the southern hemisphere, the Antarctic Continent? And why after 6000 years of cohesive civilizations, which saw the birth of new, secondary migrations and scientifically assisted explorations of his planet, did he still fail to reach Antarctica until a generation ago?

This question can only be answered by returning again into the earth's distant past, but this time moving back far beyond the appearance of man, beyond even the appearance of warm blooded mammals to the beginning of the age of the great reptiles. Here, slightly less than 300 million years ago, in the latter stages of the Carboniferous period, the earth is entering into a new geological era, the Permian. A huge proto-continent known as 'Pangea' (from the Greek—all earth), drifting sluggishly on the earth's mantle of hot viscous rocks, is breaking up, forming two vast supercontinents, one in the northern hemisphere, Laurasia, the other in the southern hemisphere, Gondwanaland. It is here within this southern supercontinent that Antarctica has its origins.

The Mesozoic supercontinent of Gondwanaland.
The Transantarctic Mountains were once continuous with the mineral-rich areas of eastern Australia and the Rand in South Africa; the Antarctic Peninsula was once linked with the Andes

Gondwanaland comprised, apart from Antarctica, the whole of present day South America, Southern Africa, India, Australia and possibly New Zealand. Its initial formation as part of Pangea occurred during Pre-Cambrian times, the earliest geological period, and therefore the rock platform constituting the shield of Greater, or Eastern Antarctica, is over 500 million years old. Eastern Antarctica, comprising the bulk of the Continent, is quite distinct from Lesser or Western Antarctica, which has a different geological history. The shield of Eastern Antarctica is composed of ancient metamorphic and intruded rocks. On top of these rest younger, sedimentary rocks—marine muds and shales, freshwater deposits, broad coal seams and sandstones. Together they make up a layer of rocks about 8200 feet thick laid down between 200 and 400 million years ago. Referred to as 'The Beacon Series', they form one of the most important geological structures of the Continent for they contain much of the valuable fossil evidence of Antarctica's past. In some areas of the Trans-Antarctic mountains, the exposed, near horizontal bands of rock with their different fossils read to the trained eye like the pages of a book. The 'Beacon' rocks have in turn been injected by later volcanic activity, evident today in the broad bands and sills of fine-grained dolerite. This rock, being harder than the sandstones, has been more resistant to the long ages of erosion and weathering and has been left as prominent horizontal platforms. Both the Pre-Cambrian shield and the 'Beacon' rocks have been subjected to the mountain-building episodes of the last thirty-five million years resulting in the spectacular exposure of the series in the Trans-Antarctic mountains. When pieced together, the various rock structures of the Continent reveal a remarkable story of Antarctica's past history and its movement across the surface of the earth.

Following long geological ages of stability, Gondwanaland began to break up about 180 million years ago, and the various pieces which today form the southern continents started the long drift towards their present configuration. This process, known as 'continental drift', continues, and with the passage of time the relationship of the continents will alter again.

The rocks of Eastern Antarctica reveal an enormous range of climatic conditions prevailing at different periods in its history. Between 250 and 300 million years ago, and some 100 million years before the break-up, an ice age, perhaps similar to the present one, covered a large part of Gondwanaland. During the Mesozoic Era, about 100 million years ago, arid, hot, sandy desert conditions prevailed. Between these two extremes, the fossils found in the sedimentary rocks of the Beacon Series—the ferns, horse-tails, cycads, shrubs and trees, freshwater crustacea and the most recent and exciting finds, the bones of reptiles and amphibians—all speak of warm, life-enhancing conditions. Even more recent fossils of the early Tertiary period, between sixty and seventy million years ago, indicate that beech forests and palm groves once flourished in the lowland plains of an ice-free Antarctica.

The geological history of Western Antarctica is very different. It has a much more broken topography, including the chain of mountains extending into the long, curving spine of the Antarctic Peninsula, that in turn continues in the isolated island groups of the Scotia Arc joining eventually, via submarine ridges, the Andes of the South American Continent. In this region the earth has undergone tremendous stress, the whole region being subjected to repeated volcanic eruptions, leaving geologists today with a complex series of rock structures to unravel. In Mesozoic times, the land was often raised far above sea level. Fossil records show that plants resembling ferns, swamp vegetation and mixed conifer forests spread over the area with an attendant population of flies, beetles and freshwater molluscs.

About seventy million years ago, a particularly violent series of crustal upheavals, accompanied by major volcanic eruptions, poured out vast quantities of molten rock into the surrounding area, marking the beginning of the formation of the Scotia Arc and the islands that lie along the west coast of the Peninsula. The whole area then rose out of the sea only to be slowly eroded away again by millions of years of weathering. Folding and faulting continued, accompanied by volcanic activity. Around thirty-five to forty million years ago, the South Shetlands, the South Sandwich group, the coastal mountain ranges of continental Western Antarctica and the remote Bouvet and Peter I islands appeared. The history of Western Antarctica is particularly disturbed compared with that of its Eastern counterpart. The South Shetlands and the South Sandwich Islands remain volcanically active, the eruptions on Deception Island in the late 1960s being a reminder of this, and the whole area is relatively earthquake prone.

Having followed in broad outline the Antarctic Continent's

formative processes from the huge supercontinent of Pre-Cambrian times to a period around forty million years ago, the emphasis slowly shifts from events taking place within the earth to those above it in the atmosphere. Here crucial developments would gradually fashion Antarctica into the unique and beautiful continent it is today.

Throughout the greater length of the earth's history, probably around 5000 million years, the polar regions remained free of permanent ice, and the global climate varied in human terms from comfortable warmth to uncomfortable heat. Ice ages, such as that of the Carboniferous and Permian periods in Gondwanaland, were the exception. This situation altered in the most recent periods of geological time and the change is more or less coinciden- tal with the beginning of the Gondwanaland break-up. At that time, the mean surface temperature of the earth is believed to have been about 20°C. Since then it has fallen steadily to just over 10°C, half what it was 150 million years ago. The polar regions, although ice-free, always remained cooler than the equatorial regions, because they received their sunlight at a lower angle, and in this general downturn of temperature the poles cooled more rapidly than the equatorial regions and the temperature gradient between them became steeper. This factor alone was sufficient to cause the formation of permanent ice caps in the polar regions, but the glacial advancement was encouraged by other simultaneous events.

Climatologists now believe that the glaciation of the polar regions was assisted by the gradual alteration in the distrubution and relationship of landmasses to oceans. If the poles became either land-locked as in the Arctic, or surrounded by ocean as in the Antarctic, this caused a major change in the circulation of both atmosphere and ocean, preventing the warmth carried by the simple north/south ocean currents from reaching the poles. With the poles located in mid-ocean, as they were for much of the period prior to the Gondwanaland break-up, there was very little chance of permanent ice forming.

The onset of glaciation in the Antarctic dates back about thirty-eight million years. This is earlier than scientists had orig- inally supposed, making the Antarctic ice sheet far older than any ice in the northern hemisphere. The climate immediately preceding the onset of glaciation was a cool temperate one in Antarctica, which at this time was still connected to Australia and

South America. Forests extended across the lowland areas and no glaciers existed even in the mountains. Evidence for the formation of the first glaciers comes from analysis of deep ocean cores, where ice-rafted sediments deposited from melting icebergs can be traced indicating the presence of sea-calving glaciers. Accompanying fossil evidence shows that beech forests grew over a wide area. The landscape and climate at this time probably resembled that found today in Southern Chile and Tierra del Fuego.

The initiation of these first glaciers began as Australia parted from Antarctica. The intervening ocean increased the moisture content of the atmosphere resulting in heavier snowfalls breaking over the Antarctic mountains. This, coupled with declining temperatures, triggered off the development of permanent snowfields and the formation of glaciers. The crucial event which turned the Antarctic from a cool temperate region of high glaciers and lowland forests into a major ice sheet was the separation of South America from Western Antarctica and the opening up of the Drake Passage. This happened about twenty-two million years ago allowing a strong westerly atmospheric circulation to develop and a dynamic circumpolar ocean current to sweep unimpeded around a totally isolated continent. The westerly circulation lowered temperatures further and increased snowfall, accelerating the pace of glacier formation. The ice age was assured. The present ice sheet covering Eastern Antarctica became established between eleven and fourteen million years ago. Its appearance caused further reductions in temperature over a wide area accompanied by a marked northward expansion of the seasonal sea ice and iceberg limits.

The formation of the ice sheet covering the fragmented archipelago of Western Antarctica occurred much later, probably between four and five million years ago, and coincided with a further period of cooling and expansion of the sea ice. The influence of the cold circumpolar ocean also extended northwards towards its present surface demarcation, the Antarctic Convergence. The ice sheet of the Continent as a whole soon reached its maximum extent, marked now by the edge of the submarine continental shelf. At its most extensive the ice sheet spread between 60 and 180 miles beyond its present coastal limits. In the Victoria Land mountains, numerous 'dry valleys' indicate that the ice sheet was once considerably larger than it is today. Glaciers once filled the dry valleys burying many of the surrounding mountains to within a few hundred feet of their summits. Nunataks which poke through the ice cap in places are the peaks of mountains similarly buried today. The huge ice-carved submarine troughs of the Weddell and Ross Seas, and the continental debris left scattered all over the ocean floor tell us that the ice sheet was once aground here, moving slowly across the sea bed.

For the last four million years the Antarctic ice sheet has continued to fluctuate. Some glaciologists believe that several of these interglacial periods precipitated the total collapse of the Western Antarctic ice sheet which, unlike that covering Eastern Antarctica, rests on bed rock below sea level. The stability of the ice sheet is maintained only as long as sea level does not rise or the weight of the ice does not decrease. A change in either of these results in an 'ice-surge' when the heart of the ice sheet is eaten away within a few centuries or even decades precipitating a catastrophic collapse of the entire ice sheet. Such an event occurred at the end of the last ice age in the northern hemisphere: 8000 years ago the Laurentide ice sheet covering Hudson Bay collapsed and disappeared in little more than 300 years.

The possibility that the Western Antarctic ice sheet may be approaching a similar collapse in the present interglacial period cannot be discounted. It could happen as a response to a rise in world sea level brought about by the recession of middle latitude ice sheets in the northern hemisphere, or from a doubling over the next fifty years of the carbon dioxide content of the atmosphere from the increased burning of fossil fuels. This could produce the necessary climatic warming in the polar regions sufficient to cause an 'ice-surge' of the Western Antarctic ice sheet, raising the ocean levels of the world by at least sixteen feet. Disastrous as the effects of this would be they would be insignificant compared with the combined melting of the ice sheet in Eastern Antarctica. If this happened, the oceans would rise almost 200 feet destroying nearly all our major cities and agricultural lowland areas. For at least two-thirds of the world's population it would be a catastrophe.

The Eastern Antarctic ice sheet, firmly supported on land, is much less prone to changes in climate or alterations of sea level. It has been calculated that a massive warming of the southern polar climate, with a rise of 20°C in mean temperatures, would be required to initiate such a flood. Since it has survived all previous interglacial periods there is little chance of any significant change taking place so long as the Continent remains centred on the South Pole. In time, of course, Antarctica will drift on from its present position and the climate of the earth will continue to alter. As in the past these changes will take place over hundreds of millions of years, a length of time so far removed from the human scale of thinking that, like the past, we are only able to contemplate them with a detached fascination, trying to picture what the future holds for our world. We can be sure that, whatever else may happen, such changes will be as far-reaching in their profound effect upon our planet as anything that has occurred in the past.

An ice sheet, whose origins stretch back thirty-eight million years, entirely overshadows the recent emergence of the human race. In the same way an individual human being standing alone on the high polar plateau, in the middle of that same ice sheet, feels utterly insignificant. The ice sheet is five and a half million square miles in area, almost twice the size of Australia. The ice reaches a formidable depth; an average of 6500 feet, while in some places as much as 12,000 feet covers the land beneath. Entire mountain ranges larger than the European Alps, with peaks rising over 10,000 feet are completely buried. Antarctica is by far the highest of the world's seven continents, its average elevation is 7500 feet. And the cold bites deep in Antarctica, deeper than anywhere, for it is by far the world's coldest continent. In summer the plateau temperature averages around minus 30°C. In winter, in the perpetual darkness of the polar night, it falls to an average of at least minus 60°C. The world's lowest temperature has been recorded here, minus 89.6°C at Vostok, the Soviet station at a height of 11,500 feet on the Eastern Antarctic ice cap. More surprising perhaps, Antarctica is a desert, an ice desert, an arid, white wasteland where less moisture falls annually (in frozen form) than in the Sahara. The blizzards are storms of wind-blown snow, suffocating drifts that blast along from one end of the polar plateau to the other for days and weeks on end. Nothing lives here and man cannot survive without a constant and adequate supply of food, shelter and warmth. Today at the South Pole, inside the comfortable, artificial environment of the American 'Amundsen–Scott' Base, these essentials, and far more besides, are available in plenty, flown in from New Zealand via McMurdo Sound by transport aircraft. But step outside for a moment, experiencing in the process a temperature change of as much as

100°C, and it is not hard to understand why, in 1912, Scott, starving and exhausted, wrote in his diary, 'Great God! This is an awful place, and terrible enough for us to have laboured to it without the reward of priority. Well, it is something to have got here, and the wind may be our friend tomorrow.' All that lies between the presence of man here now and the eternity of ice is the foothold of technology artificially balanced at the end of a precarious lifeline.

Descending from the high interior of the Continent to the coastal margins of Antarctica, the climate is modified, the environment less hostile, but the difference is only relative. Temperatures are higher. On a few days in summer they will rise several degrees above freezing-point and rain sometimes falls. But in winter, snowfalls are heavy and at times persistent. In maritime Antarctica

1: A mean monthly surface isotherm (°C) in January (after Taljaard *et al.*, 1969).

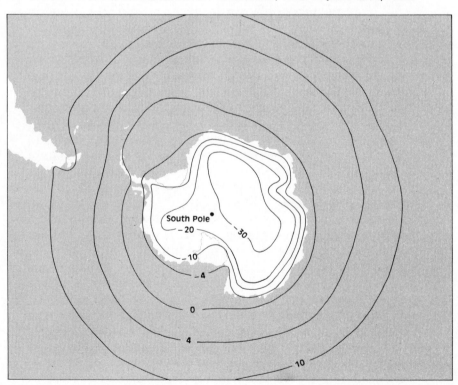

the influence of the Southern Ocean is felt to full effect, its vigorous storm centres passing frequently around the Continent. Glaciers squeeze through the mountains and spread out into massive piedmonts and ice shelves. They act like waterfalls for the cold, heavy air of the plateau that comes plunging down to the coast, creating winds of terrifying speeds. These are called 'Katabatics' and can reach speeds in excess of 200 mph. Wind is the most significant factor in Antarctica's climate. When combined with the extremely low temperatures it kills very rapidly. Along most of the coastline winter darkness is shorter, in some places only several months of soft twilight, but at this time the ocean freezes over far beyond the northern horizons. This effectively doubles the size of Antarctica's ice sheet and forces away almost all life from its shores. And the Southern Ocean, which surrounds

2: **Mean monthly isotherms (°C) in July (after Taljaard *et al.*, 1969).**

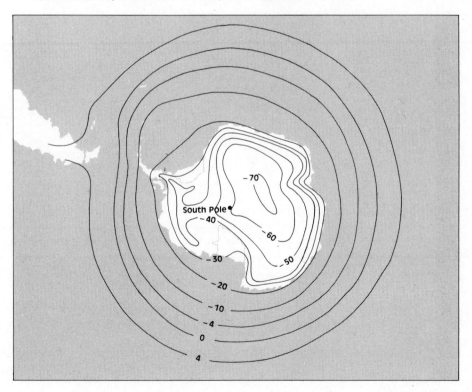

and separates Antarctica from the rest of the world, makes it the
most isolated of all the continents. South Africa lies almost 2500
miles to the north, Australia over 1500 miles and South America,
the nearest land, is still nearly 600 miles distant.

Antarctica is then, by definition, a place of superlatives where
Nature has aligned her forces in their most imposing, most majestic combination. It is the highest, coldest, driest, windiest, most
isolated continent, surrounded by an ocean which is the stormiest,
most ice-infested stretch of water on earth. These are the forces
which, throughout his evolution and for almost all of his recorded
history, denied man all knowledge of Antarctica and made his
recent access to it such a difficult adventure. Cut off from the rest
of the world the Continent echoed no human voices, carried no
human marks, shadowed no human form until the dawn of the

3: Mean annual surface temperatures in Antarctica (°C). After John and Sugden (1975).

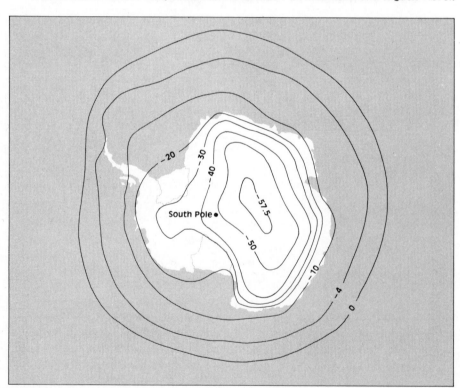

1 Entering the Southern Ocean – the 'roaring forties'.

2 South of the Antarctic Convergence – the first cold breath of Antarctica.

3 Entering the pack-ice – view from the bridge.

4 B.A.S. research ship *Bransfield* in the pack-ice.

5 British Antarctic Survey Base, Signy Island, South Orkneys (1976).

6 Halley Bay 3, Brunt Ice shelf – base construction 1974. Steel tunnels will house base complex which will quickly be buried by ice and eventually crushed. Rebuilding takes place about every 10-12 years.

7 Mt Liotard, Adelaide Island,
Antarctic Peninsula.

8 Dog team sledging out from Stonington
Island 1971. Antarctic Peninsula.

present. Today it is the least developed, cleanest environment on earth with a population density of one man for every 7000 square miles, compared with seventy people for every square mile for the earth as a whole. But statistics convey so little and facts seem to become meaningless when one actually arrives in Antarctica for, despite the severity of the climate and the rigours of its environment, nothing can prepare one for the overwhelming beauty of it all—it is simply breathtaking. But behind the beauty of the polar landscape lies its vulnerability; behind its powerful interplay of elements, ice, rock, wind and cold, now lies the challenge of man.

PART II
THE SECOND WAVE

New Men, New Motives
Science takes the Lead

When James Clark Ross returned from the Antarctic in 1843, interest turned towards the Arctic which had always been the historical focus of European polar ambitions.

For over fifty years Antarctica remained undisturbed by human presence. A few sealers still roamed the Southern Ocean and by the 1870s a partial recovery of some colonies warranted a brief resumption of the industry. But the slaughter was sporadic and short-lived, the profits hardly justifying the effort.

So a kind of peace had returned but it was no longer the peace of innocence. Antarctica had been broken into and innocence defiled. It was the sad and ominous silence hanging above a fearful void that marked this temporary absence of man.

As the nineteenth century drew to a close, the traditional whaling grounds in the Arctic were becoming unreliable through overexploitation. Antarctica began to look increasingly attractive as an alternative and the first exploratory whaling voyages were made in the 1890s.

Ross's expedition had been primarily an outstandingly successful scientific voyage which laid the foundation stone for scientific exploration in Antarctica. If the expedition laid the foundation stone, then Joseph Hooker was the founding father of Antarctic science. Hooker was to become one of the nineteenth century's greatest scientists and from the time of Ross's expedition, where his outstanding work as a naturalist formed the basis of his reputation, he constantly urged that science must play the central role in any future attempts to gain a foothold on the Continent. Hooker died at the age of ninety-four, living long enough to see the age of science inaugurated in Antarctica, when he had the pleasure of advising both Scott and Shackleton, leaders of the first major land-based expeditions at the beginning of the twentieth century.

Also poised on the threshold of this new era in Antarctica were the whalers and it is from among their ranks that the man emerges who was actually to provide the necessary practical stimulus for the new motives emerging in Antarctic exploration.

Carsten Borchgrevink, a young Norwegian, had emigrated to Australia in 1888. In 1894 he was working as an itinerant teacher when he decided to sign on as able seaman to one of the first exploratory whaling voyages into the Ross Sea. As a whaling expedition the voyage was a failure but it enjoyed the greater distinction of being the means by which man first set foot on the Continent.

After thirty-six days in the pack-ice the expedition ship, the *Antarctic*, reached the coast of northern Victoria Land on 16 January 1895. On the 24th with the ice conditions improving the *Antarctic* arrived off Cape Adare and at 2 am the following morning, having rowed inshore through the ice of Robertson Bay, seven men landed on the Continent of Antarctica. On a narrow pebble beach beneath the dark cliffs of Cape Adare they stood deafened by the roar of ice-filled surf. They looked on an awesome sight of mighty glaciers descending through clouds from mountains guarding an inhospitable, totally unknown region. It was an extraordinary moment, the significance of which was not lost on Borchgrevink. Leaving the rest of the party he walked alone along the shore, making a collection of rocks, seaweed and jellyfish. Before departing they also killed several penguins and seals as specimens. In all they were ashore about two hours.

In Melbourne local scientists and members of the Australian Antarctic Committee were impressed by Borchgrevink's collection and they listened carefully to his accounts of the area surrounding Robertson Bay. However, when he suggested that they should finance a further expedition, his appeal fell on deaf ears. But Borchgrevink had already made up his mind that he was going to return to the Antarctic as the leader of an expedition that would winter at Cape Adare and explore the land beyond the mountains they had seen. For the next three years he dedicated himself to this ambition and in 1897 he finally raised enough money. Borchgrevink's employer at this time was the wealthy British publisher, Sir George Newnes. Newnes backed the expedition and contributed £40,000 towards its costs. His one stipulation was that Borchgrevink call it 'The British Antarctic Expedition', despite the fact that all but three of its members were Scandinavians. In this there was the first whiff of nationalistic fervour which was soon to find expression in Antarctica at a time when European empire building was approaching its zenith. Borchgrevink, within sight of his dream, was undisturbed by this demand. The expedition ship, *Southern Cross*, left London on 23 August 1898.

'It was a scene terrible in its austerity,' wrote Louis Bernacchi the Australian physicist, 'that can only be witnessed at that extremity of the globe; truly a land of unsurpassed desolation.' Bernacchi spoke for them all when the *Southern Cross* arrived at Cape Adare on 18 February 1899. Their base—two prefabricated wooden huts joined together—was established in ten days. Borchgrevink called it 'Camp Ridley' after his mother. The *Southern Cross*, after almost foundering in a storm, departed on 2 March. She left behind ten men and seventy-five dogs, Samoyeds from Siberia, intended for the inland journeys.

On 15 May the sun set and throughout the ten weeks of darkness that followed they spent their time playing chess and cards, reading, arguing and listening to their musical box. Outside violent storms alternated with the frozen silence of the polar night when the Aurora flickered overhead. They maintained a detailed meteorological log—in August the temperature fell to minus 43°F —but most of the other scientific work in zoology, geology and magnetics came to a halt. 'We were getting tired of each other's company,' wrote Borchgrevink, 'and began to know every line in each other's faces . . . the darkness and the silence in this solitude weighs heavily on one's mind. The silence roars in the ears. It is centuries of heaped up solitude.'

With the return of the sun sledging began. Unfortunately, access to the polar plateau, which they could see from Robertson Bay, was denied them by a matrix of glaciers and sheer cliffs which fell directly into the sea and no one possessed the mountaineering skills which would have allowed them to break out of the bay. So they made a series of shorter journeys over the sea ice around the immediate coastline.

These first short forays on the fringe of the Continent were sufficient to give warning of the dangers that lay ahead. Several times they narrowly escaped death on heavily crevassed glaciers. One man walking alone actually fell head-first sixty feet down a crevasse and only managed to climb out using a penknife to cut steps. Men and sledges broke through the sea ice and there was a constant risk of being swept out to sea as the ice drifted about in the unstable weather. Caught in a sudden blizzard one party almost froze to death and only survived by bringing the dogs into the tent to help keep themselves warm.

Camp Ridley was buffeted by a succession of violent hurricanes, stones cascading off the nearby cliffs onto the roof of the hut. A candle left unattended set fire to one of the bunks and they only just managed to put it out, while on another occasion they were nearly asphyxiated by carbon monoxide fumes escaping from a faulty stove. But the event which overshadowed everything was the death of the biologist, Nicolai Hanson. He had become ill during the winter and grown steadily weaker until he eventually died on 14 October. He was probably the first victim of scurvy in the Antarctic, a disease which was to figure prominently on the early expeditions. They buried Hanson on the summit of Cape Adare where, as Bernacchi reflected, 'amidst profound silence and peace, there is nothing to disturb that eternal sleep except the flight of sea birds.'

The *Southern Cross* returned at the end of January 1900 and within a few days Camp Ridley was deserted. The ship then sailed for Ross Island and the ice shelf last seen by Ross. Here Borchgrevink with two companions sledged south for ten miles, setting a new record at 78° 50' south. The dogs performed excellently on the immense, featureless plain of drifting snow. It was a curious prefiguration in miniature of the great journey other Norwegians were to undertake a decade later when Roald Amundsen sledged to the Pole.

On his return to England, Borchgrevink might reasonably have expected a hero's welcome, but he found his reception muted. He had fallen foul of the establishment as represented by the geographical and scientific authorities who believed he had diverted attention and much needed funds from their prestigious British National Antarctic Expedition, scheduled to leave the following year under Scott's command.

Borchgrevink's achievements were not publicly acknowledged for thirty years, when he was finally awarded the Patron's Medal of the Royal Geographical Society. However, the men from the 'Northern Party' of Scott's second expedition wintered at Cape Adare in 1912 and they came fully to appreciate Borchgrevink's courage and the value of his pioneering efforts.

The objectives of Borchgrevink's expedition had been those of science and exploration and although in this respect his claims are modest, his observations were extremely useful to the expeditions that soon followed and above all he had proved that it was possible for man to winter on the Antarctic Continent. His expedition had experienced most of the major hazards that would have to be faced if man was going to advance beyond the shores of the Continent. During the next twenty years—the 'heroic age'—these hazards were faced and overcome, but Antarctica exacted a heavy price in return.

4

THE EMPEROR'S EGG
The First Winter Journey

The winter journey had long been the ambition of Edward Wilson, head of the scientific staff and Scott's confidant and second-in-command. As doctor, zoologist, ornithologist and artist, he possessed one of the finest combinations of skills of any man ever to visit the Antarctic, to say nothing of the personal qualities of the man himself. Raymond Priestley, the geologist on Scott's Northern Party, once said that Wilson was the nearest thing to a saint that he had ever come across in his life.

Wilson first went south with Scott on the *Discovery* expedition in 1901 when he became fascinated by the Emperor Penguin. A sledging party had reached Cape Crozier on the eastern side of Ross Island during the later part of October, the Antarctic spring, and discovered the first recorded rookery of Emperors. About 400 birds were on the sea ice and the party had great difficulty in reaching them across the heavily crevassed outfalls of the ice shelf. Eventually however, they succeeded in returning with three specimen chicks and a few eggshells. Wilson, intrigued by their findings, thought that the penguins probably bred on the sea ice and, most fascinating of all, that they must lay their eggs unusually early in the season. Eager to return to the rookery himself, he asked Scott for permission, but his request clashed with his leader's plans for the 'Southern Journey' in which he, together with Scott and Shackleton were to go as far south as possible across the Ross Ice Shelf. Wilson's disappointment is obvious from his diary, but at the same time he concedes the expedition's larger objective.

'The skipper says there is not time for me to go and hunt for them, but Koettlitz is going instead. I am afraid this long southern journey is taking me right away from my proper sphere of work to monotonous hard work on an icy desert for three months, where we shall see neither beast nor bird, nor life of any sort nor land and nothing whatever to sketch. Only I think we must, and I hope we shall, come to land when we have travelled south on the Barrier for a month or so. Anyhow it is *the* long journey and I cannot help being glad I was chosen for it. If we come across anything but Barrier, it will be exceedingly interesting.'

They were in fact to reach latitude 82° 17′ south, chart over 300 miles of unexplored coastline and set a new furthest south record. Wilson had to wait ten years before the opportunity arose again for him to realize his ambition. Even then he had the greatest difficulty in persuading Scott to let him go, taking with him two of the best sledging men who would be needed on the march to the Pole, the start of which was little more than three months away. In the intervening years Wilson had developed the theory that if a party of men could visit the Cape early enough in the season, it would be possible to secure the eggs of the Emperor, the most primitive bird in the world, and that a study of the embryo might provide a missing link in the evolution of birds from their reptilian ancestry.

They set out for Cape Crozier on the morning of 27 June 1911, Wilson, 'Birdie' Bowers and Apsley Cherry-Garrard, just five days after they had celebrated Midwinter. This date is of more importance on the Antarctic calendar than Christmas, marking as it does the day on which the sun begins to return south again from the northern hemisphere, bringing with it the promise of an end to the long polar night. However, as they left the warmth of the hut, night was still very much with them. No one had ever before considered, let alone attempted, travelling in the depths of the Antarctic winter. The hazards were simply too great. There was hardly a breath of wind and the thermometer registered 15°F. A few minutes before they left, Ponting came out and photographed them in front of the heavily laden sledges.

Man-hauling two nine foot sledges, one tied behind the other, they set out shortly after eleven in the morning. It had proved impossible to load all their equipment and rations onto the normal twelve foot sledge, so they had reduced everything as much as they could. Even so, the combined weight of these sledges was almost a quarter of a ton, a daunting prospect for such a journey. For a while they were accompanied by a small party from the base, but by the middle of the afternoon the last of them had turned back for the safety of the hut, leaving the three alone to face the sixty-five miles to Cape Crozier.

That evening, as they made their first camp, the difficulties of the journey facing them began to make themselves apparent. They were used to being able to make camp quickly, taking pride in having their tea boiling within twenty minutes of throwing off their harnesses.

'But now it didn't work,' wrote Cherry-Garrard. 'We had already realized that cooking under these conditions would be a bad job, and that the usual arrangement by which one man was to cook for the week would be intolerable. We settled to be cook alternately day by day. For food we bought only pemmican and biscuit and butter; for drink we had tea, and we drank hot water to turn in on.'

That first day was the best they were to have. The second day —day only by the clock, for darkness prevailed throughout—they rounded Cape Armitage and came under the cold flow of air blowing off the edge of the ice shelf. Cherry's fingers got frost-bitten and were soon painfully blistered. That night the temperature plunged to minus 56°F.

It took four or five hours to strike camp before they could begin each day's march. Their clothes and harnesses were frozen solid, so that two of them would have to force the other into his gear by slowly bending each piece into the appropriate shape. At night when they finally got into their sleeping bags, the cold was so severe that they couldn't breathe through the normal opening and, closing the bags over their heads, their breath then froze into the skin of the bag forming an effective seal. Consequently the air stagnated and their respiration rate increased until they gasped like marathon runners. With deathly cold without and near suffo-cation within they were lucky to snatch a few fitful moments of sleep. Frostbite was a constant hazard. Wilson continually checked whether they should stop and camp or could risk going on for a while longer.

'A wrong decision meant disaster, for if one of us had been crippled the whole party would have been placed in great difficult-ies. Probably we should all have died.'

The bay between Cape Armitage and Terror Point is subject to long periods of calm weather; the blizzards that blow in the near vicinity are deflected by local topographical features and consequently the snow accumulates undisturbed to a great depth. As the temperature falls the lying snow crystals start to combine until eventually the whole surface takes on the quality and texture of dry sand. The effect is similar to walking in sand dunes; the feet sink and slide at every step in an effort out of all proportion to the task. Imagine then these three, experiencing a similar sensation but at minus 50°F, in the dark and trying to pull two awkward and heavily laden sledges. Very soon the wrenching strain became intolerable, and there was no alternative but to relay each sledge turn and turn about. For every mile advanced they now travelled three to attain it. When the faint midday twilight disappeared they had to retrace their tracks by candlelight. All the time the temperature was falling steadily until the thermometer registered between minus 60° and minus 70°F. They travelled ten miles that day but only advanced just over three. During the night the temperature fell to minus 75°F—107 degrees of frost. Cherry was kept awake all night by a succession of shivering fits, so severe that he imagined his back was going to break with the strain. By morning he was exhausted, but Wilson was more comfortable while Bowers snored loudly!

Lieutenant Henry Robertson Bowers, known as 'Birdie' to the others on account of his extraordinary beak-like nose, was not among the shore party when he joined the *Terra Nova*. But during the long voyage south he proved to be an amazing workhorse and this, coupled with his knowledge of the expedition's stores and a capacity for organizing them down to the finest detail, brought him more and more to Scott's attention. He was a simple, straight-forward man, holding a broad, unobtrusive faith. He had great tenacity in the face of difficulties and supreme self-confidence in overcoming them. Nothing seemed capable of shattering his optimism, an invaluable asset on any expedition and particularly this one. On their arrival in the Antarctic, Scott transferred Bowers to the shore party and Bowers relieved him of much of the burden of organizing the stores and equipment. Short of stature—Bowers was only five feet four inches tall—Scott described him as 'the hardiest traveller that ever undertook a polar journey'. His endurance of the most severe conditions, his apparent indifference to cold were nothing short of astonishing, particularly as he joined the expedition straight from service on the Persian Gulf.

Now, with one hundred degrees and more of frost each night, the only heat there was came struggling up to them from the primus flame. The cold was so intense that, after emerging from the tent one morning and turning his head, Cherry found he couldn't move it back again; his clothes had frozen solid in an instant, and he had to sledge the rest of the morning with his head cocked to one side. After this they were all careful to bend into a pulling position before they were irretrievably frozen in.

1 July found them halfway between Cape Armitage and Terror Point, in the middle of the windless expanse of the bay. They began to suffer hallucinations from loss of sleep and from the continual straining of their eyes in the dark. Relaying their sledges, the depressions of their previous footprints appeared instead as mounds over which they carefully lifted their feet. Even when they realized the illusion, no amount of concentration could persuade them to abandon this painfully tiring absurdity.

It was a full week before they reached the other side of the bay, camping in the lee of Terror Point on 8 July. During all that time there had been no relief from pulling the sledges, turn by turn through the deep snow, which was sometimes up to their waists as they floundered about in the darkness and drifts. The pitiful distances they managed speak for themselves of the overwhelming odds they were battling against. On 5 July, after eight hours pulling, they had travelled one and a half miles. The day was also memorable for the lowest temperature they recorded, minus 77°F.

'That day lives in my memory,' Cherry wrote, 'as that on which I found out that records are not worth making . . . and is I suppose as cold as anyone will want to endure in darkness and iced-up gear and clothes!'

On the 6th the temperature was minus 75.8°F and they advanced a further one and a half miles. On the 7th they covered one and three-quarter miles in thick fog. The temperature had risen to minus 55°F and the relative mildness actually restored some warmth and feeling into their hands and feet. They were now travelling constantly in fog, through which the moon appeared above their heads like a Chinese lantern. As they approached the land once more, snow began to fall and the first stirrings of a breeze produced its own discomfort to add to all the others.

On the 8th they finally came out of the deep snow only to find themselves faced with a new hazard—crevasses. Stumbling about in the darkness and the fog, they imagined they saw rocks ahead of them. As they went to investigate the whole surface suddenly came alive as the ice started 'moving and splitting like glass'. The terrible noise ringing out into the darkness and the empty silent fog startled them severely in their tired, anxious state. Realizing that they were lost they pitched camp rather than risk going on. Hardly were they inside the tent than the first of a series of furious blizzards hit them. It was only a prelude of things to come. The blizzard lasted for three days but it brought one great relief. The temperature shot up to plus 9°F and Cherry wrote, 'It was not an uncomfortable time. Wet and warm the risen temperature allowed all our ice to turn to water, and we lay steaming and beautifully liquid, and wondered sometimes what we should be like when our gear froze up once more. But we did not do much wondering. I suspect: we slept. From that point of view these blizzards were a perfect Godsend.' However, they woke from time to time and lay listening to 'the unearthly banging' of the ice underneath them.

Early on the 13th the wind died away, the stars, absent so long, appeared through the breaking clouds of the departing storm. They covered a remarkable seven and a half miles for the day's run, narrowly avoiding being swallowed up in a crevasse on the way, the moon coming out from behind a bank of cloud seconds before they were about to plunge into it. For two days they fought their way along the slopes of Mount Terror, picking a route between the rocks and the scree on their left and the great pressure ridges of ice pushing up against the land on their right. Several times, one or other of them broke through the lids of the crevasses that ran like invisible blue veins in every direction under their feet.

On 15 July, nineteen days after leaving Cape Evans, they finally reached Cape Crozier. Here they pitched their tent 800 feet up the mountainside, just short of a level stretch of moraine, where they planned to build a rock shelter. This would serve as a more permanent home while they investigated the Emperor colony somewhere far below them.

The thought of these three men perched on a mountainside in the darkness and utter desolation of the Antarctic winter, clawing away at the frozen ground for suitable material with which to construct their little shelter, reminds one of the sort of activities Dante reserved for his figures in hell. Certainly they were the remotest beings in all the world and their self-imposed task must rank as one of the strangest ever devised. There was a little feeble twilight, but most of the time they worked either by moonlight or with the aid of the hurricane lamp. The rocks and the gravel were frozen to the mountainside as if they had been welded together.

Only hours of laborious chipping with their ice axes eventually released sufficient quantities to begin building the walls of the shelter. It was like working on the roof of the world and in the moonlight 'the view from eight hundred feet up the mountain was magnificent,' decided Cherry. 'I got my spectacles out and cleared the ice away time after time to look. To the east a great field of pressure ridges below, looking in the moonlight as if giants had been ploughing with ploughs which made furrows fifty or sixty feet deep: these ran right up to the Barrier edge, and beyond was the frozen Ross Sea, lying flat, white and peaceful as though such things as blizzards were unknown. To the north and north-east the Knoll. Behind us Mount Terror on which we stood, and over all the grey limitless Barrier seemed to cast a spell of cold immensity, vague, ponderous, a breeding-place of wind and drift and darkness. God! What a place!'

By 20 July they had finished the shelter, finally stretching a canvas over the roof, supported by one of the sledges, and packing it down with snow blocks and rocks until they were sure that nothing would shift it. During this time they had already made an abortive attempt to reach the Emperors, but in the darkness they had lost their way and searched in vain for a route down to the ice-foot, from where the ghostly calls of the penguins came echoing up the cliffs towards them.

So, with their shelter finished and breakfast over, they set off once more to reach the Emperors. They wore crampons and walked roped together. Each had an ice axe with which to break steps or hold himself in the event of slipping, and there was much of that as they worked their way across the slopes of the Cape. After a while, further progress seemed impossible. A precipitous wall of ice confronted them and there appeared no way of crossing it. Then Wilson found a hole in the ice, just big enough for a man to push his way through and within a few minutes they all emerged into a gully where they cut a series of steps to take them out onto the ice-foot. Here the calls of the Emperors came to them clearly, a curious, metallic trumpeting sound. At last they stood there 'three crystallized ragamuffins above the Emperors' home.' It was 20 July 1911 and they were the first men to set eyes upon an Emperor Penguin rookery in the depth of the Antarctic winter.

'After indescribable effort and hardship we were witnessing a marvel of the natural world, and we were the first and only men who had ever done so,' wrote Cherry-Garrard. 'We had within our grasp material which might prove of the utmost importance to science; we were turning theories into fact with every observation we made—and we had but a moment to give.'

A moment indeed, for the twilight hours were already turning to darkness and there were signs of a break in the weather approaching from the south. Wilson and Bowers went down onto the ice among the penguins. Cherry stayed on top of the ice-foot with the rope ready to help them back. They collected five eggs and killed three birds for the oil which they needed to replenish their blubber stove.

In 1902, the visitors from the *Discovery* had reported around 2000 Emperors gathered at Cape Crozier. This time they counted only about one hundred birds and Wilson was puzzled. Where were all the others? He thought that the main body of the rookery had probably been blown out to sea, for the ice conditions that season seemed to be particularly unstable. In the light of recent knowledge however, it seems more likely that Wilson had in fact descended the cliffs at a point some distance from the main rookery, and that what he found was a satellite gathering of birds, a number of which are known to oscillate around the main breeding colony.

As darkness fell they scrambled back to the shelter and by the time they reached it they were crawling along, feeling their way across the rocks. Only three out of the five eggs survived the ascent, the two that Cherry carried in his mitts broke in his anxiety to reach safety before nightfall. They had been out since three o'clock that morning in a temperature hovering between minus 20° and minus 30°F. A nasty little breeze which eddied about the cliffs and cornices made it feel much colder, quite enough to cause the Emperors to huddle together down on the ice.

Exhausted, but satisfied by the achievements of the day, they settled back in the warmth of their stone hut. Flensing one of the Emperor skins they started cooking their supper over the blubber stove. This gave out such a furious heat that they were soon black with soot and half choking in the fumes. The blubber stove was a messy, unreliable type of cooker, but the use of it was absolutely vital for they had only one tin of oil left for the return journey, and the difficulties of that they viewed with increasing apprehension. The blubber spluttered wildly and without warning a spot of boiling oil caught Wilson in the eye. The pain was indescribable and he lay in agony all night wondering if he had lost the sight of

9 *Opposite page* Baying the Moon.

10 View from the crow's nest entering the ice-fields of the Ross Sea.

11 *Opposite page* The abandoned whaling station at Prince Olaf Harbour, South Georgia.

12 *Opposite page* A whale catcher abandoned on the stocks at Husvik, South Georgia.

13 Echoes of War – Top: The familiar slogan here painted on a rusting corrugated shed at Prince Olaf Harbour South Georgia by passing ship's crew in 1968.

14 Below: The whaling gun with its explosive harpoon mounted on a concrete plinth outside the old Manager's house at Husvik, South Georgia.

15 The last measure indicating that there are 3 metres of whale oil left in this tank at Husvik.

16 At the height of Antarctic whaling – the flensing deck of a factory ship in the Southern Ocean during the 1950s. (photo courtesy W. MacLaughlin)

17 & 18 Final resting places: Top: Sealers' and whalers' graveyard overlooking entrance to Possession Bay where Captain Cook landed on South Georgia in 1774. Bottom: A cemetery for whales – thousands of whalebones washed ashore on a South Georgia beach.

19 Collapse of the whaling industry – the deserted manager's house at Prince Olaf Harbour overlooks the wreckage of the station.

20 Fur seals, once the target of immense slaughter, now play unmolested around old 'trypots' once used for extracting oil from another target species, the Elephant seals.

it. Outside the sky was full of racing clouds blotting out the stars and squalls of snow swept along the mountain slopes.

During the night the wind rose to a full gale; the canvas roof billowed away from the supporting sledge rafter despite the weight of rocks and ice cemented together on top of it and the lashings anchoring it down. In the morning the wind abated and they spent the rest of the day packing the roof down further with everything they could lay hands on. They also brought the tent up and pitched it beside the shelter for cooking in. While these most basic needs for survival had to be attended to there was no chance of returning to visit the Emperors. By evening the wind had died away leaving a hushed, ominously becalmed world. Overhead dense banks of cirrus veiled the stars and moved rapidly across the sky.

Early on the morning of the 22nd, they were awakened by a series of violent gusts, each preceded by a flat calm, the stillness of which seemed to gather a malevolence that sprang upon them in the next blast. 'Ten minutes and it was blowing as though the world was having a fit of hysterics,' Cherry wrote. 'The earth was torn in pieces; the indescribable fury and roar of it all cannot be imagined.'

As the wind increased to a hurricane the tent was plucked away from the ground and blown off into the swirling darkness. They fought their way across the few yards to where the tent had been. Miraculously the ground was still littered with their belongings. They searched frantically around in the drift, passing whatever they found back into the shelter. The hurricane, now screaming with terrifying force, continued all day. In the middle of preparing a meal the blubber stove collapsed and they had to finish cooking on the primus, using up their dwindling stock of precious oil. This was the last hot food they had for two days.

Drift and dust from the moraine was funnelling into their shelter. They tried plugging the holes with spare clothing but each piece was sucked in followed by a renewed blast of dust and snow. The blocks of ice that had weighted down the roof worked loose, and with each gust another one was carried off. The freed canvas smashed up and down over their heads, the ground beneath them shook and the walls trembled. They lay there for another twenty-four hours, dazed and numbed. Saturday moved into Sunday, and Wilson, whose sight had mercifully remained unaffected by the accident, managed to write in his diary, 'quite the funniest birthday I have ever spent.' They celebrated with a little tin of sweets which Bowers had salvaged from amongst the wreckage of the tent floor. Wilson was forty years old. Less than a year later both he and Bowers would be lying dead many miles to the south, killed by circumstances even more desperate than those which threatened them now. Without warning the roof was gone. Rocks and gravel cascaded down and over them swept stinging, suffocating, blinding drift thrashing them with the full force of the storm.

'The top of the door opened in little slits,' wrote Cherry, 'and that green Willesden canvas flapped into hundreds of little fragments in fewer seconds than it takes to read this. The uproar of it all was indescribable. Even above the savage thunder of that great wind on the mountain came the lash of canvas as it was whipped to little tiny strips.'

Both Wilson and Bowers were out of their sleeping bags when the roof went, and as they dived for this last remaining cover, they dragged the drift in with them, where it slowly started to melt. The temperature was around zero and quite warm by comparison with the severe cold of the journey. As they lay there in their bags, unprotected except for the reindeer skin and their tattered clothes, the seeping warmth they felt presented a curious paradox in the midst of this terrible storm. These winter blizzards often last for a week or more and they must have expected to lie there until they either starved or froze to death.

Sunday ran its fearful course and merged somewhere into Monday without respite. They huddled together, the drift covering them, and every now and then they had to shake it free before it suffocated them where they lay. They couldn't talk for even if they shouted at the tops of their voices the storm ripped the words away even before they were formed.

In the early hours of Monday morning the hurricane showed the first signs of abating. Several more hours passed. They measured the time in gusts and lulls, the lulls slowly growing in duration until they could talk once more without great effort. In the dark they managed to light the primus, holding the groundsheet over their heads and blocking the draught as best they could with their bodies.

'Very slowly the snow in the cooker melted, we threw in a plentiful supply of pemmican, and the smell of it was better than anything on earth,' wrote Cherry. 'In time we got both tea and pemmican which was full of hairs from our bags, penguin feathers, dirt and debris, but delicious. The blubber left in the cooker got burnt and gave the tea a burnt taste. None of us ever forgot that meal: I enjoyed it as much as such a meal could be enjoyed, and that burnt taste will always bring back the memory.'

Dawn crept over the mountain, spreading a miserable, sullen light, enough they decided to warrant a search for the tent, though none of them believed in the sense of that, but then sense was now something pressed to its very limits by any idea they might cling to for hope.

It was 'Birdie' who found it, lying in a hollow at the bottom of a steep slope about half a mile from their rock shelter. Incredibly it was still in one piece. Only the poles were broken; the tent itself, carried by the wind like a closed umbrella, had survived without a tear. It was the moment which makes the telling of this story possible. As Cherry commented, 'Our lives had been taken away and given back to us.'

With the recovery of the tent and the weather again threatening to close in, they now decided to make for home, or rather Wilson, who was nominally in charge, made the decision to return without delay. Bowers still wanted to have another go at the Emperors, but in their desperate state this would surely have sealed their fate. Wilson, who had given his personal pledge to Scott to return them all safely, was not about to raise the stakes any higher in this gambling of their lives. However, a fresh blizzard raged for a further thirty-six hours and it was not until 25 July that they were able to make a start. They had moved little more than a mile before the wind rose again to hurricane force and they had to camp once more. Their predicament was serious. They had only one can of oil for the return journey and, if these blizzards continued to pin them down, the odds against them getting back were slim indeed.

A major source of discomfort and a real concern was the state of their sleeping bags which, as well as being distorted by weeks of icing-up, were ripped and shredded to a point where it is difficult to understand what shelter, let alone comfort or warmth, they could have afforded. Wilson wrote, 'I still kept my down lining in the bag though it was flat as sheet tin and about as warm and soft, but it held my reindeer skin bag together, which otherwise would have come in two pieces across the middle. My bag was broken at both ends as well as two big rents across the middle and the head eventually shrunk so hard and so immovably that I couldn't close the flap over.'

Sleep, so essential for men attempting to travel under difficult conditions, eluded them increasingly. As usual Bowers was better off than the other two, of whom Cherry suffered the most, but the ordeal was beginning to tell on them all and without warning they fell off to sleep in the middle of cooking or eating, or writing up the daily log, heads lolling senselessly forward into the pemmican or across the cooker and they had to prod one another constantly to stay awake. Eventually they started to fall asleep even while they marched.

On the 26th, they covered between five and six miles, the distance uncertain as they got into heavy pressure, stumbling about from ridge to drift in the dim half-light that blurred everything into grey and formless shapes. This was the pressure caused by the shelf-ice coming up against the slopes of Mount Terror.

All the next day they continued to fight their way through similar terrain. They continued marching in the darkness, long after the twilight in the middle of the day had vanished again below the northern horizon. They travelled by ear and by touch like a party of blind men 'for both sound and the touch told one much of the chances of crevasses or of safe going'. But despite this nightmare situation they still fell down one crevasse after another and in one Bowers was nearly lost when a whole bridge collapsed, leaving him dangling in his harness over the bottomless pit. The other two inched him back to safety, the exhausting, nerve-racking effort leaving them frostbitten in a temperature of minus 46°F.

The temperature had been dropping steadily since they left Cape Crozier and on the night of 28 July, as they began crossing the great bay again, it plummeted to minus 66°F. Cherry wrote, 'The day's march was bliss compared to the night's rest, and both were awful. We were about as bad as men can be and do good travelling: but (and this is surely the most remarkable aspect of this whole extraordinary story) I never heard a word of complaint, nor, I believe, an oath, and I saw self-sacrifice standing every test.' Later he could reflect, 'How good the memories of those days are. With jokes about Birdie's picture hat: with songs we remembered off the gramophone: with ready words of sympathy for frostbitten feet: with generous smiles for poor jests: with suggestions of happy beds to come. We did not forget the Please and Thank you, which means much in such circumstances, and all the little links with decent civilization which we could still keep going. I'll swear there was still a grace about us when we staggered in. And we kept our tempers—even with God.'

They were three days crossing the bay, turning out at five thirty in the morning and not turning in until ten at night, of this some twelve hours in the harness, pulling in temperatures that never rose above minus 40.

At last, on the evening of 31 July, they sledged off the shelf-ice and, pulling once more around Cape Armitage, they made direct for the shelter of the old *Discovery* hut. Here they found a new, dry tent, which they pitched inside and with a fresh supply of oil let two primus stoves throw out all the warmth they could, while they sat dozing between mouthfuls of thick, unsweetened cocoa. 'We were very happy,' wrote Cherry.

At three in the morning they were packed up and ready to make the last fifteen miles to the hut at Cape Evans, but Nature, as if to remind them of her omnipotence, defied them with a final gesture of rising wind and drift; a farewell, a salute even, which held them back a further seven hours. But to these men on the thirty-sixth day of their ordeal, such a delay was no more than a passing inconvenience, a flutter in the majestic progression of the Antarctic winter night, whose terror and whose beauty they had witnessed and somehow lived through.

When they finally staggered into the hut at Cape Evans, they were looked upon as 'beings who had come from another world'. They had achieved, in Scott's words, 'the hardest journey ever made'. All that had stood between them and the Antarctic night had been the ragged clothes they stood up in, a few basic provisions and a broken tent hauled on a sawn up sledge.

Forty-six years later, but in the autumn and not the winter of 1957, Sir Edmund Hillary and a party of three men, taking time out from the Trans-Antarctic Expedition, re-enacted the journey to Cape Crozier. They took with them a copy of Cherry-Garrard's book *The Worst Journey in the World* as a guide and perhaps as a reminder of the incredible difference the intervening years had witnessed in Antarctic travel. On reaching the Cape, the party searched an area of several square miles in high winds and sub-zero temperatures. They were astonished when quite suddenly they came upon the remains of a rock shelter. The walls, although collapsed and severely weathered, still stood almost two feet above the surrounding moraine, while between the rocks they could see the faded remains of green Willesden canvas. Inside the walls they discovered part of a sledge, thermometers and a thermos flask in good condition, and a scientific case belonging to Dr Wilson. It was a remarkable discovery and an impressive reminder of the courage and tenacity of the men who had left them there.

And what of the purpose of it all, the original objective of securing the Emperor Penguin eggs, from which Wilson believed the missing link in the evolution of reptiles into birds might be deduced? The Natural History Reports of the British Antarctic Expedition were not published until 1934. In them Dr C. W. Parsons, who examined the embryos in detail at the British Museum, commented,

'Taking a broad view of the facts as they have been adduced, both from a consideration of the unique group of three Emperor Penguin embryos and of the series of Adélie embryos, it must be stated that neither has added greatly to our knowledge of penguin embryology.'

Was it all then a waste of time, an unnecessary risk for a doubtful scientific objective? I don't think so.

'If you march your Winter Journeys,' wrote Cherry-Garrard, 'you will have your reward, so long as all you want is a penguin's egg.'

5

SCOTT AND AMUNDSEN
Poles Apart

Scott was very much a man of his time, typical of his generation and society, but so were Shackleton and Amundsen and all the men they took with them to the far south. Shackleton however had much more of the rebel in his nature than Scott and this he used effectively in complementing his outstanding gifts as a leader. Amundsen had the practical advantage of a Scandinavian upbringing, whose education included living and travelling in a cold climate as a normal state of existence. It was a foundation upon which he would later build his life as a professional polar explorer. But we would be wrong to ignore the broader underlying values which these men shared; values inherited from a scarcely questioned morality abiding in English Victorian society and in Calvinistic Scandinavia, both coloured by a strictly European view of the world. That view may be seen by us now as a mirage but, to those who lived under its impressive shadow, it was as real to them as our own mirages are for us today.

Almost five years younger than Scott, Amundsen was just twenty-five years of age when, as mate of the *Belgica*, he had wintered through the first Antarctic night. Young as he was, Amundsen had already resolved on polar exploration as a profession in preference to a medical career which he had lately abandoned. He set himself to master every aspect of such a life. He began by making solo ski trips across the deserted mountains and plateaux of his native Norway in winter, challenging and dangerous enterprises in themselves, for which not a few of his friends thought him foolhardy. He then went to sea, enduring the rigours of life under sail. This equipped him with the necessary qualifications and experience for Adrien de Gerlache to sign him on as mate of the *Belgica*. It was one more step in Amundsen's

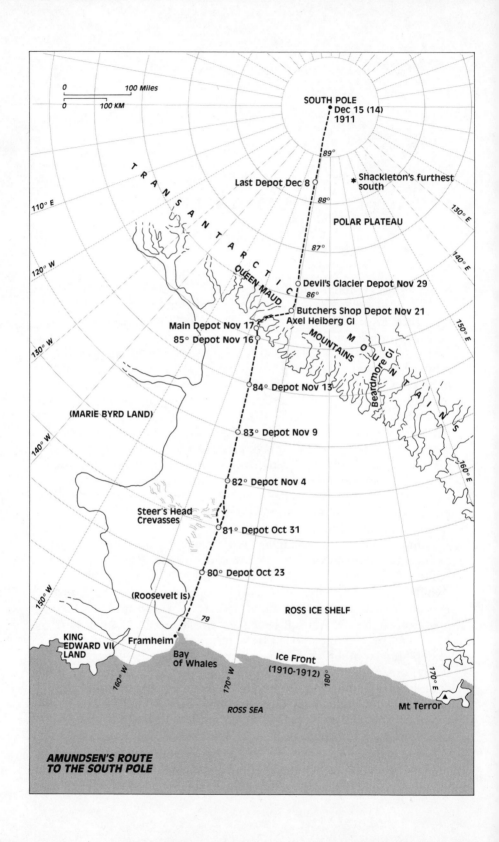

SOUTH POLE
Dec 15 (14)
1911

89°

Last Depot Dec 8 ○   * Shackleton's furthest
                                  south

88°

POLAR PLATEAU

87°

Devil's Glacier Depot Nov 29
86°

Butchers Shop Depot Nov 21
Axel Heiberg Gl

Main Depot Nov 17
85° Depot Nov 16

84° Depot Nov 13

MOUNTAINS

Beardmore Gl

(MARIE BYRD LAND)   83° Depot Nov 9

82° Depot Nov 4

Steer's Head
Crevasses   81° Depot Oct 31

80° Depot Oct 23

(Roosevelt Is)   ROSS ICE SHELF

79

KING
EDWARD VII   Framheim
LAND
                  Bay
                  Of Whales   Ice Front
                                     (1910-1912)

                                                        Mt Terror

ROSS SEA

**AMUNDSEN'S ROUTE
TO THE SOUTH POLE**

T R A N S A N T A R C T I C

QUEEN MAUD

110° E

130° E

120° W

140° E

87°

150° E

130° W

140° W

160° E

150° W

160° W

170° W

180°

170° E

0   100 Miles
0   100 KM

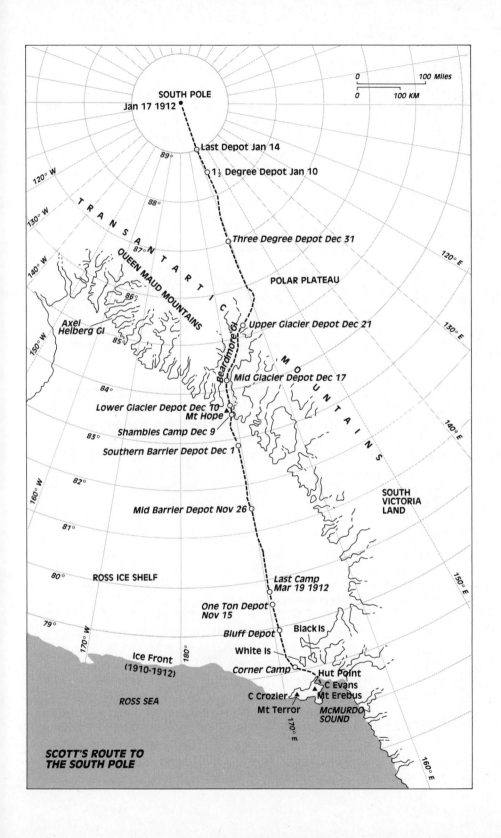

SCOTT'S ROUTE TO
THE SOUTH POLE

SOUTH POLE
Jan 17 1912

Last Depot Jan 14

1½ Degree Depot Jan 10

89°

120° W

130° W

T R A N S A N T A R C T I C

QUEEN MAUD MOUNTAINS

88°

Three Degree Depot Dec 31

120° E

140° W

87°

POLAR PLATEAU

150° W

86°

Axel
Helberg Gl

85°

Upper Glacier Depot Dec 21

130° E

Beardmore Gl

M O U N T A I N S

Mid Glacier Depot Dec 17

84°

Lower Glacier Depot Dec 10
Mt Hope

Shambles Camp Dec 9

140° E

160° W

83°

Southern Barrier Depot Dec 1

82°

SOUTH
VICTORIA
LAND

87°

Mid Barrier Depot Nov 26

80°

ROSS ICE SHELF

150° E

Last Camp
Mar 19 1912

79°

170° W

One Ton Depot
Nov 15

Black Is

Bluff Depot

180°

White Is

Ice Front
(1910-1912)

Corner Camp

Hut Point
C Evans

ROSS SEA

C Crozier
Mt Terror

Mt Erebus

McMURDO
SOUND

170° E

160° E

carefully formulated preparations towards turning himself into an undisputed authority on polar exploration. Under de Gerlache he familiarized himself with the techniques of scientific exploration. By this time, Amundsen had his sights set firmly on the Arctic as his theatre of activity. Upon returning from the Antarctic he went straight to Hamburg, where he studied terrestrial magnetism at the Marine Observatory under its director Dr George von Neumayer, internationally renowned scientist and champion of polar exploration in general, and of the new expeditions to Antarctica in particular.

A few days before mid-summer in June of 1903, Amundsen set sail from the port of Christiana, modern-day Oslo, in his tiny 100 ton cutter-rigged ship, the *Gjoa*. His destination was the North-West Passage, whose navigation had eluded the efforts of the greatest explorers for over 300 years. On the same day, Scott's ship, iced in for her second year in the Antarctic, was subjected to a furious mid-winter blizzard and Scott was complaining of the ventilation and condensation problems.

After a hazardous voyage, Amundsen had reached, by the autumn of 1903, King William Island. This was a sort of halfway house through the complicated puzzle of islands that form the Canadian archipelago. Here he found a safe and sheltered anchorage which he called Gjoa Haven, where he made his base for the following two winters, winters that covered perhaps the most important months of Amundsen's life. While Gustav Wiik, his magnetic observer, carried out the scientific work, Amundsen embarked on a series of journeys which, more than any other single undertaking, gave him the necessary experiences upon which he was able to build the skills and knowledge that would one day take him to the South Pole. Here in the Arctic, along the east coast of Victoria Island, he sledged for many months with the Eskimos. He learnt their way of travel, their techniques for survival, which were derived from the accumulated experience of thousands of years of living in the Arctic environment. Most important of all, he studied and practised their methods of handling and feeding dogs, methods which he was then able to adapt and improve upon for his own particular requirements. If the South Pole in 1911 was ever a race, then Amundsen had already won that race by the invaluable experience he gathered off the coast of Victoria Island in the Arctic winters of 1904 and 1905. Following a third winter which he spent at King Point near the mouth of the MacKenzie River, Amundsen sailed the *Gjoa* into the Pacific Ocean in the summer of 1906. He had become the first man to navigate the North-West Passage. It was just ten years since the voyage of the *Belgica* and now he had achieved the first of his polar ambitions. All his thoughts and efforts were being concentrated on the exploration of the Arctic and, unlike his friend Nansen who was turning his thoughts towards the Antarctic, Amundsen had no inclination to sail in that direction. But for another explorer, the American Robert Peary, who had fixed his sights on being first at the North Pole, it seems that Amundsen's plans would have remained unaltered.

Ever since returning from the Antarctic in 1904 Scott had been quietly planning a second expedition to 'finish off the job', as he put it. The British National Antarctic Expedition had been a remarkably successful enterprise and, in the words of its patron Sir Clements Markham, 'never has any Polar expedition returned with so great a harvest of results'. Few would quibble with that statement, for there is little doubt that it ushered in a new age, when science became aligned to exploration in a flourishing relationship which promised a wealth of new knowledge. For this development Scott should take full credit. It was a contribution which has influenced decisively the course of Antarctic affairs. The gradual maturing of Antarctic science and its elevation to a unique international status owes much to Scott's pioneering efforts to gain for it a special place. Today, it can be seen as a living memorial to the man and his belief in its importance. No matter what the obstacles in his path, Scott determined to give his scientific staff the best that was available. And he saw that they had the greatest possible chance of utilizing the time and facilities of the expedition. His insistence in these matters enabled his scientists to carry forward a programme of research, on both his expeditions, that remained unrivalled until the internationally co-ordinated efforts of a dozen countries made their unprecedented assault on Antarctica nearly fifty years later.

Ironically it was Scott's determination that his second expedition was to be first and foremost a scientific venture that precipitated him into a crisis of divided aims, unforeseen and unexpected, which he was unable to resolve successfully and which led him down the road towards disaster.

But the seeds of eventual disaster lay further back than this. The first serious attempt on the South Pole had been made on the *Discovery* expedition 1901–04. On 30 December 1902 Scott, Wilson and Shackleton reached 82° 16' south on the Ross Ice Shelf opposite an imposing glacier-filled rift in the Trans-Antarctic mountains which they named Shackleton Inlet. They were 270 miles out from Hut Point, their base on Ross Island, and 238 miles further south than anyone had been before. They were also closer than anyone had yet travelled to either pole, north or south. They were out for 93 days making a round journey of 960 miles. They had discovered 350 miles of new coastline, the spectacular mountain range that separated the ice shelf from the continental plateau. These were the facts and figures of their geographical attainment but the real significance of the 'Southern Journey' lay in the crucial effect it had upon the men themselves and the manner in which exploration moved forward from that point. The 'Southern Journey' shaped the future, for it was during these months that Scott lost all faith in dogs as a means of transport. Through a combination of inexperience and incompetence all three men failed to understand what was required of them in the efficient use of dog teams on extended journeys. They had set out with nineteen dogs and five sledges. They returned pulling the remaining sledge themselves, all the dogs having died or been shot to put them out of their misery. It does not seem to have occurred to them that the dogs were starving to death as well as themselves. As far as the British were concerned this experience led directly to the abandonment of the safest and most efficient means of reaching the pole in favour of first ponies, and then men themselves, harnessed to the sledges as draught animals. Such was Scott's disillusionment and misunderstanding that he was able to write,

'It will be seen therefore, that our experience has led me to believe that for sledge work in the Antarctic Regions there is nothing to equal the honest and customary use of one's own legs.'

And later he reflects with confidence upon this near disastrous journey in a passage which reads almost like a declaration of intent,

'I have endeavoured to give a just view of the use of dogs in polar enterprises. To say that they do not greatly increase the radius of action is absurd; to pretend that they can be worked to this end without pain, suffering, and death is equally futile. The question is whether the latter can be justified by the gain, and I think that logically it may be; but the introduction of such sordid necessity must and does rob sledge-travelling of much of its glory. In my mind no journey ever made with dogs can approach the height of that fine conception which is realized when a party of men go forth to face hardships, dangers, and difficulties with their own unaided efforts, and by days and nights of hard physical labour succeed in solving some problem of the great unknown. Surely in this case the conquest is more nobly and splendidly won.'

With the successful conclusion of Scott's *Discovery* expedition and while the rest of the world was acclaiming its great achievements, Amundsen noted quietly,

'There must be some misunderstanding or other at the bottom of the Englishman's estimate of the Eskimo dog's utility in polar regions. Can it be that the dog has not understood its master? Or is it the master who has not understood the dog?'

Aside from their failure with the dogs, Scott, Wilson and Shackleton arrived back half-starved and in desperate physical condition which was being aggravated by the advance of scurvy. Shackleton particularly had suffered a severe breakdown in his health. Despite a rapid recovery upon his return, Scott insisted on invaliding him home on the relief ship. The relationship between Scott and Shackleton had become increasingly strained on the journey to the point where each man came thoroughly to dislike the other. Temperamentally they were complete opposites and only polar ambition united them. In sending Shackleton home, Scott inadvertently made out of him an adversary every bit as dangerous as Amundsen would be in 1911. As he sailed away from Ross Island, Shackleton vowed he would return with his own expedition and with the explicit aim of reaching the South Pole. In an extraordinary display of determination and courage he almost succeeded.

Shackleton was back in the Antarctic in less than five years. Together with three companions, Adams, Marshall and Wild, he came within an ace of reaching the South Pole when on 9 January 1909 they stood at 88° 23' south, less than 100 miles from their goal. Facing overwhelming odds, narrowly escaping death on numerous occasions and suffering increasing privation, Shackleton pioneered a route to the pole across the ice shelf, discovering and ascending the mighty Beardmore glacier and then striking south across the polar plateau at over 10,000 feet. The greater part of their 1500 mile journey was carried out by man-hauling. There is little doubt that Shackleton could have reached the Pole, but had he gone on none of them would have lived to tell the tale. His decision to turn back in the face of success was as courageous as the journey itself. It was perhaps one of the hardest decisions any explorer has had to make but for Shackleton, heroic failure was better than posthumous glory. 'Better a live donkey,' he said, 'than a dead lion'.

Now Scott could only follow in Shackleton's footsteps, but nevertheless those 100 miles remained and Scott took the hopes of a nation with him when the *Terra Nova* sailed from Cardiff docks on 15 June 1910. On 6 April of the previous year, Peary claimed to have reached the North Pole. No one at the time could have guessed what possible connection this achievement was to have on those whose plans had always centred on the opposite pole. To plant the British flag at the South Pole was one of the objectives of Scott's expedition, but not it seems an objective which would in any way interfere with the scientific programme. The Pole was to be incorporated into the overall plans and was to be achieved by a kind of natural progression towards that end. But, if the attainment of the Pole was secondary to the scientific aims of the expedition as far as the Royal Geographical Society and the expedition members themselves were concerned, this was not the case with the general public and the press. They saw the main object as the Pole. The mood of the public in the early years of this century can best be likened to that which prevailed in recent years, when man was attempting to land on the Moon. The Antarctic was the Moon of Scott's day. So, amid great celebration and cheering crowds of well-wishers, the expedition set sail for the Antarctic, via South Africa, Australia and New Zealand.

Less than two weeks later on 9 August, Amundsen's ship, the *Fram* on loan from Fridjof Nansen, slipped, almost unnoticed, out of Christiana harbour. 'Quietly and unobserved we went out of the fjord at dusk,' wrote Amundsen. Although he had by then taken into his confidence his brother, the ship's captain and the two senior members of his expedition concerning their real destination, the rest of the world including all his crew still believed that the *Fram* was en route via Cape Horn and the Bering Straits for her four-year drift with the ice across the Arctic Ocean. In view of the unprecedented criticism and outraged feelings that were expressed, mostly in England it must be added, when Amundsen announced his change of plan, it is as well to realize why he acted as he did. The reason was one of finance. When the news came of Peary's attainment of the North Pole, many of Amundsen's financial backers lost interest in his Arctic drift, whose main significance for them had been the prize of the Pole. Amundsen realized if he was to secure their financial resources for his four-year venture then he had to act quickly, doing something dramatic in order to regain their interest and confidence, sufficient for them to advance the funds which were absolutely essential if his Arctic work was to continue.

On 6 September the *Fram* anchored in Funchal Roads off Madeira. Here, Amundsen informed the whole crew of his temporary change of plan. He asked them if they agreed to it and told them that any man who did not was free to leave. Their answer was unanimously in favour. Madeira was their last port of call. On 9 September they set sail direct for the Antarctic and from that moment they would be incommunicado with the rest of the world. Amundsen's last act before leaving civilization was to send a short cable to Scott, informing him of his intentions.

'Beg leave to inform you proceeding Antarctica.
                                                    Amundsen.'

The *Terra Nova* arrived in Melbourne on 12 October and here the cable was handed to Scott. The effect was shattering. It was soon followed by newspaper reports in which Amundsen was quoted as saying that he was going 'to compete in a race for the South Pole'. Although, to his credit, Scott quickly composed himself and appeared calm before the press and public, there is little doubt that privately the thought of Amundsen in the Antarctic, with the declared aim of being first at the South Pole, profoundly disturbed him. Suddenly he realized that no matter what his own plans might be, Amundsen had thrown down the gauntlet and the world was watching to see what he would do. Scott felt the honour of his country had fallen squarely on his shoulders and the burden was tremendous. He never admitted this publicly and to all intents and purposes continued on his original course, apparently unaffected by the presence of such a formidable challenger. This was as well, for he had a difficult time restraining the angry feelings expressed by the men on board the ship, some of whom reacted very strongly to the news. A few were quite outraged that Amundsen should dare to sneak into the Antarctic in such an underhand manner. But outwardly at least, Scott remained calm and unruffled and this must have required immense self-discipline in the circumstances.

Amundsen's own feelings at this time were quite straightforward, in keeping with the man himself. It would appear that he had no conception of the hornets' nest he was stirring up by the announcement of his plans. In his book, *The South Pole*, a masterpiece in understatement for such a brilliantly executed journey, Amundsen wrote,

'Nor did I feel any great scruples with regard to the other Antarctic expeditions that were being planned at the time. I knew that I should be able to inform Captain Scott of the extension of my plans before he left civilization, and therefore a few months sooner or later could be of no great importance. Scott's plan and equipment were so widely different from my own that I regarded the telegram that I sent him later, with the information that we were bound for the Antarctic regions, rather as a mark of courtesy than as a communication which might cause him to alter his programme in the slightest degree. The British Expedition was designed entirely for scientific research. The Pole was only a side issue, whereas in my extended plan it was the main object . . . Our preparations were entirely different, and I doubt whether Captain Scott, with his great knowledge of Antarctic exploration, would have departed in any point from the experience he had gained and altered his equipment in accordance with that which I found it best to employ. For I came far short of Scott both in experience and means.'

At the time that Amundsen left for the Antarctic, there were three other expeditions on their way as well as his own and Captain Scott's. The Germans under Filchner were active in the Weddell Sea, Mawson was leading the Australians to Kemp Land and the Japanese were also on their way to the Ross Sea. An American expedition under Bob Bartlett, Peary's Captain, fell through at the last moment. Of these, Douglas Mawson's Australian Antarctic Expedition achieved considerable results in extending knowledge of a vast area of Eastern Antarctica, previously unknown. Mawson's expedition is also of interest because Scott had originally asked him to join the British effort as geologist, but Mawson, encouraged by Shackleton, preferred to organize his own venture which was a highly scientific affair. Mawson himself was involved in a harrowing journey upon which he lost both his companions

21 *Diaz* and *Albatross*, old whale catchers abandoned and now vandalized at Grytviken, South Georgia's first whaling station opened in 1904.

22 Tabular iceberg swathed in frost smoke formed by cold air coming into contact with a relatively warm sea.

23 *Previous page* The *Greenpeace* in a blizzard at the Bay of Whales, Adelie penguins in foreground.

26 *Opposite page* Mt Liotard, Adelaide Island, at sunrise from Leubeuf Fjord.

24 Drift blowing off the corniced ice cliffs of the Brunt Ice shelf near Halley Bay.

25 Approaching the Caird Coast, Weddell Sea – the coastline is miraged under an evening sky while a large tabular iceberg breaks the horizon at right.

27 Immediately before the sea begins to freeze the water takes on a curious opaque and oily appearance.

28 Pancake ice – one of the most beautiful stages in the freezing of the sea.

31 Pancake ice forming in the Weddell Sea – the dark shape of a tabular iceberg breaks the horizon.

29 Bergy bits and Growlers carried along in the current of the Lemaire Channel, Antarctic Peninsula.

30 *Following page* Brash ice in the Ross Sea – the result of storms breaking up large floes and areas of pack ice.

and almost all his food and then survived a lone march, 165 miles back to his base across some of the most forbidding terrain on the Continent. A significant factor in Mawson's plans was his belief in dogs and his reliance upon them for his main means of transport.

The story of Scott's Last Expedition after its arrival in Antarctica is well known. It has been retold in many books and in many languages throughout the world and it has lost nothing by repetition. As a saga of exploration and a salute to undaunted heroism it probably forms some of the most widely read literature in the long history of man's struggle to penetrate the unknown quarters of the earth. But of the causes of the disaster that befell the polar party, less has been written until more recent times. Coming as it did, on the eve of the First World War, the tragedy provided a much needed symbol of sacrifice for those about to send millions to their deaths. In the course of the conflict a psychological monument was raised to Scott and his companions which, once erected, stood above all criticism for many years to come. But in reality this was no compliment to Scott and a disservice to his achievements, for those who follow should be aware of their predecessors' mistakes so that they might be avoided in the future.

From the moment of his arrival in the Antarctic, Amundsen's plan went precisely according to a timetable he had worked out in Norway the previous year. The *Fram* reached the Bay of Whales on 14 January 1911, one day earlier than he had predicted. 400 miles to the west Scott was already establishing his base at Cape Evans on Ross Island in McMurdo Sound where he had arrived on 4 January. Amundsen's choice of the Bay of Whales for his base 'Framheim' was a shrewd judgement and typical of his thorough preparation. It was perhaps the single, most daring decision of his life as an explorer. The ice front of the Ross Ice Shelf was an active zone of calving, where bergs regularly broke off and drifted away. No explorer in his right mind would think of establishing his base in such a place—four years earlier it had frightened off the irrepressible Shackleton. But Amundsen had studied and compared all the accounts ever written concerning the 'Barrier', from the first reports of Ross in 1841 to those of Borchgrevink, Scott and Shackleton. He came to the conclusion that while the ice front had altered considerably along the greater part of its length, as much as forty or fifty miles in some places, at the Bay of Whales there appeared to have been very little movement by comparison. Its position had remained almost constant. Intuitively, he reasoned that this stability was accounted for by the ice shelf being grounded in the near vicinity and that this therefore justified him in risking the establishment of his base in the Bay. The advantage in taking such a risk was considerable. It placed him almost sixty miles nearer the Pole than Scott, and it gave him an unimpeded route due south across the relatively level surface of the Shelf. Scott had to detour around Ross Island before he could strike directly for the Pole. Discounting the different means of transport employed by Scott and Amundsen, this difference of sixty miles under Antarctic conditions of travel was a critical one.

Amundsen's party of nine, all expert skiers and dog handlers, landed with 116 dogs, 19 more than they had started out with from Norway. Greenland huskies carefully selected and chosen from the Eskimo settlements, they were all in prime condition after the long voyage. By 11 April Amundsen had established a series of depots at each degree of latitude across the ice shelf as far as 82° south. These depot laying journeys, so crucial to his plans for the assault on the Pole the following season, were carried out with remarkable speed and efficiency. The depot at 80° south, almost 100 miles out from Framheim, contained nearly two tons of provisions. The return journey from this depot was made in two days—an average speed of fifty miles a day. Even for dogs such speed was unusual and it augured well for the polar journey. The two other depots at 81° and 82° south contained about half a ton each of provisions, including large quantities of seal meat, invaluable as a known antidote to scurvy.

Thus Amundsen's party could settle down to their winter sojourn secure in the knowledge that, at intervals up to 230 miles south across the ice towards the Pole, three tons of provisions were safely cached and awaiting their arrival on the Polar journey. By contrast, Scott had managed to establish only one significant depot before the winter closed in. This was One Ton Depot, 150 miles out from Cape Evans and thirty-five miles short of its originally intended position in 80° south. That the depot was laid short was due to the failure of Scott's preferred means of transport, namely ponies, which were in poor condition and constantly bogging down in the deep snow. This did not augur well for the polar journey.

After a costly false start on 8 September, in which they suffered frostbite and lost a dog in temperatures down to minus 69°F, Amundsen finally set out for the Pole in fine clear weather on 19 October 1911. He was accompanied by Helmer Hanssen, Sverne Hassel, Oscar Wisting and Olav Bjaaland. They had four sledges, practically empty because of the depots which had been laid, and fifty-two dogs—thirteen per sledge. They reached the depot at 80° south in four days, often riding on the sledges and averaging twenty-five miles a day. Here the sledges were loaded with 880 pounds of supplies each and the teams rested here for two days. Amundsen now set their pace at seventeen miles per day. This they managed easily and setting off on the 25th they reached the 82° depot on 3 November. Regarding the distance, 'we could easily have done twice this,' comments Amundsen.

Over 450 miles away to the north-west, Scott had only just started out. He had already delayed his departure owing to the inability of the ponies to withstand the cold that prevailed earlier in the season. While Amundsen with his dogs was going south like the wind, Scott was lamenting the breakdown of his motor transport, 'three black dots to the south,' he wrote on 4 November, 'which we can only imagine are the deserted motor with its loaded sledges . . . the dream of great help from the motors is at an end.'

Amundsen meanwhile, after a further rest, set out once again on 6 November from 82° south. Shortly after leaving the 80° depot the party started erecting snow beacons, first at nine mile intervals, then at six and now every three miles. They continued to do this all the way to the foot of the mountains which they reached on 16 November. Here in 85° 5′ south they established their sixth depot. They had averaged twenty-three miles a day, being towed on skis behind the sledges practically the whole distance. But Amundsen had now reached the most critical stage of his journey. In completely unexplored country he had to find the most direct glacier ascent through the great range of mountains that would bring him out onto the Polar plateau over 10,000 feet above them. They had with them at this point forty-two dogs. They left enough food here for thirty days, taking with them supplies for another sixty days. It was 683 miles to the Pole and back, so that even if their average rate of travel was reduced by half, they would still have sufficient means to see them through. As with the beacons so with the provisions, Amundsen was not a man to take unnecessary risks when they could be avoided. Both he and Scott assumed the narrowest margins of safety but, unlike Scott, Amundsen then proceeded to widen these margins by doubling up and doubling up again on his calculations. Nothing was left to chance and it was more than simple prudence; it was the natural procedure of a man who knew and judged precisely the nature of the elements he was dealing with.

Between 17 and 21 November Amundsen's party pioneered their way up an immensely difficult glacier to which they gave the name Axel Heiberg, after a distinguished Norwegian patron of polar exploration. They had to double up their teams in order to pull the sledges up the precipitously steep slopes, which sometimes fell away at more than 45° to their course. They wound their way through huge chasms and across narrowly bridged crevasses with only inches to spare for manoeuvring the dogs and the sledges. Constantly they had to climb ahead, reconnoitring the glacier, trying to find a way around two formidable ice-falls which at one point appeared to block their ascent completely. From one vantage point 8000 feet up, Amundsen stopped and looked back:

'The wildness of the landscape seen from this point is not to be described,' he wrote. 'Chasm after chasm, crevasse after crevasse, with great blocks of ice scattered promiscuously about, gave one the impression that here nature was too powerful for us.' But spying the 'little dark speck' of their tent far below Amundsen, confident and undaunted, adds, 'We knew in our hearts that the ground would have to be ugly indeed if we were not to manoeuvre our way across it and find a place for that little home of ours.' And manoeuvre their way they did, finally reaching the top of the glacier at eight o'clock in the evening of 20 November. Amundsen's ascent of this unknown and highly dangerous glacier was a remarkable feat and demonstrates his skills as an explorer to the full. No one has ever ascended the Axel Heiberg since that time. But in 1962 the British explorer, Wally Herbert, leading a small New Zealand sledging party came down the glacier on the fiftieth anniversary of Amundsen's ascent. Herbert testifies to Amundsen's courage and has written in his account of this journey, 'This to me is the most impressive example of his (Amundsen's) determination in the face of an obstacle that would have turned away any lesser man.'

At the top of the glacier Amundsen camped at an altitude of almost 11,800 feet. Their latitude was 85° 36' south. Here they performed the most unpleasant, but necessary task of the whole journey and the one action which more than any other incites

Amundsen's critics. Of the forty-two dogs remaining, it had been agreed previously that twenty-four, those that were obviously the weakest, should now be killed. Each man was to kill the dogs marked out in his own team. This was done in accordance with the principles of long, unsupported sledge journeys, but it was a task which they performed understandably with the greatest reluctance. The picture so often painted of Amundsen as a cold, ruthless man devoid of feelings crumbles before his description of his own reactions as the killings were carried out. He was inside the tent cooking the food and had pumped up the primus to full pressure in the hope that he might drown the sound of the shooting.

'The pemmican was cooked remarkably quickly that evening and I believe I was unusually industrious in stirring it. There went the first shot—I am not a nervous man, but I must admit that I gave a start. Shot now followed upon shot—they had an uncanny sound over the great plain. A trusty servant lost his life each time.

'The holiday humour that ought to have prevailed in the tent that evening—our first on the plateau—did not make its appearance: there was depression and sadness in the air—we had grown so fond of our dogs. The place was named the "Butcher's Shop".'

However, the eighteen remaining dogs eagerly consumed their unlucky companions and the next day the men themselves enjoyed a meal of fresh dog cutlets. The value of eating fresh meat at this point on their journey, and of depoting the remaining carcasses for their return, was considerable with regard to combating scurvy.

After four days' rest during which time they rearranged the loads, leaving one of the four sledges behind, they set out due south on 25 November in a howling blizzard. Fed up with lying in their tents pinned down by the storm, they preferred instead to set off into the teeth of the gale. The decision to move was not lost upon Amundsen.

'When I think of my four friends of the southern journey, it is the memory of that morning that comes first to my mind. All the qualities that I most admire in a man were clearly shown at that juncture: courage and dauntlessness, without boasting or big words. Amid joking and chaff, everything was packed, and then —out into the blizzard.'

For the next week, frequently in appalling conditions, Amundsen's party battled through difficult and dangerous terrain. They christened it by names quite sufficient in themselves to conjure up a picture of the sort of travelling they experienced—'The Devil's Glacier', 'Hell's Gate', 'The Devil's Ballroom'. Of the latter Amundsen says it sounded as if they 'were walking on the bottom of empty barrels'. They made another depot in 86° 2' south on the 29th. On 3 December they reached 87° south and at last the levelling surface ahead of them looked ideal. With a light covering of snow it was excellent for both the dogs and for the men on skis.

Again, far away to the north-west Scott was still toiling hard on the ice shelf. He was barely past 83° south and making for the foot of the Beardmore Glacier. This was a vast outpouring of ice almost three times the length of the Axel Heiberg and at that time the greatest glacier discovered in the Antarctic. It was a route to the plateau which had been pioneered by Shackleton in 1909. While Amundsen was killing half his dogs, abandoning a sledge and generally lightening his loads all round, Scott was making painful progress with a veritable caravan of transport in his wake. His own and the supporting parties comprised in all sixteen men, ten ponies, thirteen sledges and, significantly, twenty-three dogs which, being fed on fresh pony meat, were doing remarkably well much to the party's surprise. Curiously, despite Scott's deep aversion to shooting dogs he does not seem to have been sensitive towards the ponies meeting a similar fate.

Scott's party came within striking distance of the glacier on 4 December, but then a blizzard with temperatures rising, incredibly, above freezing kept them confined to their tents until the 9th. Wading through snow up to their waists and bumping along over drifted pressure ridges, they reached the foot of the Beardmore. Here they established 'Shambles Camp' where the remaining five ponies were shot. The next day Scott ordered the dog teams to return to Cape Evans, some 450 miles to the north. He was not prepared to subject them to what he felt would be too strenuous a haul up the glacier, this despite the fact that they had outlasted all the other means of transport and, replenished by fresh pony meat, were simply bounding along. As the dog teams turned back, Bowers commented in his diary that they were 'wonderfully fit' and 'could do about 30 miles a day.' There were now twelve men left in Scott's party. From now on they would be man-hauling every inch of the way to the Pole and back.

On the Plateau, Amundsen was moving swiftly southwards. Between 4 and 6 December they were averaging twenty-five miles

a day and on the 7th they passed Shackleton's 'furthest south' in
88° 23'. A few miles further on they camped, building their tenth
and last depot. This contained 220 pounds of dog pemmican and
biscuits, enough for thirty days. Despite gales and blinding drift
they had made remarkable progress. The same blizzard which had
caused such havoc and delay to Scott at the foot of the Beardmore
had crept over the mountains and swept relentlessly across the
open plateau, but Amundsen with his dogs was able to carry on
and now, for the first time, the Norwegians were further south
than any human beings had been before.

'No other moment of the whole trip affected me like this,' he
wrote. 'The tears forced their way to my eyes; by no effort of will
could I keep them back . . . Luckily I was some way in advance
of the others, so that I had time to pull myself together and master
my feelings before reaching my comrades.

'We did not pass that spot without according our highest tribute
of admiration to the man, who—together with his gallant companions—had planted his country's flag so infinitely nearer to the
goal than any of his precursors. Sir Ernest Shackleton's name will
always be written in the annals of Antarctic exploration in letters
of fire. Pluck and grit can work wonders, and I know of no better
example of this than what that man has accomplished.'

They marked out the depot with sixty black flags, placed at
one hundred paced intervals and at right angles to their course.
Shackleton no doubt figured prominently in Amundsen's
thoughts, man-hauling as he had done, so close to the objective
which the Norwegians now anticipated in their conversations.
That there should have been any doubt at all in Amundsen's mind
at this stage seems to us quite incredible, acquainted as we are
with the facts in retrospect. And yet he writes:

'None of us would admit that he was nervous, but I am inclined
to think that we all had a little touch of that malady. What should
we see when we got there? A vast endless plain, that no eye had
yet seen and no foot yet trodden; or—No, it was an impossibility;
with the speed at which we had travelled, we must reach the
goal first, there could be no doubt about that. And yet—and
yet—Wherever there is the smallest loophole, doubt creeps
in and gnaws and gnaws and never leaves a poor wretch in
peace.'

This statement shows how seriously Amundsen rated Scott's
chances and that, despite his confidence in the superiority of his

own methods of travelling, he was not above acknowledging that Scott's sheer determination, like that of Shackleton, might still, somehow, carry off the prize.

On 9 December in calm, fine weather, Amundsen set off on the final stage of his journey to the Pole, now little more than ninety miles distant. They again built small marker beacons every two miles as they went. On the 10th, 11th and 12th, while Scott's dogs were bounding their way north across the ice shelf, Amundsen's teams moved easily south across the great plateau. On the 13th they camped at 89° 45′ south, about seventeen miles from the Pole. That night Amundsen awoke several times with 'the same feeling that I can remember as a little boy on the night before Christmas Eve—an intense expectation of what was going to happen.'

The morning of the 14th was fine and clear once more, 'just as if it had been made for arriving at the Pole,' wrote Amundsen. At noon they called a halt and by dead reckoning had reached 89° 53′. The dogs as if sensing journey's end 'appeared to have lost their interest in the regions about the earth's axis.' They pushed on for another three hours and then:

'At three in the afternoon a simultaneous "Halt!" rang out from the drivers. They had carefully examined their sledge meters, and they all showed the full distance—our Pole by reckoning. The goal was reached, the journey ended. I cannot say,' continued Amundsen, 'that the object of my life was attained . . . I had better be honest and admit straight out that I have never known any man to be placed in such a diametrically opposite position to the goal of his desires as I was at that moment. The regions around the North Pole—well, yes, the North Pole itself—had attracted me from childhood, and here I was at the South Pole. Can anything more topsy-turvy be imagined.'

Amundsen spent three days at the South Pole or 'Polheim' as he called his camp there. They used the dogs, taking rounds of angles and sledging backwards and forwards, until there was a criss-cross pattern of tracks in all directions, all this to ensure that they should stand as nearly as possible at the absolute Pole itself. They erected a black tent surmounted by a mast carrying the Norwegian flag and flying a pennant from the *Fram*. This as far as their observations indicated marked the spot—90° south. Inside the tent Amundsen left some spare clothing, a sextant and hypsometer case, and letters to King Haakon and to Scott. Amundsen requested that Scott should return the letter to the Norwegian King, a request that puzzled Scott; but Amundsen was taking no chances, it was a safeguard against an accident which might so easily befall them on their return journey. Sick and dispirited, Scott came across the Norwegian tent exactly one month later.

On the evening of 17 December 1911, Amundsen and his companions turned for home. They were five triumphant, fit and happy men who, with sixteen healthy dogs (two had died since the 'Butcher's Shop') pulling two sledges, now faced the 900 mile return journey. 'Scott will be here sooner or later,' remarked Amundsen, but he could not have imagined under what terrible circumstances those other five men would arrive. (The remark is often attributed to Amundsen in numerous publications. However, in *The South Pole* Amundsen actually says, 'I assumed [Scott] would be the first to visit the place after us' p133 *The South Pole*). On the day that Amundsen left the Pole, Scott was still struggling up the long crevassed path of the Beardmore Glacier where, according to Bowers, 'I have never pulled so hard, or so nearly crushed my inside into my backbone by the everlasting jerking.' From now on, the contrast in fortune between Amundsen's homeward bound party and that of Scott, still 300 miles out from the Pole, becomes greater almost by the mile until one is left aghast at the difference.

Amundsen decided they would keep to a daily run of fifteen miles geographical. This gave them an effortless five hour journey each day, following the beacons they had set up on the outward course. On Christmas Eve they reached the depot in 88° 25' south. This 'was at once taken down and divided between the two sledges. All the crumbs of biscuit were carefully collected by Wisting the cook for the day . . . I doubt whether anyone at home enjoyed his Christmas dinner as much as we did that morning in the tent.'

Christmas Eve found Scott, still accompanied by his last supporting party numbering now eight men in all, at 85° 35' south. They marched over seventeen miles on Christmas Day and rounded off the occasion with their own dinner celebration which included a small plum pudding, a dessert of caramel and crystallized ginger. This was hardly a feast which could be expected to sustain men enduring the sort of conditions they were faced with. Lieutenant Evans, Scott's second-in-command and leader of the last supporting party, noted that 'the two teams in spite of the Christmas spirit, and the "Happy Christmas" greetings they exchanged to begin with, soon lost their springy step, the sledges dragged more slowly, and we gazed ahead almost wistfully. The strain was beginning to tell, though none of us would have confessed it.' In fact they were pulling close on 200 pounds per man on rations that amounted to a starvation diet. They pushed on, reaching 87° south on New Year's Eve where they established 'Three Degree Depot' with sufficient provisions for one week. They were 200 miles from the Pole. At this moment Amundsen was only 100 miles to the east of Scott and entering the area of the Devil's Glacier, which they had passed out of a month earlier. The visibility was poor and on the 2nd there were anxious hours when they overshot their depot in 86° 22' by some fifteen miles. Hanssen and Bjaaland went back with unladen sledges. 'It was five in the morning,' writes Amundsen. 'At three in the afternoon they came back to the tent, Bjaaland running in front, Hanssen driving the sledge. That was a notable feat both for men and dogs. Hanssen, Bjaaland and that team had covered about fifty miles that day.'

They travelled now as they wished, taking no notice of the arbitrary division between day and night since it was daylight all the time anyway. On the 4th they arrived at the 'Butcher's Shop' where they had depoted fourteen of the twenty-four dog carcasses. These now provided a large meal of fresh meat for the dogs, somewhat surprised it seems by this unexpected offering. A few miles further on they camped overlooking the Axel Heiberg Glacier.

They descended the glacier in two days and Amundsen devotes but a few lines to it in his book although it must have involved tremendous hazards. They arrived at the big depot on the edge of the ice shelf in 85° 5' south at eleven in the evening of 6 January. They had left here enough food for thirty days and had taken with them supplies to last sixty. The round trip had taken just fifty-one days. From this point they headed straight out across the ice shelf for Framheim, following the beacons once again. The weather was mixed and on occasions they had blizzards and deep soft snow but they sledged quickly northwards—seventeen miles one day, thirty-four the next. Depots now awaited them at each degree of latitude. At these, apart from the standard rations, there was plenty of fresh seal meat as well.

'On our way southward,' writes Amundsen, 'we had taken a good deal of seal meat and had divided it among the depots we

built on the Barrier in such a way that we were now able to eat
fresh meat every day. This had not been done without an object;
if we should be visited with Scurvy, this fresh meat would be
invaluable. As we were—sound and healthy as we had never been
before—the seal beef was a pleasant distraction in our menu,
nothing more.'

In fact they had far more food than they knew what to do with.
The dogs were given double pemmican rations, as many biscuits
as they could eat, besides a portion of the men's chocolate ration
as well! 'We had such masses of biscuits,' declares Amundsen,
'that we could positively throw them about.'

500 miles to the south now, and 10,000 feet up on the plateau,
Scott, Wilson, Oates, Evans and Bowers were gradually narrowing
the distance to the Pole. The last supporting party had turned
back on 4 January 168 miles from the Pole, three men now instead
of four. At the last moment Scott had decided to take Bowers on
with him, making a five man party. The addition of an extra man
being incorporated into a set-up rigidly designed for four men
added a considerable burden to their troubles by way of general
discomfort due to inadequate space in the tent, and the extra time
needed for cooking. Apart from this Bowers was without skis, so
that he had to walk for the next 350 miles, the man with the
shortest legs. Their diaries all speak of the fearful toil they now
experienced. They hauled their sledge in back-breaking effort
over a surface made atrociously difficult by a continuous fall of
fine crystals. It was like walking through sand. And there was a
far more ominous note creeping in. They began suddenly to feel
the cold, being thoroughly chilled at each night's camp even
though the temperatures were not unusually low, and Scott re-
marks 'we were all pretty well done at camping.'

On 9 January, Amundsen's party was visited by two Skuas,
circling around them and settling briefly on one of their beacons.
'The first messengers from another world' he called them. 'Mysterious creatures! they were now exactly halfway between
Framheim and the Pole, and yet they were going farther inland.
Were they going over to the other side?' The 13th found them
travelling in thick weather but they picked up the 83° depot when
a break in the clouds revealed it just a few yards from where they
had been camping. On they went, men and dogs keeping up the
same relentless pace—seventeen miles one day, thirty-four the
next. On the 16th they arrived at the 82° depot mid-way across

the ice shelf. Here Amundsen writes, 'We permitted ourselves a little feast. The "chocolate pudding" that Wisting served as dessert is still fresh in my memory; we all agreed that it came nearer perfection than anything it had hitherto fallen to our lot to taste.' These were contented men with few worries, who had time to cook experimental puddings in their tent.

On this same afternoon Scott found 'a black flag tied to a sledge bearer; nearby the remains of a camp; sledge tracks and ski tracks going and coming and the clear trace of dogs' paws—many dogs. This told us the whole story. The Norwegians have forestalled us and are first at the Pole. It is a terrible disappointment, and I am very sorry for my loyal companions. Many bitter thoughts come and much discussion have we had. Tomorrow we must march on to the Pole and then hasten home with all the speed we can compass. All the daydreams must go; it will be a wearisome return. We are descending in altitude—certainly also the Norwegians found an easy way up.'

On the following day they arrived at the Pole. 'Yes, but under very different circumstances from those expected. We have had a horrible day—add to our disappointment a head wind 4–5, with a temperature −22°, and companions labouring on with cold feet and hands.' And then—'Great God! this is an awful place and terrible enough for us to have laboured to it without reward of priority . . . We have had a fat Polar hoosh in spite of our chagrin, and feel comfortable inside—added a small stick of chocolate and the queer taste of a cigarette brought by Wilson. Now for the run home and a desperate struggle. I wonder if we can do it.'

A week later at 4 am on 25 January 1912, Amundsen arrived back at Framheim, 'with two sledges and eleven dogs; men and animals all hale and hearty.' In September 1909, some time before the expedition's departure from Norway, Amundsen had predicted that they would return from the Pole on precisely that date. That they should do so seems to have become something of an obsession, whereby they actually slowed down their rate of travel from 81° south. They had covered 1860 miles in ninety-nine days. The return journey from the Pole had taken just thirty-nine days. It was by any standard a magnificent achievement and one of the greatest sledge journeys ever made.

When the sleepy occupants of Framheim awoke to their return they asked, after some hesitation, about the Pole.

'Have you been there?' Amundsen quotes their excited enquiry

—'Yes, of course,' he answered, 'otherwise you would hardly have seen us again.'

There was little delay, and five days later on 30 January Framheim was abandoned to the ice and storms of the Bay of Whales. The nine Norwegians joined those on board the *Fram* and they sailed away for the last time.

They reached Hobart, Tasmania, on 7 March, where Amundsen met Mawson, who was just going south and presented him with twenty-one of his own dogs, those that had been with Amundsen's second party in King Edward VII Land. The eleven dogs that had been to the Pole naturally remained on board the *Fram*. It was to them more than anything else that Amundsen owed both his life and his success.

There had been for several months a drought in Tasmania, and the country around Hobart was quite burnt up but, 'to our eyes,' says Amundsen, 'it was . . . an unmixed delight to look upon meadows and woods, even if their colours were not absolutely fresh.' On 20 March under blue skies, and in warm sunshine with a fair wind, the Norwegians set sail on their long voyage home. The southern winter was approaching, but the South Pole already lay 3000 miles behind them; a great adventure, but finished, already history. There was no news of Scott and none would come until another year had passed.

And so it was that on the day Amundsen sailed safely away into the wide reaches of the ocean three men, shivering, starving and exhausted, lay in the shadowy twilight of a tent listening to the raging fury of a great blizzard. The wind beat the canvas about their weary heads and the drift swept relentlessly over their tent. The sound of the storm was merciless in its unending, deafening monotony. Scott, Wilson and Bowers lay in this tent, which sixty-one days after leaving the Pole was soon to become their tomb. The daydreaming that had ended there with such devastating reality had become a nightmare of suffering and privation. On 17 February at the foot of the Beardmore Glacier, P. O. Evans had collapsed and died. The biggest and once the strongest man in the party, he had been the first to succumb to their inadequate rations. Scurvy, compounded with concussion sustained in a fall, were probably the immediate causes of his death. Oates, on 16 March, half crippled and no longer able to keep up, knowing he was done for, had walked out into a blizzard, hoping thereby to give the remaining trio a better chance of getting through. It was

Oates, alone of all the expedition, who had written to his mother,

'What do you think about Amundsen's Expedition? If he gets to the Pole we shall come home with our tails between our legs and no mistake . . . They say Amundsen has been underhand in the way he has gone about it but personally I don't see it is underhand to keep your mouth shut. I myself think these Norkies are a very tough lot . . . and if Scott does anything silly such as underfeeding his ponies he will be beaten sure as death.'

And sure as death, only four days later Scott, Wilson and Bowers arrived at journey's end, at their last camp pitched far out in the cruel desolation of the ice shelf, still over 160 miles south of Cape Evans and eleven miles short of 'One Ton Depot'. On 22 March, Scott wrote in his diary,

'Blizzard bad as ever—Wilson and Bowers unable to start— tomorrow last chance—no fuel and only one or two of food left —must be near the end. Have decided it shall be natural—we shall march for the depot with or without our effects and die in our tracks.'

This was Scott's intention as he faced the accumulative effect of his errors and their inevitable consequences. But the Antarctic had other designs. A whole week passed and then on 29 March he wrote again,

'Since the 21st we have had a continuous gale from W.S.W. and S.W. We had fuel to make two cups of tea apiece and bare food for two days on the 20th. Every day we have been ready to start for our depot *11 miles away*, but outside the door of the tent it remains a scene of whirling drift. I do not think we can hope for any better things now. We shall stick it out to the end, but we are getting weaker, of course, and the end cannot be far. It seems a pity but I do not think I can write more.

R. Scott.

For God's sake look after our people.'

The following spring, on 12 November, a search party from Cape Evans found the tent. Inside were the three bodies. Scott, in the middle, was half out of his sleeping bag. His left arm lay across Wilson, his greatest and most trusted friend. Under the bag were his diaries and between the two men lay a series of letters.

'Near Scott,' wrote Cherry-Garrard, 'was a lamp formed from a tine and some lamp-wick off a finnesko. It had been used to burn the little methylated spirit which remained. I think that Scott had used it to help him write up to the end. I feel sure that he died last—and once I had thought that he would not go so far as some of the others. We never realized how strong that man was, mentally and physically, until now.'

The search party collapsed the tent over the bodies and built a great cairn above, surmounted by a simple cross made from two skis—'a grave which kings must envy,' wrote Cherry-Garrard.

Beside the tent, buried under the snow, lay the polar party's sledge. Retrieved from this was a collection of rocks: thirty-five pounds of specimens gathered by Wilson from the moraine under the coal-measures near Mount Buckley at the head of the Beardmore Glacier. At Wilson's special request, they had dragged these rocks along to the end. Wilson realized that the traces of fossilized fern imbedded in the rocks might be of great importance to the palaeontologists who would examine them later. He was right, for they were amongst the most important scientific discoveries of Scott's last expedition. The ferns were identified as belonging to the genus 'Glossoptera' and were the first firm evidence to come out of Antarctica showing that it was once a continent of warmth and life with a flourishing vegetation.

6

SHACKLETON
'The Naked Soul of Man'

During the summer of 1913 Ernest Shackleton took a few days off from a hectic schedule to spend a quiet weekend on the Norfolk Broads with his wife and Frank Wild. Wild had been Shackleton's man ever since the day on that terrible return march from farthest south in 1909 when, suffering from dysentry, he was experiencing the most extreme hunger. Their ration of one biscuit a day, the only thing he could keep down, he ate immediately. As they were starting on the march Wild found Shackleton's hand slipping his own biscuit silently into his pocket. He attempted to resist but Shackleton forced it upon him saying quietly, 'Your need is greater than mine.' The other two men were quite unaware of this and the facts recorded in Wild's diary remained unknown until after Shackleton's death when the published extract read,

'S. privately forced upon me his one breakfast biscuit, and would have given me another tonight had I allowed him. I do not suppose that anyone else in the world can thoroughly realize how much generosity and sympathy was shown by this; *I do, and BY GOD I shall never forget it.*'

Now in a moment of peace in an English summer Shackleton and Wild were together again. It seems from this moment that Shackleton began to plan seriously for his return to the Antarctic, seizing upon the one great geographical journey that he believed remained to be accomplished, the crossing of the Antarctic Continent.

The idea of crossing the Continent was not one that had originated with Shackleton but with the Scottish explorer Dr W. S. Bruce. Bruce had led the Scottish National Antarctic Expedition in the *Scotia* from 1902–04. After wintering on Laurie Island in

32 *Opposite page* Adelie penguins.

33 A wave worn iceberg acts as a temporary platform for a group of Adelies as it floats past the mountains of Victoria Land, Ross Sea.

32 *Opposite page* Adelie penguins.

34 Adelie penguins huddling against a summer blizzard – Ross Ice shelf.

35 Hide and seek on a bergy bit – Adelie penguins, Ross Sea.

36 Adelie penguins line the shore as rough seas break on the rocks of Avian Island, Antarctic Peninsula.

37 Macoroni penguins.

39 *Opposite page* Gentoo penguin chicks.

38 Gentoo penguin rookery near Port Lockroy, Antarctic Peninsula; Mt Francais, Anvers Island dominates the Gerlache Strait beyond.

40 *Previous page* Emperor penguins with their chicks, Dion Islands, Antarctic Peninsula – the only colony known to nest on land instead of on sea ice.

41 King penguin rookery, South Georgia.

42 Mature King penguin chick prior to moulting.

the South Orkneys they had sailed through the Weddell Sea discovering Coats Land on the continental coast in 75° south. From the time of his return Bruce had been planning a trans-continental journey via the South Pole but after almost a decade of effort he could not raise the necessary funds and reluctantly abandoned the idea. When Shackleton asked if he might resurrect his plan, Bruce generously gave Shackleton a free hand and with this 'The Imperial Trans-Antarctic Expedition' was born.

Shackleton, too, met considerable opposition. He was warned that to start from a base which was, in the first place, doubtfully attainable, on a journey that depended for its success on the establishment of a depot 600 miles into the interior by an independent party starting out from the other side of the Continent, neither party in communication with each other, was, in the words of the President of the Royal Geographical Society, 'a challenge to fate which might reasonably be held at least premature even by enthusiasts for Antarctic discovery.'

Shackleton persisted and by an indomitable act of will and with ferocious energy he had, within a year, raised the funds and put his expedition together. The ship was the most important element for without a suitable vessel he could not hope to penetrate the pack-ice of the Weddell Sea. Shackleton found her in Norway. She had been designed and built only a few years previously and was constructed specifically for work in polar seas. Her name was the *Polaris* but Shackleton changed it to *Endurance* after his family motto, 'By Endurance we Conquer'.

Then at the last moment as the *Endurance* was sailing down the Thames on 3 August 1914 the First World War was declared. Despite everything, Shackleton was prepared to abandon the expedition and he cabled the Admiralty immediately, offering to put his ship, crew and any equipment that might be of use at the disposal of the Navy. It must have been a moment of the most acute frustration and despair but he need not have worried. Within an hour came the most laconic reply from the First Sea Lord, Winston Churchill. It simply read 'Proceed'.

At the beginning of November the *Endurance* reached Grytviken, South Georgia. The expedition remained here for a month making final preparations before departing on the last leg of the voyage through the Weddell Sea on 5 December.

There were twenty-eight men on board the *Endurance* which was packed tight as a sardine tin. Besides stores, instruments and equipment of all types including an experimental propeller-driven sledge there were 160 tons of coal for which extra decking space had been added at South Georgia. There were also sixty-nine Greenland huskies. Since Amundsen's success Shackleton had completely revised his views on the value of dogs for polar travel, initiating the move away from the reliance on man-hauling which had handicapped so much British polar exploration.

Within two days the *Endurance* encountered the first belt of heavy pack-ice off the South Sandwich Islands. At South Georgia the whalers had warned Shackleton that it was an unusually bad ice year but he had not expected to meet it this far north. Day after day the *Endurance* battled her way southward. Progress seemed terribly slow but on New Year's Eve they crossed the Antarctic Circle and at last on 8 January 1915 spirits rose when they met open water. Two days later the ice cliffs and snow-covered heights of Coats Land came into sight. They had reached the coast of Antarctica and by noon on the 12th they had passed Bruce's furthest south. But Shackleton was determined to push on as far along the coast as possible for every mile gained to the south meant one less crossing the Continent.

On the 15th they passed a perfect landing place where the snow sloped gently down between the ice cliffs to a natural quay of fast ice. Shackleton called the place 'Glacier Bay' and wrote, 'I had reason later to remember it with regret.' The following day an easterly gale blew up and the ice conditions deteriorated rapidly. On the 18 January the ice closed in around the *Endurance* and although they could not know it then she was trapped in an endless floating world of ice from which she would never escape.

The order to abandon ship came at four in the afternoon on 27 October. The emergency stores, the three ship's boats, the dogs and finally the men themselves moved onto the ice beside the *Endurance*.

After 281 days adrift in the ice they had moved 570 miles to the north, although in actual distance they had probably travelled close to 1500 miles as they followed through all the twists and turns the ice made. They were 200 miles from the nearest land, the Antarctic Peninsula to the west, and 360 miles from Paulet Island where there was a small stone shelter stocked with provisions. The shelter had been erected by the ill-fated crew of the *Antarctic*, Nordenskjöld's ship, which had been crushed in the ice in 1903. The stores had been left there after the men had been

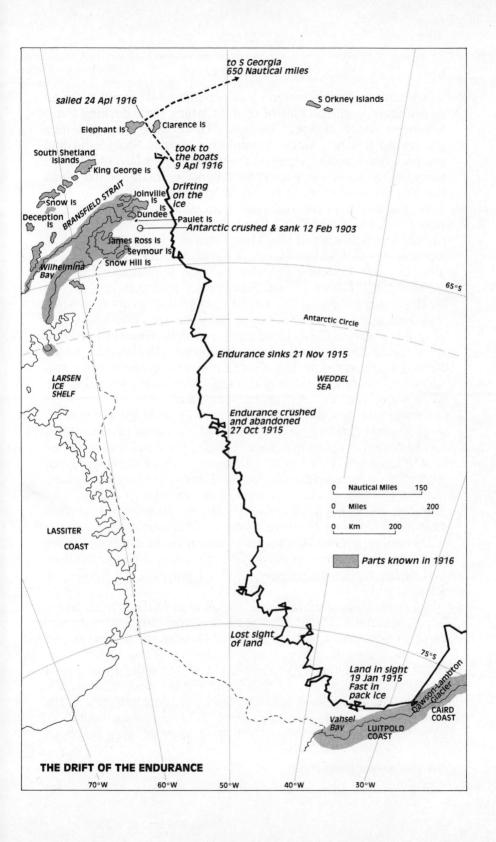

to S Georgia
650 Nautical miles

S Orkney Islands

sailed 24 Apl 1916

Elephant Is   Clarence Is

took to
the boats
9 Apl 1916

South Shetland
Islands

King George Is

Drifting
on the
ice

Snow Is

Joinville
Is
Is

BRANSFIELD STRAIT

Deception
Is

Dundee   Paulet Is

Antarctic crushed & sank 12 Feb 1903

James Ross Is

Wilhelmina
Bay

Seymour Is
Snow Hill Is

65°S

Antarctic Circle

Endurance sinks 21 Nov 1915

LARSEN
ICE
SHELF

WEDDEL
SEA

Endurance crushed
and abandoned
27 Oct 1915

0	Nautical Miles	150
0	Miles	200
0	Km	200

LASSITER

COAST

Parts known in 1916

Lost sight
of land

75°S

Dawson-Lambton Glacier

Land in sight
19 Jan 1915
Fast in
pack ice

Vahsel
Bay

CAIRD
COAST

LUITPOLD
COAST

THE DRIFT OF THE ENDURANCE

70°W   60°W   50°W   40°W   30°W

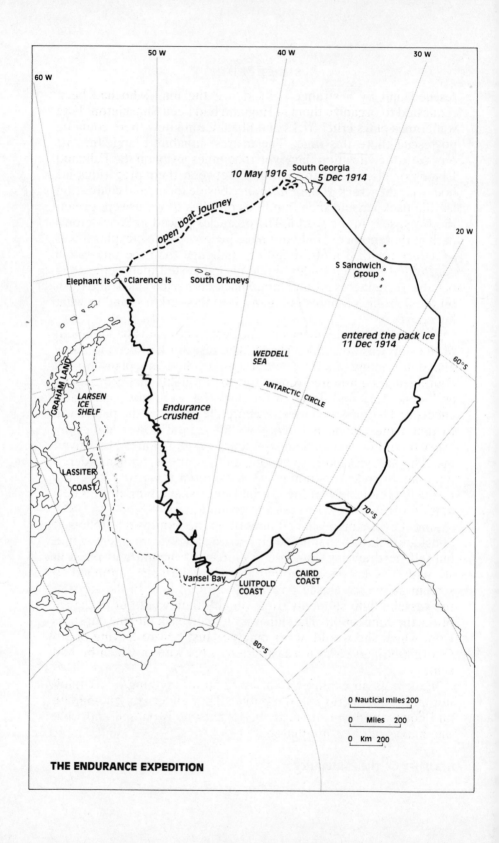

THE ENDURANCE EXPEDITION

rescued and by a strange coincidence the man who had been requested to organize them in England had been Shackleton. Fate sometimes plays cruel tricks and Shackleton knew there could be no rescue there this time. The nearest inhabited land, the last outposts of civilization, lay over 1000 miles away on the Falkland Islands or else at South Georgia. Between their precarious ice floe, with the wreck of the *Endurance* beside them, and civilization lay the pack-ice and then hundreds of miles of windswept ocean, the worst seas in the world. The obstacles placed in Shackleton's path at that moment could not have been worse. No explorer was ever faced with a more daunting challenge than the one which confronted him that night. While his exhausted men slept in the hastily erected tents around him, Shackleton paced back and forth on the floe, his thoughts going out into the darkness and to what lay ahead.

'For myself I could not sleep. The destruction and abandonment of the ship was no sudden shock. The disaster had been looming ahead for many months, and I had studied my plans for all contingencies a hundred times. But the thoughts that came to me as I walked up and down in the darkness were not particularly cheerful. The task now was to secure the safety of the party, and to that I must bend my energies and mental power and apply every bit of knowledge that experience of the Antarctic had given me. The task was likely to be long and strenuous, and an ordered mind and a clear programme were essential if we were to come through without loss of life. A man must shape himself to a new mark directly the old one goes to ground.'

And if ever a man 'shaped himself' in the months that followed Shackleton did, so that in the end no one knew from where within himself he drew his immense resources of mental and physical strength. As he paced around the floe, the ship continued to scream as the ice closed mercilessly around her. In the stern of the vessel a light suddenly came on and then went out as the ice broke the connection. The ship was plunged back into the darkness from which she would never emerge. Just before leaving South Georgia he had written a last letter to his wife in which he had said,

'Except as an explorer I am no good at anything . . . I think nothing of the world and the public. They cheer you one minute and howl you down the next. It is what one is oneself and what one makes of one's life that matters.'

With his expedition in ruins and with the dream of fresh polar triumphs smashed beyond all hope of recovery, these words so briefly written, yet expressing his profoundest belief, were to be tested to the ultimate, and not once was Shackleton found wanting or in doubt.

Within three days he had selected the safest part of the floe, about a mile north-west of what remained of the *Endurance,* moving all the stores that they could salvage, tethering out the dogs and mounting the three ship's boats on sledges ready for the journey across the ice. Shackleton called their bleak new home 'Ocean Camp'. The carpenter was kept busy at this time, raising the gunwales and decking on the boats in preparation for the open seas which they might later have to face.

With little warning on 21 November the *Endurance* finally sank. Shackleton saw her going, shouting to the men, and they all came tumbling out of the tents just in time to see the last chaotic remains of their once proud ship sliding away under the ice which, with a great sigh, closed over her as if she had never been. It was really a relief to see her go, for with her went all reminders of the past and what might have been. Now they must all look forward to whatever their frozen world had in store for them.

Ocean Camp was kept in good order. There was a regular routine of meals at which punctuality was expected in deference to the efforts of the cook and Shackleton's liking. There was no shortage of food in terms of careful rationing and, by thoughtfully grouping his men, Shackleton ensured that the most desirable atmosphere was maintained.

On 20 December Shackleton came to the decision that they must begin their journey over the ice in an attempt to reach Paulet Island. He had noticed signs of restlessness and depression in some of the men and psychologically this move concentrated their thoughts and raised their morale. He decided they must start immediately and to avoid delay they celebrated Christmas on the 22nd. It was the last substantial meal that these twenty-eight ice-bound castaways were to enjoy for over five months.

At three in the morning of 23 December they set out. The drifting ice had by this time carried them to within 200 miles of Paulet Island, and Shackleton hoped that aided by this they would make good progress towards the land. But it was slow and gruelling work. An advance party had to work ahead of those hauling the boats, clearing a path as best they could through the pressure ridges and rafted walls of ice. The boats had to be hauled in relays, sixty yards at a time, and their weight was such that the men had to stop two or three times in this distance to get breath back into their weakened bodies. The dogs came into their own, hauling the stores and what essential equipment had been saved from the ship. After a week's exhausting effort they had managed only seven and a half miles towards the island. Shackleton calculated that at this rate it would take them over 300 days to get there. They were already on short rations and what they had with them would only last for another six weeks. To himself he reluctantly admitted defeat and abandoned the attempt. The remaining stores were sledged over from Ocean Camp to their new location. Shackleton decided that they must now wait until the ice carried them into more favourable circumstances when a fresh attempt to reach land could be made. The new floe he called 'Patience Camp', a virtue which he found particularly difficult but he steeled himself to the task. The name was appropriate for they were to remain here for three and a half months.

Patience Camp was established a short distance south of the Antarctic Circle where they were becalmed for several weeks until quite suddenly a south-westerly gale sprung up and drove them northwards over eight miles in six days. On 1 February they had reached 65° 16' south. By now there was continuous daylight and on some days the sun made it unbearably hot inside the tents, a heat which Shackleton complained of, but which he remembered with longing later on. The deep snow on the floes turned to slush and everything outside and inside the tents became sodden and uncomfortable. It was the height of summer but seals were scarce and four out of the six dog teams had to be shot to safeguard the supply of fresh meat.

Throughout March they suffered a series of fierce blizzards. They were constantly at work digging out their meagre supplies from the deep drifts before they vanished for good. Food was so short now that men searched in the snow for hours to recover the smallest crumb dropped when eating. The temperatures became increasingly erratic. On some days it was so cold that they could only lie in their frozen sleeping bags shivering violently, and keeping up a constant stream of conversation in an attempt to take their minds away from frozen feet and hands. Frostbite became common, particularly amongst the men with less experience, and some of them began to despair of their situation.

Shackleton fought against this with all his strength and spared no efforts in his vigilance of each man and the manner in which they faced up to their individual battle with circumstances. Many of the men said later that, without Shackleton's extraordinary determination, his kindly but resolute insistence that they must go on, they would not have survived, so close were they to mental collapse as well as physical breakdown.

On 29 March the wind shifted to the north-east accompanied by a sudden rise in temperature, bringing rain, the first to fall since they had left South Georgia sixteen months earlier.

'We regarded it as our first touch with civilization,' wrote Shackleton, 'and many of the men longed for the rain and fogs of London.'

The floe was again converted into a morass of slush and water and conditions were as miserable as they had ever been, and now there was a new danger. With warmer waters below and a strong sun above, the two were combining to melt and undermine the great ice field on which they had travelled for so many months. Cracks and breaks were appearing in all directions and soon they were living on a floe no more than an acre in extent. A water-sky appeared on the horizon running from south-west through north to north-east and the first swell of the open sea reached them with a gentle, ominous rocking of their floe.

Dawn on 7 April revealed land to the north. This was Clarence Island about sixty miles off and partly miraged above the horizon. At first they could make out dark scree slopes and high cliffs beneath the island's snow-capped summit, but with full daylight the island seemed to melt away, turning into a huge iceberg only a few miles off, a trick played by the clarity of the Antarctic atmosphere.

Clarence Island formed an inhospitable, eastern outrigger of the South Shetlands. A little to the west lay Elephant Island, equally uninviting. Beyond these two sister islands and across a hundred miles of open sea to the south-west was King George Island, the largest member of the group. And well beyond this, Deception Island, where the whalers had a summer shore station and where emergency stores and a hut would provide sustenance and comparative safety. Indeed, there was a good chance that some of the whalers might still be there if only they could be reached in time. But the thought was impossible. Their floe was being carried relentlessly northwards into the Bransfield Strait where wind and current prevailed in opposition to their wishes; they could not hope to beat back against the wind and sea for such a distance. Their only chance was to land on Clarence Island or perhaps Elephant Island. Shackleton's greatest fear was that the ice would not break up sufficiently to allow them to launch the boats in time, and they would drift helplessly past the islands into the oblivion of the ocean beyond.

The 8th was a day of blue skies and glorious sunshine and Elephant, as well as Clarence Island, now appeared clearly on the horizon ahead of them. The swell beneath the floes increased all the time and they noticed that the slow and ponderous bergs were being left behind. They were at the mercy of the wind which might now drive them in any direction.

Towards evening the swell increased further and the floes began to crash against each other with alarming force. At 6.30 a particularly heavy shock prompted a rapid inspection of the floe. This revealed a large crack running directly under the *James Caird* and between the two other boats and the rest of the camp. Quickly, the boats were hauled over on to the main part of the floe which now resembled a rather badly mauled triangle measuring about a hundred yards on each side. Darkness fell on a turbulent sea and Shackleton was afraid the ice would be ground down into pieces, neither large enough to support them, nor scattered enough to permit access to the open sea. Night after night as they neared the end of their journey on the floe, Shackleton never slept. He paced up and down in the hours of darkness constantly watching for the first signs of a crack in the ice that would bring disaster in a moment.

Just after breakfast on the 9th, the floe broke right across the middle and straight under Shackleton's tent.

'I stood on the edge of the new fracture,' he writes, 'and, looking across the widening channel of water, could see the spot where for many months my head and shoulders had rested when I was in my sleeping bag. The depression formed by my body and legs was on our side of the crack . . . how fragile and precarious had been our resting place! Yet usage had dulled our sense of danger. The floe had become our home, and during the early months of the drift we had almost ceased to realize that it was but a sheet of ice floating on unfathomed seas. Now our home was being shattered under our feet, and we had a sense of loss and incompleteness hard to describe.'

Shackleton had prepared everything for immediate evacuation and he recognized the moment was near, but precise timing would be critical. They had to launch the boats so that they would have enough time to clear the floes before the wind and the swell slammed them shut again, trapping and crushing the boats without hope of recovery. He watched and waited, saying little, his weathered, lean face tense but determined. At one o'clock in the afternoon he chose the moment. The boats were launched and a few stores still on the floe were flung in and odds and ends of personal belongings hurriedly gathered up and bundled in together with their respective ragged owners.

'Many things,' writes Shackleton, 'regarded by us as essentials at that time were to be discarded a little later as the pressure of the primitive became more severe. Man can sustain life with very scanty means. The trappings of civilization are soon cast aside in the face of stern realities, and given the barest opportunity of winning food and shelter, man can live and even find his laughter ringing true.'

The men rowed hard and before long the three boats pulled clear of the main body of floes. They came into open water, a lake of sea surrounded by pack with a great berg in the middle set like a castle in a moat. The seas were thundering against its emerald polished sides, the waves breaking sixty feet into the air. The sight was spectacular and one which they appreciated even in their desperate plight but they had no time to stop and admire the view. Dusk was rapidly approaching and in the failing light they found a small floe on which they hauled the boats. The floe rocked precariously and they moved towards the centre where they lit the blubber stove. Soon food and warmth cheered them so that occasional snatches of song came to Shackleton's ears as he was writing up his diary.

During the night some strange misgiving prompted him to leave his tent. He started to walk across the floe and, as he did so, the sea suddenly lifted it and split it apart right under him. Muffled cries came from an adjacent tent from which a man emerged shouting that his two companions had fallen into the water in their sleeping bags. Shackleton sprang forward, flinging himself down at the edge of the crack. He saw a man in the water and managed to drag him clear just as the ice snapped together again. His companion had fortunately just escaped falling in, for Shackleton would not have had time to drag two men clear and he would have been crushed immediately. But the ice opened up once more and this time Shackleton found himself on the wrong side, the gap widening rapidly and leaving him alone on the floe in the darkness.

'For a moment I felt my piece of rocking floe was the loneliest place in the world. Peering through the darkness, I could just see the dark figures on the other floe. I hailed Wild, ordering him to launch the *Stancomb Wills*, but I need not have troubled. His quick brain had anticipated the order and already the boat was being manned and hauled to the ice-edge. Two or three minutes later she reached me, and I was ferried across to the camp.'

While all this was going on, Killer whales were cruising around in the leads between the floes and they continued to patrol for the rest of the night. They blew noisily and every now and then rose from the water staring across the floe to where the sleepless men huddled together.

For a whole week these men in their three little boats, rowing with a perseverance that has rarely been equalled, battled their way through the edge of the breaking pack and out into the wild open sea towards land. They believed they were making to the west, but a brief glimpse of the sun and a rapid observation indicated that the wind and the pack had in fact reversed their intentions and pushed them thirty miles to the east. Shackleton now decided that Elephant Island must be their haven. It was a terrible week. After constant dangers in the breaking pack where time and again men and boats came close to being crushed to pulp, they suddenly broke free of the ice on the morning of the 13th.

'Dark blue and sapphire green ran the seas,' writes Shackleton. 'Our sails were soon up, and with a fair wind we moved over the waves like three Viking ships on the quest of a lost Atlantis.'

His relief at being freed from the ice was very soon replaced by anxiety about the dangers posed by the open sea. The boats were very heavily laden with the result that they steered badly and once outside the pack, which at least blanketed the worst effects of the waves, they were constantly in danger of being swamped. Lines were attached between the boats to ensure they remained together. If they became separated in uncertain weather or under cover of darkness there was every chance that they would not see each other again. Gradually they sailed close to the land, but Shackleton feared that if they continued in the darkness they might run past the island never to regain it. His courage was tempered by caution, and the risks he took were calculated, never reckless. A sea-anchor was constructed from the oars and they hove-to for the night. The seas began breaking over them in great sheets of salty spray. It froze on contact with their clothes so that after a while they sat shivering in coats of armour, the icy breath of the Antarctic covering their faces and hair with frost, the cold driving deep into their bodies. The ice built up on the boats, lowering them dangerously in the water. All night the wind and cold cut through their ragged attire until it was almost unendurable. Added to their misery was the violent and unaccustomed motion of the boats so that many suffered acutely from seasickness. But worse than any of this was their raging thirst. They had left the ice so rapidly that they had not been able to get any aboard. Without ice they had no water to cook with, so that they were forced to eat their food cold and they had nothing to drink. Exhausted, starved, thirsty and frozen they were almost senseless. Shackleton expected that some would not survive the night. At intervals he hailed the men in the other boats and was heartened when all replied. And even in this extremity of their ordeal some could manage a cheerful remark. From the *Stancomb Wills* one man shouted that everyone was doing all right but that he would like some dry mitts. This banter brought a smile to Shackleton's face and no doubt to the others as well. He encouraged such humorous exchanges and often led off with a funny remark himself. He understood the value of humour in such distress and realized, as many others have discovered in serious situations, that it is one of the great secrets of survival. When a person can no longer laugh, they may be closer to death than someone far more seriously afflicted but who has the ability to laugh no matter what.

Slowly, as though it might never come, dawn streaked the sky on the morning of the 14th. The wind slackened and the high white peak of Clarence Island gleamed in the first rays of the sun. A clear sky overhead promised a fine day. Despite Shackleton's fears they had all survived the night, although all of them were the worse for it and some seriously so. The oars had grown thick as telegraph poles with the ice and they and the surrounds of the boats had to be chipped free before they could set sail. Their thirst by now was extreme. In desperation they tried chewing raw seal meat and drinking the blood, but after a momentary quenching the thirst returned far worse than before, owing to the saltiness of the meat. Their tongues were swollen and their lips cracked and bleeding. Some were in delirium and cried out in their suffering. The gloomy and forbidding shore of Elephant Island drew closer to the north-west. The thought of solid land beneath their feet rose vaguely in their minds. It was imperative they should move towards the coast as quickly as they could. Frostbite was taking hold of them and rapidly becoming more serious; one man muttered that he hadn't felt his feet for hours.

Towards evening the wind sprang up from the north-east. They were still several miles off the south-east shore of the island. Within an hour, as darkness came, huge seas were running and their chance of landing was lost. If anything the night that followed was worse than the previous one. The men huddled together in the bottom of the boats getting what warmth and comfort they could from each other. Violent squalls tore at the fragile sails and the boats, coated once more in ice, plunged about in the heavy cross-seas for ever in danger of broaching by the waves. All night Shackleton remained seated at the tiller of the *James Caird* holding the painter of the *Stancomb Wills,* feeling it pull and relax in his grasp as the seas rose and fell. He had had no sleep for days but still his mind remained active, planning ahead, trying to visualize any eventuality he had not already thought of.

Dawn came with dark racing clouds and black seas topped by foaming crests. They had come close inshore by now, plunging about right under an immense cliff-face. This was land, but so forbidding that it was impossible to get ashore without being smashed to pieces on the ugly rocks that lay at the foot of the cliffs. They turned along the coast, but everywhere it presented an unapproachable face of sheer black rocks or ghostly tumbling glaciers. Eventually towards the north-west corner of the island they spied a small, wave-torn beach. It was not a very attractive landing place, but as it was the only one they had seen they must try and get ashore there. They rowed for a narrow opening in a reef where giant breakers were foaming white water on the barely sunken rocks. On a rising swell Shackleton's boat sped through the gap and beached herself on the narrow shore of storm-flung pebbles. After sixteen months they had firm ground beneath their feet again. The boats were hauled ashore and twenty-eight men gathered there, hardly daring to believe their fortune, the first human beings ever to land on Elephant Island. It was ten o'clock in the morning of 15 April 1916.

Ashore on Elephant Island Shackleton writes, 'Some of the men were reeling about the beach as if they had found an unlimited supply of alcoholic liquor on the desolate shore. They were laughing uproariously, picking up stones and letting handfuls of pebbles trickle between their fingers like misers gloating over hoarded gold. The smiles and laughter, which caused cracked lips to bleed afresh, and the gleeful exclamation at the sight of two live seals on the beach made me think for a moment of that glittering hour of childhood when the door is open at last and the Christmas tree in all its wonder bursts upon the vision.'

Labouring to bring some of the stores ashore they realized how weak they were. They lit the blubber stove and enjoyed their first hot meal for almost three days and at last there was fresh water, as much as they could drink. All were in a state of collapse and soon most were fast asleep in their makeshift, boulder-strewn camp. Shackleton had now gone without rest and with virtually no sleep for eight days. Exhausted as he was, uncertainty over the safety of their beach compelled him to carry out a search with Wild and Worsley. This revealed that during storms the beach would be completely swamped by the sea. They had to find a safer spot. With this thought Shackleton lay down upon the beach and slept for many hours, unconcerned by either wind or cold or the rough pebbles beneath him, for never was an uncomfortable bed more welcome.

From this time until 24 April Shackleton gave his whole mind to the problem of their predicament and the most likely way of effecting a rescue. In the end he had only two choices. Either they could stay where they were, or they could try and reach some outpost of life from which help could be summoned. The first choice offered no hope at all, since a search party, even if there was one, would never think of looking on Elephant Island. So he considered all the possibilities open to him from the second choice and eventually he decided that, with a few picked men, he would attempt to reach South Georgia over 800 miles away to the north-east. A journey in an open boat, a twenty-two foot 'whaler' already damaged by so much work on the ice and by the crossing to Elephant Island, was obviously fraught with hazard. They would be crossing one of the worst stretches of ocean in the world and barely a month off the middle of the Antarctic winter. They could expect nothing but tremendous seas, severe cold and great privation. Their chances of surviving the journey must be very small but there was a chance nevertheless that they might succeed. For Shackleton this was enough and he took possession of it with all the energies of mind and body that he had left. While on a reconnaissance they had discovered a safer beach along the coast to which they moved and here, lashed by furious snowstorms and tremendous hurricanes, they prepared for the boat journey to South Georgia.

The *James Caird* was selected as the vessel in which they would attempt the crossing. She weighed almost two and a half tons and was sturdier than the other boats. McNeish the carpenter set about decking her over with any scraps of timber he could muster, mostly from old packing cases, and he strengthened her amidships with the mast taken from the *Stancomb Wills*. They stocked the boat with a month's provisions for six men. If they couldn't make it in that time, they never would. To accompany him Shackleton chose Worsley, Crean, McNeish, McCarthy and Vincent. He left Wild to care for the twenty-two men who must be left behind to await rescue and live meanwhile under the upturned boats. If no rescue arrived by the spring, Wild was to try and reach Deception Island 200 miles to the south-west.

Their departure was delayed by several days of appalling weather. Shackleton feared that the pack from which they had so recently made their escape might soon surround the island and imprison them. Ice and bergs streamed past offshore as they waited anxiously for a break in the weather. On the morning of 24 April there was a temporary lull and without delay they launched the *James Caird* into the Southern Ocean.

Six men sailed out beyond the thundering surf, and soon those left waving on the beach were lost beneath the surging horizon of the sea. Five men exhausted already by a year of incredible hardship, racked by hunger and by pain, their wet clothes clinging to their bony bodies like rags on neglected scarecrows, now entrusted themselves to Shackleton's leadership in a bid for their lives and the lives of those they had left behind. For Shackleton it was the key challenge in this, his third and greatest battle with the Antarctic.

Words seem inadequate to describe the rigours of their contest with the sea. They voyaged across the ocean to South Georgia in sixteen days and lived through more in that time than most men would live through, given sixteen lifetimes. The conditions in the boat were desperate in the extreme. It was virtually impossible to stand up except by the supreme effort of holding on to the mast. They could not lie down properly because of the ballast of rocks and the food boxes in the bottom of the boat. If they did crouch down beneath the makeshift deck then water dripped on them constantly, so that everything soon became soaking wet. With luck they could sit upright in the little open well if there was room, but here the helmsman had obvious priority. He was usually so cramped after his two hours steering that he had to be lifted out of his position, being quite unable to bend either legs or arms. The sea caked everything in salt which stung their eyes and covered them in blisters, and frostbite assailed them constantly. Shackleton was reminded of the heat he had complained of back in his tent on the ice floe. They sheltered the primus as far as possible from wind and wave and, guarded by two men on either side who could save it from the worst lurchings of the boat, they managed somehow to cook their food. At the beginning of the voyage it was deathly cold and they spent most of their time chipping the ice off the sides and deck. Later, when the temperatures rose somewhat, this effort turned to hours of ceaseless bailing, the breaking seas threatening all the time to fill the boat and sink them in an instant. The size of the seas can scarcely be imagined. They are unbelievably immense even to those who have seen them in their full fury from the comparative safety of a normal ship. To Shackleton's men in their open boat, they were as monstrously impressive as men are ever likely to witness. Shackleton writes vividly of this time.

'We fought the seas and the winds and at the same time had a daily struggle to keep ourselves alive. At times we were in dire peril. Generally we were upheld by the knowledge that we were making towards the land where we would be, but there were days and nights when we lay hove to, drifting across the storm-whitened seas and watching, with eyes interested rather than apprehensive, the uprearing masses of water, flung to and fro by Nature in the pride of her strength. Deep seemed the valleys when we lay between the reeling seas. High were the hills when we perched momentarily on the tops of giant combers. Nearly always there were gales. So small was our boat and so great were the seas that often our sail flapped idly in the calm between the crests of two waves. Then we would climb the next slope and catch the full fury of the gale where the wool-like whiteness of the breaking water surged around us.'

43 Mt Erebus (3794 metres), Antarctica's spectacular active volcano on Ross Island which overlooks McMurdo Sound and the Ross ice shelf.

44 Part of the Caird Coast, Coats Land, named by Shackleton in 1915 and where he failed to land in his attempt to cross the continent.

45 Sunlight and shadow as drift spins off the ice cliffs at Halley Bay.

46 Early morning in Stromness Bay, South Georgia.

47 Moonrise at sunset over the ice cliffs near Halley Bay.

48 Katabatic winds scour down the North-East Glacier near Stonington Island, Antarctic Peninsula.

49 A gale whips spindrift high into the air where the plateau descends steeply towards the sea – Caird Coast.

50 Ice-filled surf breaks over a berg bit in the aftermath of a storm at Adelaide Island, Antarctic Peninsula.

51 Killer whales in the Ross Sea.

52 Minke whales blowing on a calm night in the Ross Sea.

53 Wilson's Storm Petrel, Signy Island.

55 *Opposite page* Fur seals on a breeding beach, Elsehul, South Georgia.

54 Weddell seal.

56 Female Fur seal, Cooper Bay, South Georgia.

57 Fur seals, Bird Island, South Georgia.

As they moved north-eastwards on their course, birds of the ocean, curious at this unknown thing upon the waves, flew around in graceful accompaniment, the little petrels and the majestic Wandering Albatross. Shackleton had his shotgun with him, but the fate of the Ancient Mariner was more real to him now than it had ever been and he was superstitious enough, despite his hunger, to refrain from killing the birds.

A week after leaving Elephant Island, the sun appeared briefly for the first time and at noon Worsley managed to get a fix on their position. This showed that they were almost 400 miles out, midway on their journey. With the help of the strong prevailing westerlies they were making good progress. As a navigator Worsley was remarkably skilled, but he was never tested so severely as on this boat journey. Later Shackleton pointed out that, but for Worsley, they would in all probability have missed South Georgia and sailed on into the South Atlantic never to be heard of again.

On the eleventh day out they narrowly escaped disaster. It was just after midnight and Shackleton writes,

'I was at the tiller and suddenly noticed a line of clear sky between the south and south-west. I called to the other men that the sky was clearing, and then a moment later I realized that what I had seen was not a rift in the clouds but the white crest of an enormous wave. During twenty-six years' experience of the ocean in all its moods I had not encountered a wave so gigantic. It was a mighty upheaval of the ocean, a thing quite apart from the big white-capped seas that had been our tireless enemies for many days.'

The wave struck them with its full force, flinging the boat forward like matchwood. In the darkness the seas crashed over them from all sides and the boat was deluged in seconds. As the wave passed they could see and feel the boat half full of water and in imminent danger of sinking. With anything they could lay their hands on they bailed for their lives. After about ten minutes, shaking from the effort, they felt the boat slowly rise to life again. Nothing had escaped the passage of the wave and everything in the boat was completely soaked. The primus was almost swept overboard and it was several long, cold hours before they could get it alight again. Miserable and wet they were all suffering from the terrible ravages of the voyage. For hours they shook uncontrollably from the cold. Both Vincent and McCarthy, who was over fifty, were on the point of collapse. Vincent, the youngest person in the boat, was causing particular concern. He lay most of the time in a semi-conscious state among the ballast in the bottom of the boat.

On the following day the weather improved slightly, but they were running short of fresh water. Most of what they had left had been contaminated by the sea as a result of an accident with the container when they were launching the boat and they had no chance of going back to replace it. Their thirst increased by the hour, worsened by the continual drenching of spray. The men begged Shackleton to increase the water ration by giving up the following day's allowance. This he refused to do although the temptation must have been great. Shackleton feared that unfavourable weather might lengthen their voyage by many days, in the event of which their need would become even greater than it was at this moment. Shackleton records that the following two days passed in a sort of nightmare, their thoughts dulled, their actions slowed and all the while the torture of their thirst increasing so that even the dangers from the huge seas receded in their minds under the agonizing desire for water. They were in a desert every bit as terrifying as that of a traveller lost in hot waterless sands; theirs was a heaving desert of cold, dark seas, where the presence of undrinkable water lent irony to their agony.

They must not run past the island, for once that happened they would never regain the land. Shackleton decided to alter course. On a scrap of torn chart, which was all they had managed to salvage from the wheelhouse of the *Endurance*, they marked a course which would bring them to a point about thirty miles down the coast from the north-western end of South Georgia.

The morning of 8 May was dark and stormy but they knew by now that land could not be far and they searched the seas ahead for any sign of a coastline. Pieces of kelp floated past and a little later two cormorants appeared sitting on a large mass of weed. These birds never flew far from land and their presence was as sure a sign from nature as if man had built a lighthouse there. Just past noon through a break in the ragged clouds, McCarthy glimpsed the soaring cliffs of South Georgia. It was the fourteenth day out from Elephant Island and Shackleton writes,

'It was a glad moment. Thirst-ridden, chilled, and weak as we were, happiness irradiated us. The job was nearly done.'

The end of their voyage might have been in sight, but their

battle with the sea was not yet won. The coast was as treacherous
for a boat as a minefield for a tank. Everywhere they looked,
huge breakers crashed around uncharted reefs and the air was
filled with the wind-driven spume. Darkness was falling rapidly
and any attempt to land would have met with certain disaster.
They had to haul off for the night. The hours dragged by, time
filled with the torment of their dreadful thirst, the cold striking
fiercely through them. At five in the morning the wind swung into
the north-west and within an hour they were being driven before
a full hurricane, powerless to control the boat. Throughout the
day the wind and the sea drove them down towards the coast.
The waves were so monstrous, the air so thick with spindrift
that they could see nothing, but the fearful sound of breakers
thundering against the unseen cliffs told them that they were in
the greatest danger. Shackleton set the double-reefed mainsail
hoping to claw off. The strain of this on the boat was terrible and
she banged about through the waves, water pouring in everywhere
and Shackleton admitted,

'The chance of surviving the night, with the driving gale and
the implacable sea forcing us on to the lee shore, seemed small.
I think most of us had a feeling that the end was very near.'

The wind had been at hurricane force throughout the day, but
just as it seemed they must be lost, it swung suddenly off-shore
and abated. They hauled away from the immediate danger of the
coast and, as they did so, the lynch pin holding the mast in place
fell out. Had the wind not subsided when it did, the mast would
have been carried away and within minutes they would have been
dashed to pieces on the rocks.

Another long dark night followed standing away from the coast,
so near, yet so difficult of approach. Would they be able to get in
the next day? Their thirst, which they had almost forgotten in the
desperation caused by the hurricane, returned to them with a
renewed intensity. There was nothing left but a pint of filthy
water, which they tried to strain through a piece of gauze from
the medicine box.

The morning of 10 May found them close to the entrance of
King Haakon Bay, a long fjord driving back between glaciers and
high cliffs. There was shelter here if they could reach it. All day
they attempted to get in, but reefs and fickle winds funnelling
down the glaciers kept them tacking about. As dusk fell they at
last found a way through, the gap between the rocks being so

narrow that they had to take in the oars and trust the huge swell to carry them safely through towards the cove they had been trying to reach since morning. Within a few minutes the *James Caird* touched the beach and Shackleton sprang ashore in his concern to secure the boat. As he scrambled about he slipped on a wet rock and fell almost twenty feet. Severely shaken and bruised he was saved from any worse injury.

It was a beautifully sheltered spot and at their feet a little stream came down the beach. They sank to their knees and drank the ice-cold water and never was refreshment so sweet as it was then to these men. They were too weak to haul up the boat and Shackleton set watches to hold the painter throughout the night. While each man in turn watched an hour at a time, the others slept. After sixteen momentous, harrowing days, they were ashore on South Georgia, achieving what seemed to have been impossible, a journey in fact far stranger than any fiction. It was just one month since they had landed on Elephant Island. It was 526 days since they had left South Georgia. Against all the odds they had succeeded in returning to the island from which they had departed so full of hopes, hopes which they saw eroded bit by bit, until there was nothing left except faith in themselves, men unarmed against the Antarctic. And having come so far and endured all things, there remained yet one final test. Help, if help there was, resided on the north coast of the island, at the whaling stations, the nearest of which was Husvik, some seventeen miles distant in a straight line. But they were on the south coast, and the south coast was deserted, and between them and the whaling station lay a great snow-covered mountain range, rising into the clouds and surrounded by crevassed and treacherous glaciers. No one had ever attempted to cross the island, and the whalers who knew it best said that it was impossible. But Shackleton knew that it was also impossible to sail the *James Caird* around the island. If they were to reach safety and bring rescue for the men left on Elephant Island, there was no alternative but to attempt the crossing.

During the following few days they sailed to the head of King Haakon Bay and established a camp in a small cave. Here they had access to the island's interior which had been denied them at the previous site.

At 2 am on the morning of 19 May under a full moon, Shackleton together with Worsley and Crean set out. Vincent and McNeish were left in the care of McCarthy; these two men were in a poor

state and Shackleton knew that any further strain might well prove
fatal. The three men took with them a couple of old socks filled
with biscuits and a few sledging rations, enough food for three
days; the primus and the small cooker filled with oil, a box of
matches half full; fifty feet of alpine rope, and the carpenter's
adze which they could use as an ice axe. That was all. They took
no tent, no sleeping bags, no extra clothing because they hadn't
any, only the wind-worn rags they stood up in.

For anyone who has looked up from the sullen South Georgia
shore towards the soaring, razor-edged peaks and the terrible
chaos of glaciers topped by swirling clouds and scoured by mighty
winds, the knowledge of the crossing made by these three men
adds a wider dimension to an already awe-inspiring sight. How
they did it, God only knows, but they crossed the island in
thirty-six hours. They were fortunate that the weather held,
although many times great banks of fog rolled in from the open
sea, creeping towards them over the snow and threatening to
obscure their way. Confronted by precipices of ice and walls of
rock they had often to retrace their steps adding many miles to
the journey. They walked almost without rest. At one point they
sat down in an icy gully, the wind blowing the drift around
them, and so tired were they that Worsley and Crean fell asleep
immediately. Shackleton, barely able to keep himself awake,
realized that to fall asleep under such conditions would prove
fatal. After five minutes he woke the other two, saying that they
had slept for half an hour.

Just after dawn on Saturday 20 May they stopped for breakfast
on a high ridge overlooking Fortuna Bay on the north coast, some
2000 feet below them, and immediately to the east were the
hills that rose behind the whaling stations of Stromness Bay. At
6.30 am Shackleton thought he heard the steam whistle at the
whaling stations used for waking the men. At 7 o'clock he knew
it would sound again, summoning them to work. The three men,
intensely excited, waited in the vast silence, watching the hands
of their chronometer close towards the hour. Suddenly the sound
of the whistle broke the silence, lifting towards them across the
snow-filled valleys in the sparkling air. It was the first sound from
the outside world they had heard since December 1914. They
started off immediately, cheered beyond belief, but the country
ahead of them was still difficult and it was not until the middle of
the afternoon that they stood on the last ridge sloping down to

Stromness Bay, the whaling station little more than a mile away. They reached this spot with the carpenter's adze, the cooker and their log book. The rope had been abandoned in a waterfall, where they also lost the primus as they climbed down through the icy cascade.

'That was all,' writes Shackleton, 'except our wet clothes, that we brought out of the Antarctic, which we had entered a year and a half before with well-found ship, full equipment and high hopes. That was all of tangible things; but in memories we were rich. We had pierced the veneer of outside things. We had "suffered, starved, and triumphed, grovelled down yet grasped at glory, grown bigger in the bigness of the whole." We had seen God in his splendours, heard the text that Nature renders. We had reached the naked soul of man.'

Approaching the whaling station they came across two small boys, of whom they enquired directions to the Manager's house. The boys did not answer but fled in terror as if they had seen three ghosts. As they walked on between the buildings and through the sheds, the men working there stopped and watched in silent disbelief at what they saw. An old man they passed and asked directions from looked at them as if he had seen the Devil and hurried off without a word. Eventually one man showed them to the Manager's house where they waited for a few minutes, flakes of snow dancing around them in the cold wind that blew between the long sheds. Presently the Manager came out. His name was Sørlle and Shackleton knew him, but the Manager recognized none of them. After a few minutes of brusque questioning he was none the wiser. Only the voice of the man who seemed to be the leader of this dirty, dishevelled trio sounded familiar.

'Well,' he asked at length, 'who the hell are you?'

'My name is Shackleton,' replied the man in the middle.

Some say Sørlle turned away and wept.

They were all eager for news and Shackleton asked, 'Tell me, when was the war over?'

'The war is not over,' replied Sørlle. "Millions are being killed. Europe is mad. The whole world is mad.'

So ended the greatest journey of escape ever accomplished. They had freed themselves from a world without men, only to discover that man was making his world an inescapable nightmare.

On 30 August 1916, Shackleton, after three attempts which were thwarted by the impenetrable pack, succeeded in reaching

the men on Elephant Island. All had survived over four months
of intense hardship. Wild had never doubted that Shackleton
would be back, and every morning from a fortnight after they had
left, he would roll up his sleeping bag and say, 'Get your things
ready, boys, the Boss may come today.'

The Imperial Trans-Antarctic Expedition, the most ambitious
polar journey ever attempted, had failed before it had hardly
begun, but Shackleton snatched from the jaws of disaster a far
greater triumph when he succeeded in bringing all of his twenty-
eight men out of the Antarctic alive. As one of his men later
remarked, 'He was the greatest leader that ever came on God's
earth, bar none.'

Within a few months the Expedition had dispersed. The men
went off to the war and not a few of them were killed soon
afterwards. Men who had survived the very worst that nature had
to offer found death at the hands of their fellow men. But then,
as Sørlle had said, 'The world is mad.'

When the war was over, there were enough men left when
Shackleton announced a new expedition who rallied round him
again, forming the same invincible nucleus. Wild and Worsley
were with him and four others who had survived the wreck of the
Endurance and the war. Together they sailed in the *Quest* to
explore the unknown coastlines of Antarctica, so much of which
still remained shrouded in mystery. They left Plymouth on 24
September 1921 and, sailing via Rio where the heat was devastating, they reached the familiar shores of South Georgia on 4
January 1922. The ship anchored off Grytviken in King Edward
Cove. As she rode at anchor in the dark waters of the little bay
in the shadow of inspiring peaks and sweeping glaciers, Shackleton
died of heart failure. It was 3.30 am in the twilight hours of 5
January 1922. He was not yet forty-eight years old.

Shackleton's death marked the ending of an era, the 'heroic
age' which had begun when he, Scott and Wilson sledged to their
furthest south and the Antarctic still held most of its secrets from
the world of men. And in a much larger sense, and in as much as
any single man can be said to close a page of history, Shackleton's
death marked also the ending of all the long ages of exploration;
ages that stretched back to the very beginnings of man's first
faltering attempts to discover the unknown regions of his planet,
lands and seas that lay beyond the immediate horizon of his life.
Although there was much that remained to be discovered in the

Antarctic, millions of square miles that no one had ever seen, the last continent had fallen to man the explorer, the explorer who faced the unknown world alone, in isolation and with few means and won its secrets by his own unaided efforts. A new age was dawning in a changed world, a brave new world from which new men, changed men, would come to the great white south, with new ideas, new inventions, new machines that would revolutionize their approach towards discovering what remained of the furthest reaches of the earth.

Shackleton was buried at South Georgia in the little graveyard overlooking King Edward Cove and the whaling station at Grytviken. Elephant seals wallow in the tussock close by and penguins strut to and fro along the shore. The granite headstone above his grave reads simply

TO THE DEAR MEMORY OF ERNEST HENRY SHACKLETON EXPLORER

Across the bay, on a rocky headland behind King Edward Point, Shackleton's men built a memorial cairn surmounted by a wooden cross. There was no inscription here, for he had inscribed his life upon the hearts of those who built it, and no words could equal their thoughts as they stood in silence, in memory of the man to whom they owed their lives.

PART III
THE THIRD WAVE

7

ENTERPRISING MERCHANTS
The Demise of the Whale

I looked upon the rotting sea,
And drew my eyes away.
The Rime of the Ancient Mariner
Part IV

Throughout written history and very probably for much longer than that, man has been the ruthless enemy of whales. The significance is that, unlike most other species, the whales' only enemy was their dangerous and unchosen adversary, man. Without him they would have remained unmolested in the oceans of the world. Unfortunately, it has been the whale's special fate to attract the most protracted and barbaric attentions of his most cunning and dangerous fellow mammal.

Evidence from cave paintings in northern Norway indicates that man has hunted the whale for at least 3000 years. From the cradle of civilization in the eastern Mediterranean, the Phoenicians pursued both the Sperm and the Right whale some 2000 years ago. However, until the end of the nineteenth century man was restricted in his warfare against the whale, as indeed he was against his own kind, by the limitations of a pre-technological age. The days of sail imposed their own restraint on what was physically possible. As a result man could pursue only a few species. At first these were the slow and playful Biscay and Greenland Right whales. The Right whale received its name because it was just that—the right whale to hunt. The large Rorquals, the Blue, Fin, Sei and Humpback were all too fast for men in small open boats armed only with hand harpoons and the whales' size, even if they had managed to kill them, would have made them impossible to handle. They also sank when killed and could not have been towed away with any tackle then available, whereas the Right whales remained floating long after death.

During the eighteenth century the Americans introduced Sperm whaling. This reached its climax nearly a century later in the 1830s. The Sperm whale was valued for its high grade oil which replaced the poorer quality 'train' oil of the Right whales, at that time rapidly declining in numbers. Oil was required for heating and lighting prior to the discovery of electricity, while the Industrial Revolution would soon be making greater and more diverse demands. It was a Sperm whale, an albino, which Melville immortalized in the form of Moby Dick, the novel being published in 1851. The narrative gives us an extraordinarily clear account of what whaling and the whaling industry involved in the mid-nineteenth century. Prompted by what he observed, Melville was already coming to some grim conclusions concerning the fate of the species.

'Whether owing to the almost omniscient lookouts at the mast-heads of whale-ships, now penetrating even through Behring's Straits, and into the remotest secret drawers and lockers of the world; and the thousand harpoons and lances darted all along continental coasts; the moot point is, whether leviathan can long endure so wide a chase, and so remorseless a havoc; whether he must not at last be exterminated from the waters.'

Despite this however, Melville believed the polar seas would provide an ultimate sanctuary for the whale.

'They have two firm fortresses,' he continued, 'which, in all human probability, will forever remain impregnable . . . hunted from the savannas and glades of the middle seas, the whale-bone whales can at last resort to their Polar citadels, and diving under the ultimate glassy barriers and walls there, come up among icy fields and floes; and in a charmed circle of everlasting December, bid defiance to all pursuit from man.'

By the mid 1850s neither the Right nor Sperm whale was any longer a commercially viable proposition in the northern hemisphere. In those regions explored in the southern hemisphere, particularly the new colonies of Australia and New Zealand, the same was true. Despite the technical disadvantages with which the early whalers had to contend, their industry both in Europe and America succeeded in bringing these species to the verge of extinction. It seemed then as if the industry had brought upon itself a catastrophic end from which recovery was impossible. In fact it was only the end of the beginning and within a few decades the plight of the industry would be altered dramatically.

In 1803, when the first great age of whaling was in its heyday, a man was born in the tiny whaling port of Tonsberg on the shores of Oslo fjord in southern Norway, who was destined to have the most profound influence on the whaling industry. His name was Svend Foyn and he became the architect of modern whaling, the saviour of a dying industry. For the whales themselves he was the harbinger of universal death.

Foyn spent the first years of his long life hunting seals in the Arctic, but his real interest seems to have been whaling and everything connected with it. For years he watched the decline of the industry and the effect of this upon the people of Norway who depended on it for their livelihoods. He concluded that only some revolutionary techniques in the actual method of hunting the whale would save the situation. Foyn, now almost sixty years old, decided to put his ideas to the test. In 1863 he ordered a ship built to his own specifications. She was traditionally schooner-rigged but fitted with a steam engine, giving her that vital auxiliary power. He called his ship the *Spes et Fides*. Steam solved the first of the whaler's problems. The large Rorquals could now be chased, but the second far more difficult problem, that of killing them, kept Foyn occupied for the next four years. They were years of constant trial and, on occasions, dangerous error. In one incident he caught his foot in a harpoon line. The harpoon was fired, dragging him overboard into the icy water where he nearly drowned. Apparently unshaken by the near disastrous episode, he swam back to the ship and clambering aboard was heard to thank the good Lord for his safe deliverance. Such incidents won him the respect and admiration of the crew, a pretty tough lot themselves. In 1868, Foyn finally produced his 'harpoon gun' and it is this invention which sealed the fate of the whales. For the first time the great Rorquals could be chased and killed. The next few years saw Foyn perfecting his deadly weapon and its effectiveness may be judged by the fact that it remains essentially unchanged in design to this day. At first, the swivel gun mounted in the ship's bows fired a double barbed harpoon. Later, the head of the harpoon was fitted with an explosive charge which detonated inside the whale's body. Foyn prevented the whales from sinking by pumping up their bodies with compressed air, keeping them afloat, marked with a flag, until they could be secured alongside the catcher.

No doubt Foyn's experiments with the explosive harpoon head were aided by the work of his fellow Scandinavian, Alfred Nobel, who had discovered the immense destructive properties of dynamite in 1866, while in England, Pastor Esmark contributed valuable information gained from his 'hobby' of pyrotechnics. That these were God-fearing men and one, as a Lutheran Minister, an earthly representative of the supreme deity, provides a macabre touch of irony to their single-minded devotion towards the means of mass destruction.

Not until the 1880s did Foyn's methods catch on among the Norwegian whalers, but when they did they quickly afforded them an overwhelming supremacy in the industry, a lead which they maintained until the mid 1950s. The second great age of whaling spread relentlessly into the southern hemisphere and came finally to the margin of Antarctic waters in 1904. But long before this, men sailing towards Antarctica had commented on the huge numbers of whales to be seen.

James Weddell was among the first explorers after Cook to remark on the activities of Antarctic whales. He did so during the earlier stages of the same voyage which later brought him to the ominously deserted beaches of the South Shetlands. In his *Voyage towards the South Pole* he makes an entry in February 1823 on the day they passed Cook's 'furthest south', which contains the following description.

'In the morning of the 17th the water appearing discoloured we hove a cast of lead, but found no bottom. A great number of birds of the blue petrel kind were about us, and many humped and finned back whales.'

The discoloration Weddell mentions we would recognize today as a swarm of 'Krill', the small, pink, shrimp-like *Euphausid* which move in dense shoals throughout the Antarctic seas, forming the rich oceanic pastures upon which the great whales feed during the Antarctic summer.

Again it is the reports of Sir James Clark Ross which aroused real interest and curiosity on the part of the European whalers in the possible harvest that might be gleaned from this remotest of hunting grounds.

On 14 January 1841, Ross was at latitude 71° south, exploring the other great Antarctic sea on the opposite shores of the Continent to the one which Weddell had discovered almost twenty years earlier.

'In the course of the day,' he wrote, 'a great number of whales were observed; thirty were counted at one time in various directions and during the whole day, wherever you turned your eyes, their blasts were to be seen. They were chiefly of large size, and the hunch-back kind: only a few sperm whales were distinguished amongst them, by their peculiar manner of "blowing" or "spouting" as some of our men who had been engaged in their capture called it. Hitherto, beyond the reach of their persecutors, they have here enjoyed a life of tranquillity and security; but will now, no doubt, be made to contribute to the wealth of our country, in exact proportion to the energy and perseverance of our merchants; and these, we well know, are by no means inconsiderable. A fresh source of national and individual wealth is thus opened to commercial enterprise, and if pursued with boldness and perseverance, it cannot fail to be abundantly productive.'

No doubt Ross himself would have been surprised at the energy and perseverance shown by the merchants some sixty years later.

In December 1842 Ross had sailed around the Continent, coming within a few miles of the islands and new land that had witnessed the slaughter of the Fur seal colonies twenty years before, and whose demise Weddell had commented on so perceptively. Sailing off Joinville Island, which lies at the north-eastern end of the Antarctic Peninsula, Ross again makes special reference to the whales, and his entry is an impressive one.

29 December: 'We observed a very great number of the largest-sized black whales, so tame that they allowed the ship sometimes almost to touch them before they would get out of the way; so that any number of ships might procure a cargo of oil in a short time. Thus within ten days after leaving the Falkland Islands, we had discovered not only new land, but a valuable whale-fishery well worth the attention of our enterprising merchants, less than six hundred miles from one of our own possessions.'

One is left marvelling at the friendly curiosity of these oceanic herds of pasturing giants towards the strange intruders sailing in their midst.

Ross returned to England in the autumn of 1843. Soon afterwards, the Enderby brothers laid plans to exploit the new-found whale fishery. They consulted Ross and he advised them to set up their operation on the Auckland Islands, south of New Zealand, which he had discovered in 1840 with the following recommendation: 'In the whole range of the vast Southern Ocean, no spot could be found combining so completely the essential requisites for a fixed whaling station.'

In 1851 the Enderbys established their shore-based whaling station in the Auckland Islands. But the attempt proved disastrous. After two seasons the station was abandoned. They had completely underestimated the treacherous weather of these southern waters. Neither, it seems, had they realized that nearly all the whales were large, fast Rorquals, and as such quite impossible to capture.

Nearly twenty-five years passed after the Enderby fiasco before, in 1874, two Scottish brothers, David and John Gray, citizens of the old whaling port of Peterhead in Aberdeenshire, published *A Report on New Whaling grounds in the Southern Seas*. In this report Ross's observations were reproduced and substantiated by extracts from among the crew's journals. Armed with this document, the two brothers hoped to find support for their plans to operate a southern whaling company. The *Report* was reprinted three times between 1874 and 1891, and it was undoubtedly instrumental in bringing about a number of exploratory whaling expeditions to the Antarctic in the closing years of the last century.

In the year 1892, four ships were fitted out for a season's whaling in the Weddell Sea. This was the famous 'Tay' or 'Dundee' whaling fleet, named after the Scottish river port from which they set sail. In the same year, the Norwegian ship *Jason* was sent south, and again in the season of 1894–95. They were puzzled by the total absence of Right whales, 'the largest-sized black whales' that Ross had reported so enthusiastically. A case of mistaken identity did not apparently occur to them. Surrounded by schools of uncatchable Rorquals, the whaling expeditions of the 1890s concluded that only Foyn's methods, using powerful harpoons and the fastest ships, would be capable of turning Antarctic whaling into the sort of profitable business all had come to expect.

Involved in these exploratory whaling voyages was the Norwegian whaling captain, Carl Anton Larsen, who had acted as manager of the *Jason* enterprise. Larsen returned to the Antarctic in 1901 as Captain of the ship being used by Dr Otto Nordenskjöld's Swedish South Polar Expedition which was carrying out exploration and geological survey along the east coast of the Antarctic Peninsula. This ship was the *Antarctic* and after considerable

58 Approaching the north coast of South Georgia.

59 Grey-headed Albatrosses nesting near Elsehul, South Georgia.

60 *Previous* The Wandering Albatross on its nest, South Georgia.

61 Black-browed Albatross with chick, South Georgia.

62 Wandering Albatrosses during part of their remarkable courtship display – Cape Alexandra, South Georgia.

63 Grey-headed Albatross.

65 *Following page* Blue-eyed shags at dawn, South Georgia.

64 Chinstrap penguins at Signy Island, South Orkneys.

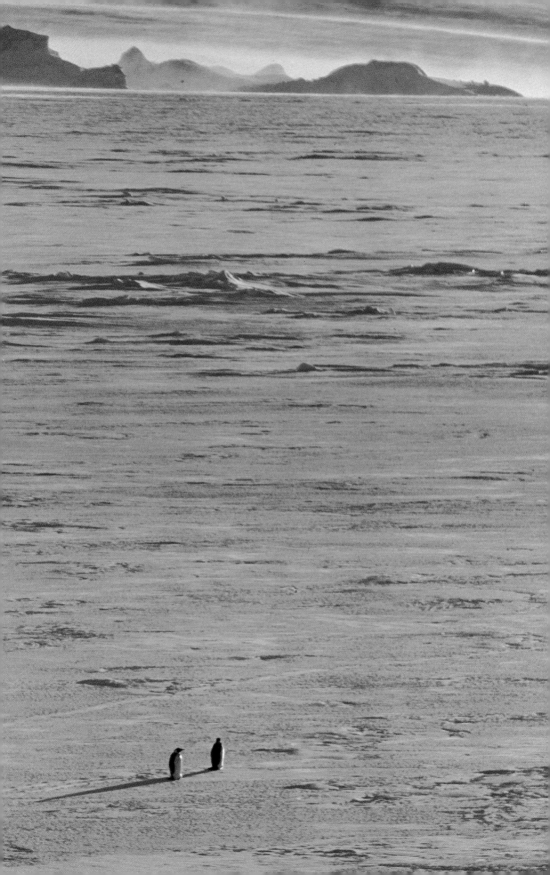

difficulties Larsen succeeded in bringing the vessel through the dangerously pressured pack-ice and landing Nordenskjöld's wintering party on Snow Hill Island. Early in 1903, the *Antarctic* made her way south again to relieve Nordenskjöld as previously instructed. The ice conditions were even worse than the previous season. The ship was trapped and within weeks crushed by the tremendous pressure. Larsen and his crew finally abandoned the sinking ship on 12 February 1903, making a hazardous journey over the pack-ice to the adjacent coast. There, they successfully survived the privations of the following winter in their improvised stone huts. After a terrible journey, Larsen and his crew eventually reached Snow Hill Island in the following November on the same day that an Argentine vessel, *Uruguay*, arrived to pick up the rest of the expedition. The lives of all had been in doubt, while Larsen and his crew had been given up for dead. It was a remarkable ending to an adventure which had involved unbelievable coincidences and providential timing, thereby saving the lives of these Antarctic castaways.

The *Uruguay* returned to Buenos Aires where a banquet was held in Larsen's honour. Afterwards, Larsen expressed his thanks publicly to all those who had helped to save him and his men. His speech was characterized by his delightfully broken English and he ended it with a simple question to his audience, a question that would influence profoundly the entire future of whaling in the Southern Ocean.

'I thank jouse vary mooch,' he said, 'and dees is all vary nice and jouse vary kind to me, bot I ask jouse ven I am heer vy don't jouse tak dese vales a jour doors—dems vary big vales and I seem dem in hoondreds and tousands.'

The ship which none other than Svend Foyn had renamed the *Antarctic* had been lost in the ice, but in that final twist of fate, her loss had brought the right man to the right place and at the right moment. Larsen was about to realize all Foyn's dreams. Within days, he was invited to enlarge on his ideas before a circle of Buenos Aires businessmen. A few weeks later he received their backing when they formed a company, appointing him as station manager. With the coupling of Argentine capital and Norwegian expertise, the 'Compañia Argentina de Pesca' established the first Antarctic whaling station in December 1904. Larsen had already chosen the site for the station on his previous voyages. It was a well-sheltered natural harbour mid-way along the north-east coast

66 *Opposite page* Emperor penguins journeying in the desolation of Antarctica near Vahsel Bay, Filchner ice shelf.

of South Georgia. The island was a British possession and the Company had to agree, after some hesitation, to take a lease of 500 acres for the site of the station, at an annual rent of £250.

The harbour, a small cove on the west side of a great fjord known as Cumberland East Bay, lay in the shadow of several high hills and a serrated, frost-shattered peak, Mount Hodges. The cove had been the favourite anchorage for an earlier generation of hunters. The huge belly-shaped 'trypots' in which the sealing gangs had refined in crude form the blubber oil of the elephant seals lay scattered along the beaches and overgrown in the tussock grass. Larsen called the cove 'Gryt Vik', 'Pot Bay', and sited his station on a level stretch of ground, immediately under the mountain at the head of the bay. The whales were so plentiful that, with his two sailing ships and a steam whale catcher, he had no need to venture further than the mouth of the fjord. A few days before Christmas 1904 they shot their first whale. It was the signal that commenced an appalling slaughter whose perpetration was as terrible as anything man has ever done to another species.

For the first few years the development of Antarctic whaling was a slow process. Right and Humpback whales still provided the bulk of the catch. They were the preferred species, pursued as the easiest target in the vicinity of South Georgia. At the end of the first decade of the twentieth century however, they were already becoming scarce, and from a practical standpoint, no longer a commercially viable proposition. So the war against the whale turned in earnest to the large Rorquals, to the Blue and Fin, but they inhabited the deep ocean far beyond South Georgia and her protected harbours.

During the years leading up to the First World War, the Falkland Islands' government, acting under instructions from the British Colonial Office, granted in all seven further leases for whaling companies wishing to operate from South Georgia. At the same time, and following a pattern similar to that of the sealing industry a hundred years earlier, the whaling companies began to expand their operations southwards and westwards. Eventually their activities encompassed the South Sandwich Islands, the South Orkneys and the South Shetlands, where the first floating factory ship, the Norwegian vessel *Admiralen*, arrived in January 1906, anchoring at Deception Island.

Inevitably the First World War disrupted the industry and

catches declined at a time when the need for whales had never been greater. Oil from the baleen whales was used for the production of glycerin which was a vital requirement in the manufacture of explosives. Thus a macabre circle of death was joined in which men slaughtered whales in order that they could slaughter each other more efficiently. Rarely has man debased his relationship with another living creature to quite such a degree as in this grotesque ritual.

Factory ships and catcher fleets increased year by year and the shore stations expanded to fill every inch of suitable ground. The timeless peace of summer in those remote harbours was replaced by the scream of winches, rasping hausers and the rip and cut of the bone saw. A ghastly underwater sunset lingered in every fjord where the whalers worked. Black furrows were ploughed at sea in the wake of catchers delivering their harvest into the flensers' practised hands. Drawing their knives like scalpels they made their own long furrows through each passing carcass. The splitting ebony skin, the folding blubber, the flesh and bones, the dark interior caverns, the intricate arterial networks that sustained the huge and wonderful lives were reduced in minutes to fistfuls of bubbling chaos in a hundred boilers; being refined for something 'useful'. This was the way the whale ended, under a stenching breeze and a pallid sky, entrails floating in the harbours, a banquet for the gulls and petrels fighting in winged bedlam through the swirling snow, red flakes and flocks of blood everywhere.

As the carnage escalated some managers realized that the industry could not continue to produce mounting profits indefinitely. They decided to offer a small proportion of the profits from the Grytviken factory to the British Government for the setting up of a research programme into existing whale stocks. Under the administration of the British Colonial Office, the 'Discovery' investigations were inaugurated. The Discovery Committee launched a detailed scientific study of the whales' ecology and the effects of whaling on the Antarctic stocks in general. In 1924 they purchased the old *Discovery* that Captain Scott had used on his first expedition in 1901. They spent the next two years working in the Southern Ocean with such success that in 1927 the ship was replaced with a new vessel, *Discovery II*, built specifically for marine biological research. *Discovery II* arrived at South Georgia in January 1930 where, at the entrance to Larsen's 'Pot Bay' now renamed King Edward Cove, the Discovery Committee had established a laboratory on the shore facing the Grytviken whaling station. The choice of location was quite deliberate, intended by the scientists to be of mutual benefit to both themselves and the whalers. In the event, it was not. Had the whalers heeded the advice and the warnings which emerged from the scientific findings, then both whales and whaling would have survived. In the end, alarmed at the increasing decline of both whales and profits, the industry did decide to take some action but it was too little and too late.

When I first arrived at Grytviken there was an old Norwegian caretaker living in the former Manager's house. He spent his days wandering silently around the buildings lost in a world of his own. For me the old man embodied the conscience of the past. Like a ghost, he seemed to be waiting for the day of the whale's return yet knowing it would never come. What thoughts, what images were in his mind, I do not know. What sounds he heard on his daily walks, rattling the locks, testing the doors and windows of those buildings he took with him to the grave. On my return to Grytviken he was no longer there. His vigil had ended and no whales had come back, except maybe in his imagination. He had returned to Norway to live out his remaining years among the mountains and fjords of his homeland.

The 1930s saw the gradual transition from shore-operated whaling stations to 'pelagic' or oceanic whaling. This was carried out by an expanding fleet of factory ships, served by their attendant fleets of catchers. They followed the whale herds through the open sea and then along the ice-edge as the whales passed southwards and then north again on their seasonal migration from the tropics and their equatorial breeding grounds. This increased mobility of the whalers made devastating inroads into the remaining whale stocks.

The idea of pelagic whaling originated in 1912 when a floating factory ship was prevented from reaching her usual harbour in the South Orkneys by heavy pack-ice. Her captain therefore decided to work his ship along the ice-edge and during that season formulated the idea of fitting the ship with a stern slipway, up which the largest Rorquals might be winched with relative ease and safety to the flensing deck. Some years passed before his idea was tested, due largely to the fact that there was no pressure at that time to move out into the open sea. But from the mid-1920s onwards, more and more ships left the shelter of the Antarctic islands for this new, highly profitable style of whaling. Initially, old ships were requisitioned and modified, but later new ships were built incorporating the stern slipways.

In 1923 Larsen led a successful expedition aboard the new factory ship, *Sir James Clark Ross*. They spent the first season in the Ross Sea and in the following two seasons the ship more than doubled its oil production. This gave a much needed boost, bringing pelagic whaling in on a grand scale. By 1930, whaling had spread from its modest shore-based beginnings at South Georgia to become a highly efficient, ocean-going industry encompassing the whole Southern Ocean.

Throughout the 1930s the slaughter increased remorselessly. By 1934 the average seasonal toll exceeded 30,000 and the decade of unprecedented killing that was to follow opened with a record catch of 40,874 whales in a single season. In the 1937–38 season almost 55,000 whales were killed. This horrific total was achieved by thirty-one factory ships and 256 catchers, while the 1931 total had employed forty-one factory ships and slightly fewer catchers. The efficiency of the industry was increasingly apparent, but another crucial and alarming feature was becoming evident at the same time. More whales were being killed, but less oil was being produced, while the proportion of Blue whales, the primary target, had slipped from eighty percent of the total catch to less than sixty.

The writing was clearly on the wall, and yet man continued to hunt down the last scattered remnants of the once great whale herds. As a consequence he was forced to turn from the largest species towards the smaller ones. In the 1970s the Soviet Union began operating a 32,000 ton factory ship, *Sovetskaya Rossiya*. This was the largest and most sophisticated vessel of its type in the world and, with the aid of every possible technological development including helicopter spotting teams, the whales although widely scattered stood little chance of going undetected. In 1931 over 1000 Blue whales were destroyed at South Georgia alone. In the season prior to the abandonment of Grytviken in 1965, the industry managed to find and process only four. With this they realized that they could no longer go on with the killing. They closed the factory and 'protected' the Blue whale after fighting against such legislation for years.

In 1946, the United Nations set up the International Whaling Commission. It is an impressive sounding title but the Commission was sadly lacking in the ability to carry out the legislation its scientists recommended. Most of the appeals made to its members, the whalers themselves, by the scientists who had served on the Commission's behalf, were either ignored or treated with contempt. The Commission introduced the Blue Whale Unit (BWU), replaced by species quotas in 1974, by which it sought to limit the catch by a unit of oil production rather than by the number of whales killed. One Blue whale was then supposed to represent two Fin whales, two-and-a-half Humpbacks, six Sei whales and so on. A total quota was fixed for each season and, as soon as this was reached, whaling, in theory, would cease. But these general quota limits proved useless. A species limit should have been introduced long before the Blue whale had been hunted to the verge of extinction, and the same pattern was repeated as the whalers selected their 'replacement species'—the next one down the line in order of size. Yet, in retrospect, none of this would have had the desired effect, for the seasonal quotas set by the whaling industry itself were in every instance too high. The advice of the Commission's scientists went unheeded and they had no actual authority with which to control the whalers' independent, commercially biased assumptions.

By the early 1960s the statistics available to the scientist were prodigious. They came not only from their own long and patient research, but also from the catch summaries being received by the Central Bureau of Whaling Statistics based at Sandjefjord, Norway. These summaries were transmitted weekly during the season from the whaling fleets in the Antarctic. From this highly organized information network, it was possible for the scientists to predict with extreme accuracy the actual quota that would result from the coming season's whaling. For instance, in 1963 the whalers set their quota at 10,000 Blue whale units, but the scientists insisted that they would achieve at an absolute maximum 8500 units. The result was 8429. By this time of course, it was the Fin whale that had to provide the bulk of the BWU. The scientists again predicted on the results of the '63–64 season's catch, that the actual number of Fin whales caught the following season would be 14,000. It was 13,853. Obviously such accuracy was more than the inspired guesswork the scientists were accused of by some unscrupulous members of the industry with a large stake in the diminishing profits.

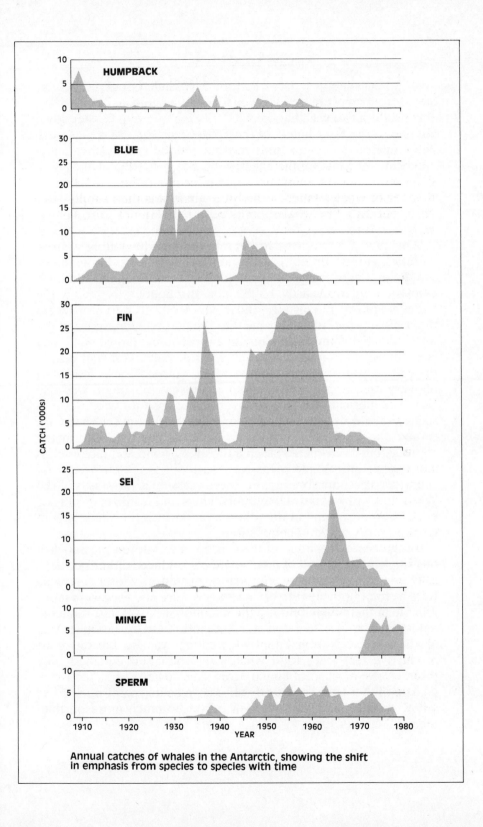

Annual catches of whales in the Antarctic, showing the shift
in emphasis from species to species with time

In the decade after 1955, the total Fin whale population plummeted from an estimated 110,000 to less than 40,000. The predictable result of this was that the whalers went one step further down the line to the Sei whales. In the 1963–64 season, 8695 Seis were killed against an upper limit recommendation of 8400, already indicating a decline for this species on an estimated total of 20,000. In the same season, the Blue whale went unmolested for the first time in sixty years. But the moratorium had come pitifully late. Throughout the entire world only eight Blue whales were sighted in that season.

Whatever the reasons had been in the past for killing whales, there was no longer any justification for continuing the slaughter a moment longer. The vested interests of a declining but stubborn industry were not easily halted and throughout the 1970s the killing went on. Financially, those who stood to lose more were the companies selling whale meat to the pet food industry and the fur trade, but many other manufacturers complained that they were at risk if whaling ceased. High grade baleen oil was used in the production of paints, soaps and margarine; lower grades of oil were used widely in the tanning industry. Whale oil was also used as a lubricant for machinery and as a base for wax products such as shoe-polish and polishes for everything from car bodywork to household surfaces. Oil from Sperm whales was used in the manufacture of cosmetics, such as lipsticks, hand and face creams and suntan oil. Whale meat was, and still is, eaten in several countries, most notably Japan, where it assumes the status of the Westerner's roast beef. Detergents, glues and fertilizers from the bones were just some of the other uses to which the whale was so ignominiously made to contribute.

By the late 1960s none of these products required the sacrifice of a single whale for all of them could be produced either synthetically or from a naturally occurring substance. Moreover these were becoming cheaper to obtain and produce and they were more reliable in their availability to the manufacturer. Of oil-producing industries listed by the Food and Agriculture Organization (FAO) of the United Nations, that of whaling was by far the least productive. In 1968, total whale oil production equalled only three-tenths of that obtained from sun-flower seeds, and one quarter of that from rape seed, while soya beans, palm-nuts, corn, tallow, herring and anchovies all produced much more oil than the whaling industry.

In 1978 a unique protest by an unfamiliar category of Russian dissident was received by the British press. In an open letter, an anonymous Soviet scientist accused the Russian whalers of a 'crime against nature' in their violation of the current quotas established under the International Convention for the Regulation of Whaling. The letter, typed in Russian on a Russian character typewriter, stated that 'The Captain . . . and the National Inspectorate are breaking the laws of the whaling industry. As a result of the 1977/78 season there were obtained higher than the quota of whales: 1095 Sperm whales, 167 Sei whales, 654 Minke whales. And they are similarly hunting young animals and females accompanying their young. Scientists must prevent the cruelties. Stop the murderous crime against nature. I ask you to print my letter in the press.' It was signed 'a scientific worker' and posted in the Canary Islands, where the Russian whaling fleet docked for a few days on their way home to the port of Odessa on the Black Sea. The accusations of this scientist illustrated how flagrantly the rules of the Commission were being violated under a monitoring system that could be so easily abused. Russia and Japan, the 'big two' whaling nations, are both members of the IWC and the monitoring system was operated by an exchange of observers from each country aboard the other's ships. The figures to which the Russian scientist referred amounted to a total overkill of almost 2000 whales on a combined IWC Russian Japanese quota of 12,369 whales for the 1978 season. But if the two nations were conniving with each other, then the overkill was at least 4000 whales a season. This sort of illegal action represented a serious escalation of the threat already posed to the remaining whale stocks, which were arrived at on the so-called 'true' returns.

It was this and other similar evidence in the 1970s that prompted conservation organizations worldwide to re-double their efforts on an issue which they had been fighting for years without success. The World Wildlife Fund, The International Union for the Conservation of Nature, Friends of the Earth and Greenpeace began campaigning vigorously for a total moratorium on all whaling. Greenpeace in particular took the fight out of the conference room onto the high seas where, in a series of dramatic non-violent confrontations with the whalers, they exposed to the world the iniquities of the continuing slaughter. They were the 'shock troops' of a revitalized conservation movement and nothing like it had been seen before. Public opinion was outraged and this was mobilized in a number of peaceful but vociferous demonstrations. The media in particular played a crucial role in promoting what was seen as a kind of 'David and Goliath' battle, except that David was without even his catapult. This tactic of taking direct action at sea whilst intensifying the political battle in the conference room introduced a powerful new factor into the lobbying process which was being undertaken inside the meetings of the International Whaling Commission. During this time first Fin whales were completely protected in the Antarctic in 1976 and two years later this protection was extended to Sei whales. Despite Commission regulations that required a three-quarters majority in favour of any protective legislation the conservationists persuaded a growing number of countries sympathetic to their cause, and not engaged in whaling themselves, to join the Commission. At the 1982 meeting this tactic paid off when the Commission voted to suspend all commercial whaling from 1986. Despite this moratorium, 5569 whales, mainly Minkes, were killed in the 1985–86 season. IWC countries had voted 25 to 1 to give protection to Minke whales.

On the face of it this was an unprecedented victory for the conservationists, but they are under no illusions concerning the apocryphal nature of the moratorium. A nation need not accept the majority vote—it can simply leave the Commission, which has no legal powers of enforcement. Several nations, whilst agreeing to the moratorium in principle, have insisted on their own scheduling. Thus the Soviet Union said it would cease whaling in 1987, the Japanese the following year. Norway has said it will not stop until 1990. However, both Norway and Iceland, which stopped commercial whaling in the early 1980s, have said they will continue with 'scientific' whaling. This is allowed under the terms of the Commission and purports to allow whales to be caught for scientific analysis and research. Unfortunately scientific whaling provides a convenient loophole through which any nation may continue to kill whales whether for scientific purposes or otherwise. Greenpeace argues that further research demanding whale carcasses is unnecessary. The scientists have already had sixty years of that form of research and there is far more interesting work to be done with living creatures. The moratorium, which lasts only for a period of ten years, is far from the intended victory the conservationists are seeking. Faced with such an unpredictable future which rests on such a tenuous agreement, the conservationists will have to remain constantly vigilant and maintain pressure within the Commission.

As long as man continues to view any recovery in whale stocks as a signal that commercial whaling may again become practicable the whales will never be safe, their continued existence permanently in doubt. The problem ultimately is a moral and ethical one, requiring of man a sensitivity and range of values which, sadly, the savage, self-interested nature of his past does not leave him well-equipped to undertake. The desire for this change of heart which is expressed by many people is, on the other hand, our only source of hope, and we must continue to believe in its transformative power.

Towards the end of the Second World War, when the last major phase of whaling began, there were around 100,000 Blue whales living in Antarctic waters. By 1970, twenty-five years later, American scientists estimated that probably no more than 500 remained. That certainly constituted commercial extinction and, because of the whale's particular life cycle, characterized by its slow pattern of development, it cannot be said with any certainty that such a small remnant population will not eventually disappear for ever, for there are no signs as yet of a recovery. In the last fifty years over two million whales have been slaughtered and beyond that millions more, but the numbers become meaningless when all we have left is a few hundred or a few thousand of any particular species.

The Blue whale is the largest creature to have inhabited the earth since the dawn of life. Even during the age of the great reptiles like Brontosaurus and Brachiosaurus, nothing approached the proportions of the Blue whale. It would require a herd of twenty-five African elephants, the largest land animal in the world today, to equal its mature weight—an average one hundred and twenty tons. But impressive as these statistics are, there are reasons for being concerned at the plight of the whales which are far closer to the heart of man. Living in their dark, oceanic world, separated from us in a place man had always regarded with fear and surrounded with myth and superstition, our age-old hostility has prevented us from enjoying any friendly association with them until very recently. It seems ironic that, as the species comes perilously close to extinction, a few men are making the first tentative moves towards understanding their remarkable ocean-going life.

Whales, like us, are warm-blooded animals. They breathe the same air that we depend on. They have a mouth, two eyes and two ears. The eyes are not very sensitive, picking up light and objects in general rather than in detail, but the ears are wonderfully constructed, being their principal means of navigation, locating food, maintaining contact with each other and providing advance warning of any danger. The ears are only slightly less sensitive than those of the bat—the most sensitive ear in the animal kingdom. Whales mate and reproduce their young in the same way as man and, judging from eye-witness accounts, the ritual of love-making means as much to them as it does to us. The cows suckle their young calves, protect them from danger and generally show a degree of devotion comparable to the human mothering instinct. It was an instinct which during the early days of whaling often proved fatal. The cow will not leave her calf even when it is dead. Learning this, the whalers would, where possible, kill the calf first, in order to be sure of securing the real target, the mother.

Sound recordings made of Humpbacks, Right and Blue whales have been particularly rewarding. The sounds are hauntingly beautiful to the human ear, but what the whales are communicating to each other across great stretches of ocean remains a mystery. The whales' 'songs', as they have been appropriately described, have been heard by man since he first ventured across the oceans. Ships' logs contain references to strange sounds whose sources could not be identified and as such they were incorporated into the mythology of the sea. Awoken from their weary sleep the sailors in that earlier, quieter age of sail heard above the creaking timbers and the wash of the sea those ethereal songs coming to them out of the unknown. How much more they might have feared and maybe respected those sounds had they realized that beneath them the creatures that they thought of as mindless beasts, fit only for their cargo of oil, were everywhere in intelligent communication with their fellows.

Whatever memorial man might choose for the whale, none can ever exceed that of his handiwork now littering the deserted shores of South Georgia. The beaches, cluttered with the bleached and weathered bones of whales, remind one of those other cemeteries with their massed white crosses; the rotting, wind-tormented buildings murmuring across a wasteland of corrugated rust; silent flensing plants that echo to the solitary footstep; the floating docks half sunk with cranes flung skyward like the spires of wrecked cathedrals; catchers stranded on their slipways or funnel-deep in mud and weed; the blubber boilers, bone cookers, separators and fertilizer plants; the whole machinery of death surrounded by walls of empty-bellied tanks, whose booming to the touch sounds like the tolling of funereal bells. And the fluttering of a curtain with its faded flowers by a plastic rose above a table where the meal still waits, abandoned beside a window left open more than twenty years ago. These are the images which speak of man's destruction, his true epitaph to the whale, contained in these disfigurements of iron and steel, of cloth and bone and botched upon a landscape of incomparable beauty. Surrounded by these things I have felt the immensity of the tragedy played out between men and whales, the enormity of the crime against nature and the shame such deeds compel. And I have felt fear, fear because faced with those demonic ruins and their ghostly presence, I was forced to recognize how impotent seems the desire for life when faced with the desire for profit, power and even death. I am haunted by the deeds of men I cannot know and fear such deeds are within us all.

> For the sky and the sea, and the sea and the sky
> Lay like a load on my weary eye,
> And the dead were at my feet.

8

WAR AND PEACE IN ANTARCTICA

Although the storm broke far away from the shores of Antarctica, it was not long before the first waves began rolling in towards the Continent. As the nations of the beleaguered world were plunged into warfare in the closing months of 1939 the Antarctic, untroubled by the conflicts of man, might have reverted to its former peace much as it had done during the First World War. Since 1918 however, and hastened by an escalation in technology which had resulted from that war, the pace of events had so quickened that despite its remoteness and indeed, because of it, Antarctica was drawn into the conflict.

Between the two world wars the United States had taken the leading role on the Antarctic stage. Both in the scale of their operations and in the introduction of new technology the Americans ushered in the mechanical age in Antarctica and further consolidated science as the Continent's principal export. Richard E. Byrd, already famous for his pioneering flight over the North Pole in 1926, was the explorer who spearheaded this new attack upon the Continent. On his first expedition to Antarctica in 1929 he became the first man to fly to the South Pole from his base 'Little America' on the Bay of Whales. The Pole journey that had taken Amundsen, leaving from the same spot, three months to complete in 1911, and from which Scott had failed to return, took Byrd a mere sixteen hours.

On his second expedition in 1933, Byrd returned to Little America with fifty-six men, three aircraft, a variety of tractors and snow-mobiles, 153 sledge dogs and what has been described as 'an absolute mountain of scientific equipment'. Significantly, Byrd was the first explorer to initiate radio communications with the outside world thus ending, in both sense and reality, the total isolation of Antarctic exploration up until that time. But it was the use of aircraft that completely altered the concept of Antarctic exploration, setting a pattern which has been followed ever since. Great lifeless distances which had been such a daunting prospect to the early explorers could now be covered quickly, in relative comfort, and with comparative ease. These flights opened up a new perspective on the Continent in the form of aerial photography and map-making. A journey that would have taken months and years by traditional methods was suddenly possible within days and even hours. Between 1933 and 1935 Byrd added enormously to our knowledge of Antarctica, discovering new mountain ranges and much of the plateau which forms continental western Antarctica. He proved that the Ross and Weddell Seas are not connected and in measuring the depth of the continental ice cap gave the first indications of the incredible load of ice which covered the Continent.

It was on the strength of these achievements that Byrd launched his third expedition within a decade in June 1939. President Roosevelt appointed him commanding officer of the United States Antarctic Service Expedition, a government backed project for which Congress had appropriated funds amounting to 350,000 dollars. This interest by the American government in the Antarctic, the first such interest shown since the explorations of Charles Wilkes over a century before, was prompted by awareness of political factors which had been coming increasingly into play with regard to those nations which had been actively engaged in Antarctic exploration since the First World War. Now, as Byrd put it on the eve of the Second World War,

'The origin of the Antarctic Service Expedition of 1939 may be stated broadly to be due to the desire to place the United States in possession of full and up-to-date knowledge with regard to the geography and natural resources of the Antarctic, especially the hitherto unknown sector in which the extreme south-eastern part of the Pacific Ocean abuts on the continental land mass of Antarctica. Other countries—Great Britain, Australia, France, Norway —claim sovereignty over parts of Antarctica, and it is incumbent on us to be prepared with information for whatever policy concerning territorial rights the Government may decide upon.'

Byrd's expedition had two ships, four aircraft, fifty-nine men and a large number of dogs and several tractors for the overland surveying and geological work. The old base at Little America was under attack from the moving ice shelf and a large part of it was already crushed beyond hope of reoccupation. Conditions in the vicinity generally indicated that the site had become unsafe so a new spot several miles away was chosen to establish the base. Once this was done, the ships sailed to Marguerite Bay on the south-western approaches to the Antarctic Peninsula. Here at Stonington Island another base, 'East' base, was established. Byrd proposed that the whole coastline, almost 1700 miles long between Little America and Stonington, should be overflown and photographed during the following two seasons with ground parties working towards each other at the same time. The expedition lasted until the end of March 1941 when the base at Stonington was finally evacuated with some difficulty due to severe ice conditions off the Peninsula. A few months later the United States was precipitated into the Second World War with the Japanese air attack on Pearl Harbor.

In the United States the Secretary for Defense was already indulging in a little sabre-rattling when he stated in 1939 that 'considerations of continental defense made it vitally important to keep for the twenty-one American republics a clearer title to that part of the Antarctic continent south of the Americas than was claimed by any non-American country.'

On the outbreak of the Second World War only one sector of the Continent, that part in which the Americans had been primarily active, remained unclaimed. For the rest, the British, Norwegians, Australians, French and New Zealanders all laid formal claims to sovereign rights over the respective territories. These effectively divided the Continent into pie-shaped wedges, narrowing smoothly from the irregularities of the coastline towards the Pole. The validity of the claims varied, but they were all established with some degree of authority since each nation and particularly the Australians, British and Norwegians could claim to have carried out long-term activities in the areas under question. These claims, which had gone largely uncontested during the years of the armistice, began to be called into question as the world slid towards renewed hostilities.

In 1938, Germany dispatched a well-equipped expedition to the Antarctic using a specially designed ship, the *Schwabenland*. The expedition was led by Captain Alfred Ritscher and was personally sponsored by Field Marshal Goering. The *Schwabenland* sailed

69 *Following page* A rising blizzard on the Fuch's Ice Piedmont, Adelaide Island.

67 Husky sledge dog.

68 On the Nordenskjøld Glacier, South Georgia, with the peaks of the southern Alardyce Range beyond.

70 Ice cliffs at the edge of the Ross ice shelf – here about 130ft above the sea.

71 Iceberg in the Ross Sea.

to that sector of the Antarctic where Norway had been active both in whaling and in exploration. With two aircraft, which could be launched from the ship by means of a catapult, they flew over and photographed 135,000 square miles of territory in three weeks, dropping liberal quantities of Swastika flags as they went. Alarmed and angered by this brazen incursion into what Norway regarded as her sector of the Antarctic, King Haakon, in a formal proclamation made on 14 January 1939, claimed for Norway the whole sector of the Continent between 20° west and 45° east. The claim was given immediate support by the four other claimant nations. Three days later, the Third Reich claimed the same territory for Germany, calling it 'Neu-Schwabenland'.

There was considerable concern that the German expedition, whose personnel were drawn almost entirely from Air Force and Navy ranks, had been more interested in the use that might be made of the hydrographical and meteorological observations for future Antarctic-based wartime raiders than in geographical discovery for its own sake. The concern was soon justified. The Second World War brought home the fact that Antarctica could no longer be ignored as either a political or a strategic issue. National rivalry was intensifying and exploration, hitherto the province of individuals with little interest in, or taste for, political dealing, was brought increasingly under government control, while the tentacles of power-politics and bureaucracy from far away lands began slowly to unfurl themselves over Antarctica.

As had been feared, the Germans based a small fleet of raiders in remote coves of the Antarctic islands from which they could attack shipping in the South Atlantic. One frigate, the *Pinguin*, managed to capture an entire Norwegian whaling fleet and sank over 136,000 tons of British shipping before she was herself sunk in 1941. Afraid that the Germans might use the large coal bunkering and fuel facilities intended for the whalers on Deception Island, the British sent in a small task-force to destroy them. There was also an urgent need for more accurate weather forecasting for the approaches to the Drake Passage and a forecasting office was established by the Royal Navy at Port Stanley in the Falkland Islands.

Meanwhile, 400 miles away on the South American mainland, Argentina and Chile, neutrals in the world conflict, were about to complicate matters further. The war was going decidedly in Germany's favour at this stage and these two South American nations considered the moment opportune to assert territorial sovereignty over the sector of the Antarctic immediately south of Cape Horn on the far side of the Drake Passage, namely the Peninsula and that tract of the Continent at the head of the Weddell Sea stretching south to the Pole. Apart from the claim bringing these two countries into conflict, it clashed seriously with that already lodged by Britain as early as 1908—the first territorial claim made in the Antarctic. But with the defeat of Britain and the dissolution of her Empire apparently only a short time away, this was not expected to cause any serious problems.

The South American claims were made on the grounds of geographical proximity and, in the case of Argentina, by continuous occupation of the meteorological station on Laurie Island in the South Orkneys which, thanks to the generosity of the Scottish National Antarctic Expedition, they had taken over after the expedition had vacated it in 1904. Chile formally laid her claim in 1940 and Argentina in 1942. In the same year the Argentine Government sent out its first Antarctic expedition to back up its claim by occupation of bases on the Peninsula. The expedition was composed entirely of military personnel.

In 1943, with the tide of the war beginning to turn in the Allies' favour, Britain considered the threat to her Antarctic territory sufficiently serious to warrant the mounting of a Naval operation. This was code-named 'Tabarin' and was intended to counter Argentine activities and re-establish British sovereignty in the areas between 20° and 80° west. HMS *Caernarvon Castle* was sent south and in the 1943–44 season two bases were established, one at Port Lockroy on Wiencke Island on the west coast of the Peninsula, and the other at Deception Island, whilst the following season a sledging base was established at Hope Bay. The commanders at each base were sworn in as magistrates with overall responsibility for the area under their jurisdiction. The Base Commander also acted as official Postmaster, a Post Office being of key importance in establishing the validity of a claim in International Law.

When they arrived at Deception Island the British found brass cylinders containing notes claiming Argentine possession. These were removed and the notes politely returned via diplomatic channels to Argentina. The following year the British returned only to find their previous traces of occupation removed and the Argentine flag painted prominently on a number of rock faces. In turn these were painted out and this time the British re-established their base and stayed put. When the war came to an end it was clear that a delicate and potentially dangerous political situation had developed within the area of the three conflicting claims. 'Tabarin' was changed to a peacetime role becoming The Falkland Islands Dependencies Survey (FIDS—the acronym still applied to British personnel in the Antarctic). FIDS marked the commencement of the first continuously maintained Antarctic Expedition, which has since become the British Antarctic Survey, its name being changed on 1 January 1962.

The end of the war also marked a resurgence of American activity and in 1946, with Byrd once again in command, the biggest expedition ever mounted returned to the Ross Sea and Little America.

The operation, known as 'Highjump' using facilities made available by America's vast war output, included a fleet of thirteen ships, one an aircraft carrier, and also a submarine, twelve long-range aircraft and a number of smaller planes, several helicopters and a large number of tracked vehicles. The expedition brought over 4000 men into the Antarctic in a single season, more than had stepped ashore in the entire fifty years since Borchgrevink's landing in 1895.

'High jump' was an enormous undertaking with the ships strung out around the entire Continent. But it over-stretched itself and its scientific value was not in proportion to its size or its cost. Tens of thousands of aerial photographs were taken, but lack of ground control made over half of this effort worthless from the point of view of accurate map-making. On the other hand it clearly represented a further escalation in man's involvement with Antarctica.

By 1948, the British had expanded their field of operations with a total of seven permanently manned bases along the Peninsula and on the islands to the north. They were beginning to build up an on-going, comprehensive scientific programme. Surveying and geological parties were engaged on an extensive exploratory project and round-the-clock meteorological observations were radioed regularly to the central data collecting office at Port Stanley. In the same year, Deception Island was made the centre of a large Argentine Naval exercise in a display of military strength guaranteed to raise the political temperature. There were retaliatory moves by the British who tore down some of the Argentine huts on the island. In the South American capitals there were even rumours of war. In 1949 however the three powers agreed not to send Naval vessels south of 60° except to relieve their respective bases. At an international level the situation appeared volatile—a curious contrast to the atmosphere most often prevailing in the Antarctic itself. At Deception Island, where the three countries maintained bases almost within shouting distance of each other, it was normal practice for a number of years for the issue of sovereignty to be settled by a series of football matches, the winning team being entitled to claim the island in its country's name until the next match. A darts championship was held with a similar object and the various national emblems exchanged and adorning the different huts testified that the men on the spot, left alone, could find their own solution to the problem. Sometimes political wrangling produced farcical results. Each season the different bases would be visited by their relief ship. When the Argentine ship arrived for instance, the Commander of the British base would go on board to deliver a note of protest to the Captain complaining of his violation of territorial waters without prior permission. This formality having been observed, the Captain and his crew would be invited ashore for a party. Much drinking, laughter, smiles and singing was forthcoming within a few hours. The following day both sides with sore heads would wave farewell for another season. The habit proved harder to break in the end than the political deadlock and the same uproarious parties are still a special feature of base reliefs, happily minus the protest notes.

In 1947, the British Government invited both Argentina and Chile to submit their claims along with their own to the International Court of Justice in The Hague. Both countries declined and after a further rebuffed invitation in 1955, they insisted their sovereignty was so clear that no third party could cast judgement over what they regarded as a domestic issue.

The early 1950s produced a period of worsening tension over the Antarctic sovereignty issue fuelled by the emergence of a popular nationalist regime in Argentina. These were the years of Antarctica's Cold War, a softer mirror-image of the greater division developing between East and West after the defeat and partition of Germany. The wrangling, the protest notes, the tearing down of huts, the altering of previously accepted place-names, the constant repainting of flags, the football matches, all of this went on much like a mad hatter's tea party. Then in 1952, at Hope Bay, where British and Argentine bases stood within a few hundred yards of each other, an over-zealous Argentine officer suddenly opened up with a machine-gun over the heads of an incoming British relief party. Fortunately no one was hurt. On receipt of an angry protest note delivered to the Argentine Foreign Office, they calmly brushed the incident aside, saying the firing had been meant as a friendly greeting! However, the offending officer was hastily relieved of his duties, doubtless protesting his patriotic intentions. The following year the Argentine party decamped from the immediate vicinity of the British base on Deception Island, just in case there was any chance of a repeat performance.

The potentially serious consequences of these incidents could no longer be ignored by the international community, where the dispute was beginning to generate proposals with far-reaching implications.

As early as 1948, the United States had proposed that the small group of nations, excluding the USSR, which had been involved in Antarctic exploration and research should merge their claims and interests, establishing a condominium. The US suggested that the whole area be placed under United Nations Trusteeship and in so doing made the first move towards solving the political status of the Continent. The proposal, not surprisingly, fell on deaf ears, largely because the Soviet Union had not been invited to participate in the discussion, and it was therefore adamant that it would not recognize any solution concerning the future of Antarctica, particularly a solution in which it had taken no part.

Considering the remarkable turn of events over the next ten years, the apparently intractable difficulties caused by national rivalry and boycotting of meetings could not have presented a more inauspicious beginning for those attempting to solve the problem. The situation was nothing short of chaotic, the obstacles overwhelming, progress non-existent.

It was the imaginative gesture of a Swedish glaciologist, Professor H. W. Ahlmann, which, if we are to look for an event which marks the beginning of the political evolution of Antarctica, presaged the dawning of a new era. Before the war, Ahlmann had been searching for the cause of the recent recession of the Arctic ice. He argued that if this was due to global alterations in climate and not merely to local fluctuations, then there should

also be evidence for this in the Antarctic. Reports of considerable
ice-free areas from Ritscher's 1939 expedition suggested that this
might be the case and was worthy of proper scientific investigation.
Together with Dr H. U. Svedrup, Head of the Norwegian Polar
Institute, Ahlmann developed his ideas and, with the help of
the Scott Polar Research Institute at Cambridge, England, the
Norwegian-British-Swedish Expedition 1949–52 came into being.
In the course of its three-year stay, the expedition completed an
impressive amount of work and was probably the most productive
Antarctic expedition since those of Scott and Mawson in the
'heroic' era. One of its most notable achievements was the com-
pletion of the first seismic traverse of the inland ice sheet to a
height of 9000 feet. At that point the sounding indicated a massive
thickness of ice—a depth of 7000 feet. For the first time man
could begin to build a profile of the hidden land beneath the ice.
But undoubtedly the real significance of this expedition was its
international character. Three nations working harmoniously
together, unimpeded by either political or strategic restraints,
brought home a wealth of results. In Antarctica at least, there
was more to be gained for all in co-operation than in conflict. It
seemed such an obviously simple lesson and its implications were
not lost on other nations with their own interests in Antarctica.

1953 marked the turning-point in Antarctica's political status,
a watershed in international co-operation that has no precedent.
It was the year in which the International Committees met for
initial discussion and formulation of their ideas for the International Geophysical Year which was planned to run from 1 July
1957 to 31 December 1958.

The idea of an International Geophysical Year was first
suggested by Dr Lloyd Berkner at an informal meeting of scientists
at the home of James Van Allen in America in April 1950. Berkner
had accompanied Byrd as a radio engineer on his 1929 expedition.
His idea was first conceived as a Third International Polar Year.
The First Polar Year had taken place in 1882–83 when eleven
nations dispatched expeditions to the Arctic. Berkner suggested
that a Third Polar Year should concentrate its efforts in the
Antarctic. Advances in technology and scientific instrumentation
also made it desirable to press ahead with the plan as soon as
possible rather than wait for the half-century gap which seemed
to separate the Polar Years by tradition rather than by design.
A combined international assault was both apt and timely in

Antarctica. With discussion his idea soon evolved to become a year of simultaneous planetary observations covering a wide spectrum of scientific disciplines.

With the convening of the first meeting of the Special Committee for the International Geophysical Year in Brussels in July 1953, the idea was transcribed into a provisional programme, drawn up and based on the proposals of twenty-three nations. Antarctica was singled out for special attention and some of the major geophysical problems to be tackled involved the structure and volume of Antarctica's ice sheet, its effect upon the world's weather and its relationship to the upper atmosphere. Beyond this, attempts were to be made to unravel the mystery surrounding the Aurora, with special attention being paid to the ionosphere.

Concurrent with the planning of the IGY, moves were still being made in the political arena to settle the long-standing disputes bedevilling the Antarctic. In February 1956, Arthur Lall, Indian permanent representative to the United Nations, put forward a proposal similar to that of the United States in 1948. Inspired by New Zealand's desire to move the situation forward, Lall requested that 'the question of Antarctica' be included on the provisional agenda of the General Assembly. India wanted to secure international agreement for the development of Antarctic resources for peaceful purposes, for non-militarization of the area, banning of nuclear weapons testing, and reference of future disputes to the International Court. The New Zealand Prime Minister was looking for a form of United Nations Trusteeship for the Antarctic which would become a 'world territory' under the control of the UN, and that any arrangement for international control should have the approval of the United Nations. Several countries, including Sweden, expressed interest in this plan, but India's proposal was finally withdrawn, largely because of opposition from Chile and Argentina, and lack of support from the United States and Britain.

By 1956, plans were well-advanced for the International Geophysical Year. Sixty-seven countries were now involved across the world, whilst in Antarctica twelve nations had agreed to undertake a co-ordinated programme of research. Of these, seven countries consisted of the original claimant states. The other five, Belgium, Japan, South Africa, the United States and the Soviet Union, had varying interests but had laid no claims. The participation of the two Super-Powers, the principal Cold War protagonists, was one of the greatest political coups to come out of the IGY. Not everyone endorsed their joint participation, fearing that this would only lead to the Cold War being extended to Antarctica. Australia, in whose sector the Soviet Union had been assigned IGY base sites, was particularly worried. The raising of the Soviet flag in Antarctica on 14 February 1956 to celebrate the twentieth Congress of the Soviet Communist Party reportedly caused deep alarm and anxiety among members of the Australian Parliament in Canberra. This led to fears that the Russians might be planning to use Antarctica as a base for ICBM sites, a fear only finally allayed by the International Antarctic Treaty.

Between them the United States and the Soviet Union mounted by far the largest operations in Antarctica. The Americans began moving in supplies in the 1955–56 season. The operation was called 'Deepfreeze' and was again under the overall command of Admiral Byrd. Seven bases were established in this season between the Ross Sea and the Filchner Ice-shelf in the Weddell Sea. Over 3000 men, 200 aircraft, 12 ships and 300 vehicles were involved. The most difficult operation involved the construction of a base at the South Pole, which began on 19 November 1956. The buildings were ferried to the Pole by C-124 Globemaster aircraft, at that time the world's largest freight-carrying aircraft. Prefabricated sections of the buildings were parachuted down, to be assembled by an advance building party—the first men to stand at the South Pole since Scott forty-five years before. It was a display of technological power and confidence symbolizing the new age and the new men arriving in Antarctica. That buildings would one day rain down upon the Pole from the sky would, to Scott and his men, have been an unimaginable dream, the stuff of science fiction. Thus was the gulf between past and present widened.

By the time the beginning of the International Geophysical Year arrived, Rear-Admiral George Dufek, who had taken over command from Byrd, estimated that the United States had spent some 245 million dollars just getting themselves established in the Antarctic. It was a far cry from the days of Scott's *Discovery* and Shackleton's *Nimrod*.

Meanwhile the Russians, back in the Antarctic for the first time since Bellingshausen, were mounting the Soviet Comprehensive Antarctic Expedition. This had sailed from the Baltic in November 1955 in the ice-breaker *Ob* and the refrigerator ship *Lena*. Like the Americans they carried a large fleet of aircraft and during the following year they established five bases with the help of nearly 500 men. Towards the end of the Geophysical Year itself, they opened a sixth base at the Pole of Relative Inaccessability. At 82° 6′ south, 54° 58′ east, this was the point on the Continent furthest from any coastline, and standing at over 11,000 feet its location was as inhospitable as the name suggested.

Altogether sixty bases were established around and across the Antarctic Continent and on the Antarctic islands. During the Geophysical Year, there were more men working in the Antarctic regions than there had been in all the years together since Captain Cook had first circumnavigated the Continent in 1773. As a result of this huge effort, science had more answers to old questions and more new problems for which answers had yet to be found than anyone would have thought possible at the outset of the Geophysical Year. The United States alone shipped home more than twenty-seven tons of scientific data. The idea of the Antarctic as the world's greatest natural scientific laboratory was well on the way to becoming a reality.

A great proportion of the research involved programmes of a largely static nature carried out in the immediate vicinity of each base. However, some of the more exciting results were obtained from the numerous ice-traverses which spread out in many directions, often far into the continental interior. Of these, the boldest and most imaginative was that of the Commonwealth Trans-Antarctic Expedition under the leadership of Sir Vivian Fuchs. This expedition planned to cross the Continent from the Weddell Sea to the Ross Sea via the South Pole, following a route similar to the one which Shackleton had proposed in 1914.

For two years prior to the actual crossing, preparations gradually went ahead, sometimes with the utmost difficulty, as in the case of establishing the forward base, 'Shackleton', at Vahsel Bay on the Filchner Ice-shelf. The advance expedition ship *Theron*, only the second vessel to attempt a passage to the head of the Weddell Sea since the *Endurance*, was beset for thirty-three days before finally reaching the bay. At the close of the season, after the *Theron* had departed, blizzards lashed the area, breaking out the fast-ice on which the stores had been dumped and much still remained. As a result the advance party lost all their coal and a large part of the fuel and food supplies needed to sustain them through the winter, which they spent in a converted wooden crate, previously used for transporting one of the Snow-Cats. Under cramped and uncomfortable conditions they battled through the winter, slowly erecting the base hut for the arrival of the crossing party the following season.

When the relief ship arrived in January 1957, the establishment of a small advance base 300 miles inland towards the Pole began immediately. It was named 'South Ice' and its construction was only made possible by the use of the expedition's aircraft, a small, single-engine Otter. In much the same way that the Americans had established their base at the South Pole, but on a small scale, the Otter flew in the necessary materials, one ton at a time, a total of twenty flights. Whilst this was under way on the Weddell Sea side of the Continent, a New Zealand party under Sir Edmund Hillary had arrived in McMurdo Sound and were preparing to reconnoitre a route 700 miles out towards the Pole from their quarters at Scott Base on Ross Island.

Fuchs left Shackleton on 24 November 1957. The advances that had come to polar exploration in the forty years since Shackleton's Imperial Trans-Antarctic Expedition were much in evidence, and when they finally set out from South Ice on Christmas Eve they had eight tracked vehicles, Sno-Cats and Weasels, which when fuelled carried 320 gallons of petrol between them. On sledges they pulled a further 5200 gallons, some twenty-one tons of fuel. The lubricants, tools and spare parts required to ensure this caravan kept on the move totalled another two tons. There were also one and a half tons of food and half a ton of paraffin to cook it with, and another seven tons of camping equipment and scientific instruments including half a ton of explosives for the seismic shots, one for every thirty miles all the way across the Continent. They pulled out of South Ice with thirty-two tons of provisions and equipment, enough, together with some advance air-drops, to last the one hundred days which Fuchs calculated it should take them to complete the journey. An additional feature of this historic crossing and a concession to traditional and proven methods of polar travel was the use of two dog teams which were employed to reconnoitre a safe route for the vehicles along the greater length of the journey.

Fuchs had a tough time getting to the Pole from Shackleton. Tractors and sledges often broke down through the treacherous surfaces and on several occasions came close to being lost down cavernous crevasses. Whilst Fuchs was struggling towards the Pole, the Otter, fitted with an auxiliary fuel tank, made a non-stop flight across the Continent from Shackleton to Scott Base via the Pole, a 1600 mile flight. The RAF team of four led by Squadron Leader John Lewis were the first to fly across Antarctica via the Pole.

On 19 January 1958, Fuchs arrived at the South Pole after 855 miles in which four of the vehicles had been abandoned along the way, not reluctantly, but as part of the pre-arranged plan. Hillary was there to meet Fuchs, having arrived on 4 January after a spirited dash of 500 miles from Depot 700, using Ferguson tractors, which had not been designed to cope with the high-altitude conditions of the plateau. The American 'Amundsen–Scott Base' with its home comforts, hot showers and iced beer presented an extraordinary contrast to the crossing party, who had driven across an unbroken, white horizon for fifty-seven days. At the Pole there were some attempts to persuade Fuchs to abandon his crossing because of the advancing season. He could fly out and come back next year and complete the journey. Fuchs had none of that, realizing that if he gave up now he might never be able to get back again.

After four hectic, crowded days preparing for the last and longest leg of the journey, they set off for Scott Base on McMurdo Sound, 1250 miles away. Happily it proved a much less arduous run than that to the Pole and after a journey totalling 2180 miles they accomplished the first surface crossing of Antarctica on 2 March 1958.

Despite the difficulties and dangers, the Commonwealth Trans-Antarctic crossing was completed with almost military precision, and, despite its obvious and fundamental differences, there are about this achievement echoes of the past, coincidences with that other great explorer of precision, Amundsen. Although one man went to the Pole and back and the other went on to cross the Continent, both men predicted with uncanny accuracy the time their journeys would take, and when one considers almost fifty years separated them it is even stranger that both lasted exactly ninety-nine days.

Fuchs carried with him Captain Scott's watch, worn on a leather thong around his neck, and, true to the aspirations of that man, he doggedly pursued the expedition's scientific programme to the very last even when, on occasions, it must have been tempting to cut things short and push on. One result of his patient persistence

was the first complete profile from sea to sea of the Continent which
lay beneath the ice. The seismic soundings revealed huge mountain
ranges completely buried under the ice and separated by undulating
valleys and, in places, deep trenches that fell hundreds of feet below
sea-level. Sometimes the mountain peaks they travelled over were
not far beneath them, in other places the depth of ice was over 6000
feet. Together with the long traverses carried out by the Americans,
Russians and French in other parts of the Continent, a picture began
to emerge from which scientists could draw two important conclusions. One, that there was much more ice in Antarctica than
anyone had previously suspected, and two, that, despite the differences in the rocks between East and West Antarctica, the land
beneath this ice was indeed one great continent.

If Antarctica was throwing up surprises for science, the success
of the IGY effort also took the politicians by surprise. The twelve
nations, by agreeing to shelve their political differences and work
together on a mutual, co-operative scientific programme, had
created in Antarctica a unique international circumstance. There
arose accordingly the strong desire that this spirit of co-operation
should continue and enable the general programme of research
to move forward.

At a conference called on 2 May 1958, the United States
proposed to the other Antarctic IGY participants that they should
join 'in a treaty designed to preserve the continent as an international laboratory for scientific research and ensure that it be
used only for peaceful purposes.'

Sixteen months of intensive discussions followed and many
doubts and fears were expressed concerning the feasibility of such
a Treaty. For many it was too bold, an unrealistic plan that would
degenerate into a dangerous new crisis. In the United States, with
a Presidential Election pending, certain senators voiced great
uncertainty while some were openly hostile. Senator Clair Eagle
of California wanted consideration of the Treaty postponed until
after the election, stating:

'The new administration which will have the responsibility of
conducting the foreign policy of this nation for four years should
have the opportunity of passing on the provisions of this important
treaty. The treaty involves an area as big as the United States of
America plus all of Europe. For all practical purposes, it disposes
in perpetuity of the relationships of this nation and other major
nations to the vast continent of Antarctica.'

High on the list of doubts was the widespread suspicion that the Russians would not abide by the terms of the treaty and would flout it, turning it to their own ends, and move in and take over. Many were not convinced by the argument that Antarctica was militarily and economically valueless. 'How does anyone know it will remain worthless?' asked a Senator from the State of Georgia. He had a point, and twenty years later he might have received a different answer to his question.

Clearly the formulation of a plan to safeguard the peace of Antarctica and the interests of scientific co-operation had many obstacles and trenchant opinions to overcome. Certain compromises had to be made along the way in the interests of securing a treaty that would be acceptable to all concerned, but the guiding principle of preserving peace in Antarctica for the international advancement of science with benefits for all was never allowed to falter. The coaxing of politicians at home and the long rounds of negotiations abroad, involved some of the most brilliant diplomacy of modern times. A succinct analysis of the treaty came from Herman Phleger, who led the American delegation at the negotiations, when he wrote:

'This treaty for the first time in history devotes a large area of the world to peaceful purposes. It is the first treaty which prohibits nuclear explosions with adequate inspection.

'It is the first treaty to provide freedom of scientific investigation over large areas and it constitutes a precedent in the field of disarmament, the prohibition of nuclear explosions and the law of space.'

The International Antarctic Treaty was finally signed in Washington by the twelve nations active in the Antarctic during IGY on 1 December 1959. It came into force on the 23 June 1961 for an initial period of thirty years, at which point it may be reviewed by the nations concerned. Throughout these years of unremitting international tension, characterized by increasing political instability, peace has been maintained, indeed strengthened, in Antarctica. Contrary to what sceptics believed was an impossible dream, the dream has turned into reality. Antarctica became a continent without conflict, allowing man the chance to grow a little, moving a first hesitant step beyond the boundaries behind which he has hidden in fear for so long.

The Antarctic Treaty, an eleventh hour gamble in a world overshadowed by the constant threat of nuclear holocaust, social and environmental catastrophe, has so far succeeded where all else has failed. It is more than a practical demonstration of a concept capable of unifying men of diverse creeds in an environment which they mutually respect. It is, in a universal sense, a reflection of the soul of man in its longing to be free and in its search for the key to that freedom, to the lost paradise which he knows he must regain, or perish. Today, Antarctica symbolizes man's aspirations towards that freedom and all that is most noble in him. Whether he has the strength to continue further towards a greater realization of his dream, or whether he will turn back into the darkness of the surrounding world, his brief experiment with the 'new age' extinguished by the nightmare realities of the present, only the strength of his desire to be free, his belief in the possibility of the impossible, will provide an answer.

A memory. A day dark and grey, the sea wild and black beneath a sky of storms. A cold, harsh wind blowing down a long black beach, at either end distant breakers hammering on white rocks. At my feet, swirling sand and snow. Huddled in small groups, men with their heads bowed beneath upturned collars turn their backs to the weather. Out in the bay, a small red boat plunges through the waves towards us and beyond it a ship appears mysteriously out of the mist, riding impatiently at anchor. And breaking suddenly between the clouds, a shaft of sunlight races along the beach until our faces become golden, our expressions fixed in each other's eyes like a flash photograph. Laughter, smiles, many strange words. Hands reaching out for hands, arms around each other. Bottles of Vodka, of Whisky, thrust this way and that, an exchange of gifts, of English cigarettes and dried fish from the Caspian Sea. A big man grasps my hand like a vice clamping over it, his eyes wide and staring. We smile at each other. We have smiled often this day and talked a little. He laughs at me a big growling laugh. I laugh, drunk from too much Vodka, and we stagger down the beach together. The red boat is waiting.

'Good-bye my English,' he roars, black waves washing over his enormous black boots.

'Good-bye, good-bye,' I shout, falling clumsily into the boat.

'I give you a push. Here we are friends. I come back next year. You come too?'

'I don't think so,' I say.

'Pity. You can tell me more about Scotland. I love Scotland,' he growls.

'And you can tell me more about Russia,' I laugh.

'Take care English.'

'You too,' I shout, but the wind is so strong we can no longer hear each other and I am feeling sick. We wave to each other for a long time, until the distance grows too much between us.

I sometimes think of him, of the photograph he showed me of his pretty wife and little daughter outside their house somewhere in the Ukraine. I wonder where he is now and if he ever thinks of me. Sometimes I wonder if I imagined it all until I look at the empty Vodka bottle. One day, perhaps, there will be another shore.

9

ASSETS UNFROZEN
The Fatal Compromise

In 1930 the writer Olaf Stapleton speculated on the future of Antarctica in a remarkable work of science fiction called *Last and First Men*. At that time Byrd had just flown over the South Pole and his activities heralded the modern scientific and technological age in Antarctica. Despite this, knowledge of the Continent was still scant and much of it rested on the work carried out by the explorers at the beginning of the century. However fantastic Stapleton's vision may have seemed fifty years ago it has more than a ring of truth to it now. I quote it because the detachment with which this future scenario is laid before us is quite unnerving if we are prepared to alter its original perspective to that of the present. It is a reminder that the gap between fact and fiction has narrowed to the point where the edges are now so blurred that the reality of the present, thanks to science and technology, is continually disappearing before our eyes in favour of the future. There is no longer substance to grasp, only the illusion of substance. Here is what he wrote.

'At the time with which we are at present dealing, means had recently been found of profitably working the huge deposits of fuel in Antarctica. This vast supply unfortunately lay technically beyond the jurisdiction of the World Fuel Control Board. America was first in the field, and saw in Antarctic fuel a means for her advancement, and for her self-imposed duty of Americanizing the planet. China, fearful of Americanization, demanded that the new sources should be brought under the jurisdiction of the Board. For some years feeling had become increasingly violent on this point, and both peoples had by now relapsed into crude old nationalistic mood. War began to seem almost inevitable. And indeed it was for the world was precipitated into a quarter of a century of devastating warfare. Forces were mobilized by this conflict however, which eventually led to the founding of the First World State and an Americanized planet where all continents save one, were urbanized. The enterprise of an already distant past had brought every land under civilization. The coasts of Antarctica . . . were permanently inhabited by those engaged in exploiting the mineral wealth of the hinterland.

'Although after the foundation of the World State the fuel of Antarctica had been very carefully husbanded, the new supply of oil had given out in less than three centuries . . . It soon became evident that even the unexpectedly rich coal-fields of Antarctica would not last forever. The cessation of oil had taught men a much needed lesson, had made them feel the reality of the power problem.'

The value of Stapleton's imagined Antarctic future lies not in its specifics, which are only a convenient means to an end, although some of these seem uncomfortably close to reality, but in his ability to understand that the impossible would indeed become possible. Considering the present relationship of mankind to Antarctica his vision in fictional form is fired like a warning shot across the bows of the future from a totally unexpected direction.

The Antarctic Treaty is a remarkable document (see Appendix 1), unique as a piece of international diplomacy and legislation, far-reaching in concept. The Treaty is often referred to as the 'model' for international co-operation and a 'blueprint' for environmental protection (see Agreed Measures, Appendix 2). Its basic provisions, were they adopted on a global scale, would initiate a transformative process for mankind's future wellbeing. Unfortunately this presupposes an ideal world. Although the Treaty is specifically designed for the Antarctic, its fundamental principles address some of the most urgent problems which confront mankind, and upon whose successful solution hangs the fate of the world. These principles can be summarized as follows:

Antarctica shall be used for peaceful purposes only and nothing of a military nature shall be allowed; nuclear explosions, the disposal of radio-active waste and any weapons testing in general are banned. Personnel may travel freely anywhere and there shall also be free exchange of all scientific information for the benefit of mankind as a whole. Territorial claims are 'frozen' for the duration of the Treaty, will not be disputed and no new claims may be established. In addition to these basic principles a further set of comprehensive agreements have been signed concerning the preservation and protection of the Antarctic environment and its wildlife and these have come into effect at varying intervals since the formulation of the original Treaty.

It is therefore not difficult to imagine the effect these agreements would have were they to be translated onto a global scale. The reference to the banning of nuclear weapons testing is particularly poignant in view of the agonizingly protracted negotiations between the United States and the Soviet Union to effect control over the arms race, nuclear weapons in general and their potential for instant genocide. Indeed nothing further can be written here outside that context, for failing its successful resolution all else becomes utterly meaningless.

So the Antarctic Treaty is a uniquely impressive piece of legislation which would appear to represent a translation of man's highest and noblest aspirations into a successful demonstration of their practical application.

The value of Antarctica's vast natural laboratory for expanding scientific research in many fields quickly became evident. The primary advantage was the Antarctic environment's natural purity, unequalled anywhere else. Therefore Antarctica could be used as a baseline for monitoring changes occurring over the rest of the planet. It is important to understand that this environmental purity underpins a great deal of the research and that without it much of the science would lose its essential value. Free of its own industrial and urban pollution and remote from the centres of civilization, Antarctica reflects global pollution levels in the snow that falls and consolidates into the ice sheet and in the wildlife, the seals, penguins and seabirds that visit its shores from the surrounding ocean. Unfortunately, the evidence being gathered in this field paints a grim picture for the planet as a whole and indicates that we are turning it into a sewer that is continually spilling over into Antarctica where the fragile ecosystem is particularly susceptible to contamination.

Detailed sampling reveals that lead for instance, a toxic metal byproduct of industrialization, has only appeared in the Antarctic snow since the early 1940s. Its increasing presence coincides with the rapid industrial expansion that has taken place throughout the world over the last four decades. The steady rise in levels of carbon dioxide and a whole range of pesticides in ice core samples during the last twenty-five years is merely an indicator of the alarming quantities we have already dumped into the environment. Pesticide residues including DDT have been found in seals, penguins and krill which forms the basis of the entire Antarctic food chain. The DDT found in penguins is an example of the insidious nature of this poison which has filtered through the planetary ecosystem all the way from its liberal and indiscriminate use as an agricultural pesticide in the 1950s prior to being banned in the developed world and then exported to the Third World. Needless to say a graphic record exists in the Antarctic snow of the radioactive fallout from the atmospheric nuclear testing programmes conducted during the 1950s and 60s. By citing these few examples, it is clear that the folly of man comes home to roost in Antarctica where he is made vividly aware of the repercussions of his thoughtless disregard for the closed natural systems of his planet.

Throughout the 1960s Antarctic scientists realized increasingly that the Continent held vital clues to the understanding of our planet in the past, the present and into the future. In the fields of meteorology, climatology and glaciology, research began to reveal the major influence Antarctica has on global climate, both in day to day weather patterns and in longer term climatic cycles. Physicists studying the upper atmosphere and inner space found that Antarctica provided them with the best place for observing such phenomena as the aurora, magnetic storms, solar wind and the earth's ozone layer. An apparent thinning of the ozone layer above Antarctica in recent years has been detected. Whether this is a naturally occurring phenomenon linked to solar activity or changing weather patterns, or an event triggered off by man-made chemicals such as spray can propellants and industrial solvents is not yet clear. Since the ozone layer is critical in filtering out ultraviolet radiation, harmful and potentially lethal to life on earth, an understanding of the cause of the ozone thinning is vital.

Antarctica also played an important role in the United States' space programme. When it was realized that the 'dry valleys' of Victoria Land, not far from the US McMurdo Station, were the nearest earth equivalent to the alien environment that would be encountered on Mars, the space scientists developed tests for the Mariner space probes, using the primitive soils of the dry valleys.

In the life sciences, Antarctica has proved to be a particularly rich and rewarding location. There are few places in the world where animals and birds are so unafraid of man and this, together with the surrounding beauty of their natural environment, gives this branch of science an additional particular appeal. Antarctica's ecosystem and that of the Southern Ocean are comparatively simple compared with those found in the temperate and tropical latitudes. However, it is this very simplicity which makes the system so vulnerable to disturbance. The relationship between the species and the short food chain linking prey and predator has therefore become a major focus of biological research. It may not be long before a single unifying concept is produced for explaining how the entire Antarctic ecosystem functions.

Microscopic insects that live inside porous rocks and can survive the extremely low temperatures of Antarctica's high interior by hibernating for 300 days a year are more than just scientific curiosities. So too are some fish which survive by virtue of a form of antifreeze in their blood. Understanding such remarkable adaptations has particular value for medical science.

Finally in the field of geology and geophysics, Antarctica turned out to be the essential piece in the earth's jig-saw puzzle of landmasses, enabling scientists to prove that continental drift was more than an attractive theory. Fossils found in Antarctica's rocks, particularly those of a small reptile called 'Lystrosaurus' discovered in 1967, coupled with the emerging science of Plate Tectonics, which explained the causes of continental drift, turned theory into fact. Continental drift is in a sense a framework that provides geologists with an explanation for the earth's evolution.

These then, very briefly, are some of the areas where research has been advancing in Antarctica in an unprecedented international co-operative effort, which has now lasted a quarter of a century. This effort has been greatly assisted and enhanced by developments in electronics, computers, satellite imagery and communications. There can be little doubt that at this point in time Antarctica presents the smiling face of science in its twentieth-century showcase.

Throughout the Treaty's first decade the affairs of nations in Antarctica proceeded smoothly. During the 1970s however, the first signs began to appear that this harmonious state of affairs might be more precariously balanced than had been anticipated. The purity of science in Antarctica was perhaps not so pure after all and in any case pressures from the outside world meant that events were in danger of overtaking a system that appeared inadequate to cope with the threat that was looming ahead. The reasons for this had their origin in the original Antarctic Treaty negotiations. In two key areas, those of sovereignty and resources, particularly mineral resources, it soon became apparent that to pursue these issues would result in the negotiations breaking down.

Seven of the twelve nations involved in the negotiations already claimed territory in the Antarctic. These were France, New Zealand, Australia, Norway, Argentina, Chile and the United Kingdom. Each recognized the other's claims but those of Argentina, Chile and the United Kingdom overlapped, a complicating factor that has remained a sensitive, potentially explosive one. The five other nations, Belgium, South Africa, Japan, the USA and the USSR, did not recognize the claims of the seven, and both the United States and the Soviet Union reserved the right to make their own claims based upon prior discovery and exploration. The sovereignty issue was overcome by the diplomatic expedient of 'freezing' the existing claims for the initial thirty year duration of the Treaty. Simultaneously, then, claims would not be renounced but neither would they be recognized depending upon the particular position of a contracting party. It was a neat sidestep politically and provided an answer all could accept.

When it came to mineral resources the issue proved to be just as delicate, particularly as it was inextricably linked to that of sovereignty. Because of the economic and political consequences resulting from any significant discovery of minerals—oil, gas, uranium, for example—it was quickly recognized that any attempt to legislate for this eventuality would undermine the entire Treaty and that no agreement would ever be reached. Whilst realizing that some significant resource might well be discovered, the possibility of this was regarded as being so far in the future as to have little bearing on prevailing circumstances. Accordingly the issue was dropped and subsequently there is no mention of minerals in the Treaty. This permitted the twelve member states to reach their historic accord.

Outlining what might be described, somewhat uncharitably, as these two defects should not detract from the Treaty's impressive and otherwise wholly inspired nature. Obviously it was better to have a couple of problems under wraps than no Treaty. At the time the threats posed by these unresolved problems seemed insignificant by comparison with all there was to be gained. This has most certainly proved to be the case and the disastrous situation that would have resulted in Antarctica in the absence of the Treaty was one of the strongest reasons for ensuring its successful implementation. The failure lay simply in the inability to recognize the speed with which events were to unfold. In a sense the very success of the scientific programmes themselves allied to, and backed up by, a rapidly evolving technology hastened the day of reckoning.

Throughout the world wherever conditions have permitted, man has exploited whatever resources he has found and were suited to his needs. In every continent save one and across the oceans man has taken whatever he wanted to sustain a world civilization that has required varied and increasing amounts of raw materials to maintain its industrial base and permit unlimited economic growth. The ocean surrounding Antarctica was no exception and its contribution to this process over the last 150 years has been considerable. With the signing of the Antarctic Treaty, science for the first time was ahead of exploitation and development. The responsibility the scientists felt towards this unique environment was soon demonstrated by the adoption of the Agreed Measures for the Conservation of Antarctic Flora and Fauna in 1964. The Agreed Measures applied to the continent and all land, including ice shelves south of latitude 60°. It did not include the high seas. In 1961 the question had already been raised concerning the future exploitation of seals. This prompted a protracted series of discussions eventually leading to the Convention for the Conservation of Antarctic Seals which was finally ratified by all the signatories to the Treaty in 1978. The Convention on seals was designed to halt the free-wheeling exploitation of the past in favour of a more rational system based on data resulting from comprehensive research. It set quotas for catch limits on Crabeater, Weddell and Leopard seals, the most numerous species, and gave total protection to the Fur and Elephant seal and to the extremely rare Ross seal. While it would appear that three species might be at risk, no new sealing industry has started and the Convention is notable for its determination to regulate sealing before it started.

However, the biggest breakthrough came in 1982 with the ratification of the Convention on the Conservation of Antarctic Marine Living Resources. The significance of this agreement is

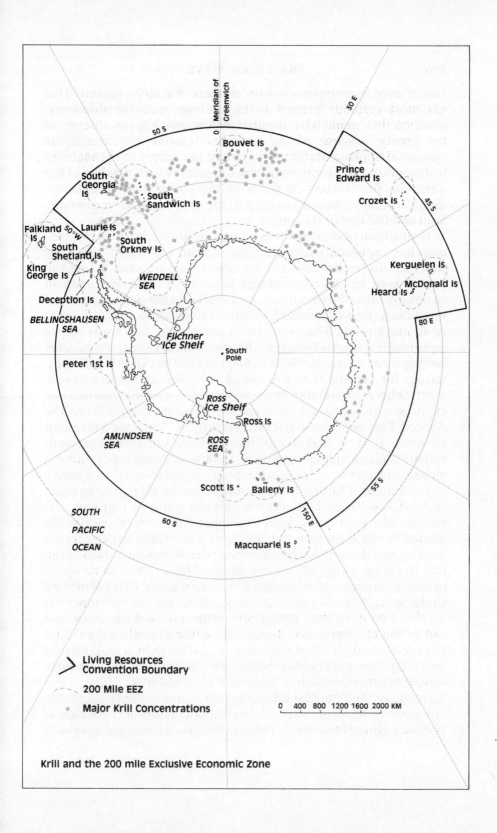

Krill and the 200 mile Exclusive Economic Zone

that it encompasses the living resources of the Southern Ocean not only within the Treaty area but south of the Antarctic Convergence, a substantially larger area and one more representative of the Antarctic ecosystem as a whole. The Convention is again designed to permit exploitation but within conservation guidelines which emphasize the rational use of resources. A number of the articles in the Convention relate to those of the Antarctic Treaty and the Agreed Measures. One of the major problems affecting the 1982 Convention is the absence of reliable data on which catch limits can be based. Estimates suggest that there may be 5000 million tons of krill in the Southern Ocean. Of this, squid are thought to consume 100 million tons annually, seals 80 million tons, fish 60 million tons, whales 43 million tons and birds about 40 million tons. It is therefore suggested that humans could harvest up to 150 million tons annually without altering the overall balance of the krill population. But this is guesswork. In an attempt to overcome this lack of vital information, the Scientific Committee on Antarctic Research (SCAR) inaugurated the Biological Investigation of Marine Antarctic Systems and Stocks (BIOMASS) in 1980, using eighteen ships from eleven nations and concentrating on those areas where krill is known to be most abundant. The hope is that eventually BIOMASS will lay down guidelines for the harvesting of krill as well as other marine organisms. It is generally accepted that the Southern Ocean, whose total fish catch could equal that of all the other oceans combined, will be exploited in the future. The intention of the 1982 Convention is to put a brake on the fishing already taking place prior to being able to set reliable catch limits for a developing industry. Over the last decade, West Germany, Poland, Argentina, Chile and the Soviet Union have been engaged in experimental exploitation of krill. For the time being, all but the Soviet Union have given up on economic grounds. Krill is technically an expensive form of protein to catch and process and marketing it as a consumer product has involved considerable difficulties. Most of the krill which the Soviet Union harvests is manufactured for animal feedstuffs. It has been calculated that to take an annual catch of 10 million tons would involve 500 vessels capable of processing 20,000 tons each. Apart from the problem of mounting a sustained operation of this magnitude, the potential impact upon the marine environment in the form of fuel oils and general rubbish poses a considerable pollution threat. However, the governing economic factors could alter at any time, and this, coupled with an improved fishing technology, would rapidly increase the pressures for exploitation. In the long term the Convention is designed to prevent future actions leading to the sort of disasters associated with the exploitation of Antarctica's marine resources in the past.

However, the Convention still assumes a perspective and set of values that is less of a break with the past than an attempt at adapting traditional practices into a scientifically acceptable form. The hope of the Antarctic scientists would appear to be that in this way they can cope with economic and political structures whose value system is firmly rooted in the exploitation ethic. The danger inherent in such a compromise becomes apparent when the original conditions under which the Convention was signed are seen by any one of the parties to conflict with an emerging set of circumstances which might demand a unilateral declaration of exploitation compatible only with that nation's self-interests. As technology makes Antarctica increasingly accessible, agreements, however well-intentioned, however carefully formulated, are in constant danger of being broken. The fact that so far all nations who abide by the Convention do so because it is in their individual interest assumes a permanence and a stability in the world which does not exist. There is no guarantee beyond the requirements of each day. But for the present the strength of the Convention rests on its internationalization of the marine resources, recognizing that they may be shared by anyone who is willing to accept its recommendations. Interestingly, another aspect of its strength is a product of the natural function of krill itself. At present these creatures are quite unpredictable in their movements so a fishing fleet can never be sure of their location or the quantity available. This makes it very difficult for any nation to declare an Exclusive Economic Zone (EEZ) in an attempt to portion off part of the resource for itself. Apart from conflicting directly with the principles of the Treaty, the area where krill is most abundant is also the area claimed by Britain, Argentina and Chile.

The conservation agreements illustrate the serious attempts being made by the Treaty nations, as represented by their consultative parties within the Treaty organization, to come to terms with the increasing pressures being exerted on the Antarctic environment by the outside world, and also on the organization itself. In broad terms the progress and success of these agreements have depended upon their formulation within a framework that accepts exploitation as inevitable and makes its policy and value-judgements in accordance with economic and political realities.

Faced with the problems posed in reaching an agreement to deal effectively with the future exploitation of Antarctic minerals, whether on land or under the sea, we move much closer to the heart of the industrial complex which lies at the core of every nation signatory to the Antarctic Treaty.

There is little doubt that since the end of World War II, the promise of resources has never been far from the minds of those responsible for directing Antarctic policy. Some have viewed the prospect as a clarion call for action to safeguard these resources as part of a global strategy aimed at upholding the industrial/economic superiority of their nation. In 1953 Admiral Byrd remarked that Antarctica was 'a vast untouched reservoir of natural resources. As we recklessly squander our natural resources in this country (the United States) we will come to need these new resources. It is imperative that they do not fall into the hands of a potential enemy.' In the 1960s and 70s the United States Government stated that it was 'unwilling to take any steps which directly reduced the freedom of American companies to go where they wanted in the Antarctic and to do whatever appeared to be commercially attractive', and that the option of the exploitation of mineral resources should remain open 'regardless of diplomatic or environmental consequences'. Others have voiced clear dissent. 'Antarctica should be left alone,' declares Dr Peter Barrett, Director of the Antarctic Research Centre in Wellington, New Zealand, 'but I also recognize that because the world is hooked on petroleum, very few people are going to listen.'

Every nation conducting research in Antarctica has become involved in the quest for the region's mineral resources, some overtly, but most covertly. During the 1950s and 60s the economic boom which the industrialized nations created meant that there were relatively large amounts of money available for research. The boom coinciding with signing of the Antarctic Treaty meant that funding for Antarctic science was readily forthcoming. While research programmes were government funded, there were few strings attached and scientists could pursue their work with a large degree of independence. The economic climate was also such that few governments took more than a passing interest in Antarctica. Although the scientists had concluded the Treaty for their own purposes, their respective governments drew benefits in other

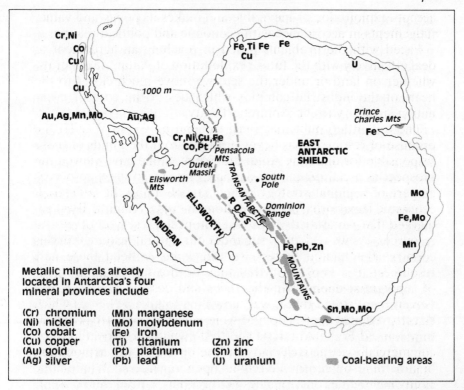

Metallic minerals already
located in Antarctica's four
mineral provinces include

(Cr) chromium	(Mn) manganese	
(Ni) nickel	(Mo) molybdenum	
(Co) cobalt	(Fe) iron	
(Cu) copper	(Ti) titanium	(Zn) zinc
(Au) gold	(Pt) platinum	(Sn) tin
(Ag) silver	(Pb) lead	(U) uranium

Coal-bearing areas

ways. Being party to such a treaty could always be cited as evidence
of political maturity and a desire for peace and co-operation,
particularly in a period marked by the tensions of the Cold War.

Then came the downturn in the world economy in the 1970s
and the first of a series of 'oil crises' which shook western governments out of their slumbering complacency. Scientific programmes
in the Antarctic came under close scrutiny and a series of financial
cutbacks followed. A number of bases were closed and research
projects cancelled or trimmed back. Suddenly governments
wanted to see some sort of return for their investment in Antarctic
science. The golden years were over and Antarctic scientists were
going to have to do something more than extend mankind's
knowledge of the world simply for its own sake if they were to
survive the austerities of a changed economic climate. Enter the
geologists and the geophysicists, whose work was open to distinctly

different interpretations depending on what you wanted to know. The dividing line between 'pure' and 'applied' research is so narrow in this area that it can be crossed without its outward appearance altering at all and it soon provided an answer to the dilemma.

Prompted by a United States National Science Foundation study in 1969 into the feasibility of oil exploitation on the Antarctic continental shelf, the New Zealand Government received several applications for prospecting rights in 1971 and 72. During the same period, numerous enquiries and several more applications were made to a number of Treaty governments including Britain, the United States and France. Under the terms of the Treaty however, these applications could not be granted and companies such as Texaco, British Petroleum and Gulf Oil had to content themselves with quietly influencing the direction of geological research from behind the scenes. Subtly, the dominating strength of the alliance between government and industry in the form of international oil corporations and other multinationals was brought to bear on Antarctic science which, lacking adequate funding, was in danger of losing its unique natural laboratory. Understandably, the majority of scientists were extremely disturbed by the prospect of this intervention since it would inevitably lead to their scientific freedom being compromised. The restrictions and secrecy involved in any commercial operation would run directly counter to the spirit and the letter of the Treaty. But it was a 'Catch-22' situation and the risk had to be accepted if new sources of finance were to be forthcoming. Geological and geophysical research, particularly in the form of seismic and aeromagnetic surveys designed to build up detailed profiles of underlying rock structures of the Continent and surrounding ocean, could easily be used in the search for resources that might have commercial value at any indeterminate point in the future.

If there is an event which can be regarded as precipitating the mineral resources issue into the open and bringing it rapidly to the top of the agenda for discussion, then we have only to look back as far as January 1973. In that year as part of a global geophysical study, the 'Deep Sea Drilling Project', the United States research vessel *Glomar Challenger* drilled four experimental holes in the Ross Sea. Three of these holes produced gaseous hydrocarbons, an initial indicator of the possible presence of oil and gas. Because the scientists in charge of the project were already well aware of the political impact of such a discovery, they had deliberately designed the drilling programme to avoid the most promising oil-bearing structures. They also had no means of capping a hole should oil be struck. With the results of their research now pointing to the likely presence of oil they immediately attempted to play down the importance of the event. They stressed that it would be premature to attach any economic significance to their discovery. However they could not refrain from saying that the situation warranted a closer examination of the Ross Sea potential.

The Ross Sea discovery made a considerable impact upon the Antarctic Treaty consultative parties who, until this point, had preferred to keep any discussion of such a sensitive topic to a minimum. Their apparent lack of urgency arose from the conviction that any need to resolve the minerals problem lay decades ahead, most probably into the twenty-first century. But the *Glomar Challenger* had changed that timescale and a series of private meetings was hastily convened in Norway in the summer of 1973. A number of experts met under the auspices of the Nansen Foundation, acting as a preliminary forum for discussion before bringing the minerals issue onto the agenda of the Antarctic Treaty meetings. As a result of the discussions in Norway it was immediately clear that widely differing attitudes prevailed between the nations involved. The *Glomar Challenger* discovery coincided with the second Arab-Israeli War and the first major oil crisis of the 1970s, and this was a sharp reminder that the accepted economic order was extremely fragile. The whole framework on which the industrialized Western democracies based their economies could no longer be taken for granted. The incentive for investigating the possibilities of alternative sources of supply prompted several governments to take action.

At the request of the Antarctic Policy Group of the United States National Security Council, a secret study of the minerals potential of Antarctica was carried out by the US Geological Survey. Much to the embarrassment of the United States Government, the results of the survey were leaked to the press. While the findings could only be regarded as best estimates based upon minimal scientific data, their disclosure was nevertheless sensational and, even when the figures produced were said to be highly unreliable, it was enough to provoke the serious attention of governments and oil companies around the world. Estimates of some 45 billion barrels of petroleum and 115 trillion cubic feet of natural gas were made for the combined potential of the Ross, Weddell and Bellingshausen Seas. When compared with the 8 billion barrels estimated potential for the North Slope oilfield of Alaska it is easy to understand why these figures provoked such a reaction. It must also be clearly understood that no one had actually found oil anywhere in Antarctica.

A further outcome of the changing emphasis in Antarctic research towards resource related studies has been a steady increase in the number of nations formulating Antarctic research programmes and establishing bases which qualify them to apply for membership of the Antarctic Treaty. It is quite clear that these nations consider the possibility of future resources sufficient justification for mounting these expensive operations. By 1986, membership of the Antarctic Treaty had risen to thirty nations. Of these, sixteen enjoyed full consultative status, enabling them to participate fully in the decision-making processes, which are conducted behind closed doors. The secrecy of these meetings makes it impossible to know what is going on and the public statements issued are rarely a reliable indicator of either the content or the general tone of the discussions.

Significant newcomers to the Treaty include China, India, Brazil and West Germany. The first three countries represent the majority of the world's population and on those grounds alone they insist that their voice should be heard and that they are seated at the table when it comes to any share out of resources. West Germany, which only established itself in the Antarctic in 1980/81 and is already a full consultative member, makes little secret of her reasons for being there. They have constructed a sophisticated research station, George von Neumayer, on the Ekstrom Ice-shelf at the head of the Weddell Sea with accommodation for thirty scientists while at the same time operating five ships in the area. They have one of the world's most advanced ice-strengthened research vessels, *Polarstern*, working in the Weddell Sea not only in summer but also in winter. They are amassing a considerable amount of data from their geophysical surveys of the Weddell Sea basin, one of the most promising areas around Antarctica for oil, and their recent discovery of gas seems to confirm this.

1000 miles to the south-west, the Soviet Union established Druzhnaya Base on the Filchner Ice-shelf in 1975. [As the book was going to press, it was reported that Druzhnaya was floating

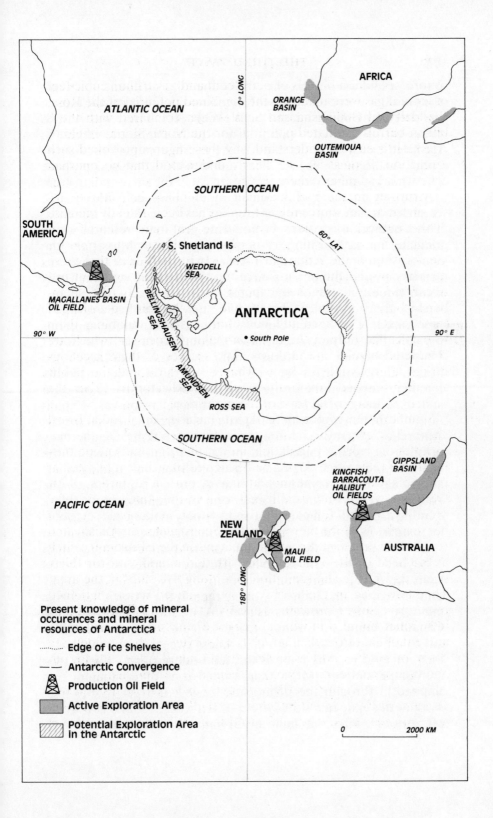

Present knowledge of mineral
occurences and mineral
resources of Antarctica

········· Edge of Ice Shelves

— — — Antarctic Convergence

⊠ Production Oil Field

▓ Active Exploration Area

▨ Potential Exploration Area
in the Antarctic

0   2000 KM

out to sea on an iceberg the size of the English county of Kent, the result of unprecedented calving from the Filchner and Larsen ice shelves at the head of the Weddell Sea. There has been a break-off of an area totalling 7000 square miles, the largest in recorded history and three times the average annual loss for the entire Antarctic ice sheet.] They did so with the express purpose of evaluating mineral resources potential in the surrounding area, particularly in the Dufek Massif in the Pensacola Mountains, regarded as a most promising area for a wide variety of minerals. This assumption is based on the geological interpretation which indicates marked similarities between the Dufek Massif and the Bushveld complex in Southern Africa, which is one of the world's primary areas of mineral resources and production. Although only some three percent of the Dufek Massif is exposed, the rest being buried under ice, the area is much larger than previously recognized. The Soviet Union's interest in Antarctic minerals parallels that of the United States although at present the Soviet Union is pursuing her interests more vigorously than the United States. Both countries are well placed to develop commercially feasible reserves in the future owing to their extensive knowledge and experience of exploiting Arctic mineral resources. Exploitation in the Arctic is widely regarded as a dress rehearsal for the Antarctic—certainly a more difficult undertaking, but already possible on technological and practical grounds. Most of the technology required for polar oil exploration and mining operations has been developed in the Arctic. Adaptation to the Antarctic requires only an extension and refinement of these existing capabilities and not an entirely new system. In a fascinating extension of this argument the Dutch geologist, Dr Maarten J. de Wit, explodes the myth that Antarctic mineral exploitation is beyond our present capability. He cites impressive examples from the Arctic where mining operations have been successfully established and maintained. Among them is the 'Polaris' lead-zinc mine on Little Cornwallis Island in latitude 77° north in the Canadian Arctic. At this remote location the winter temperatures fall to minus 50°C and there is darkness twenty-four hours a day for four months. The mine is located underground in over 1200 feet of permafrost. More than 13,000 tons of equipment was shipped in through the polar pack-ice to construct it. 240 men work at the mine in a shift system of ten weeks on and two weeks off. Another lead-zinc mine in Greenland is situated over 1000

72 Iceberg in the Weddell Sea.

74 *Following page* Under the Harker Glacier, South Georgia.

73 Ice cliffs, Ross ice shelf.

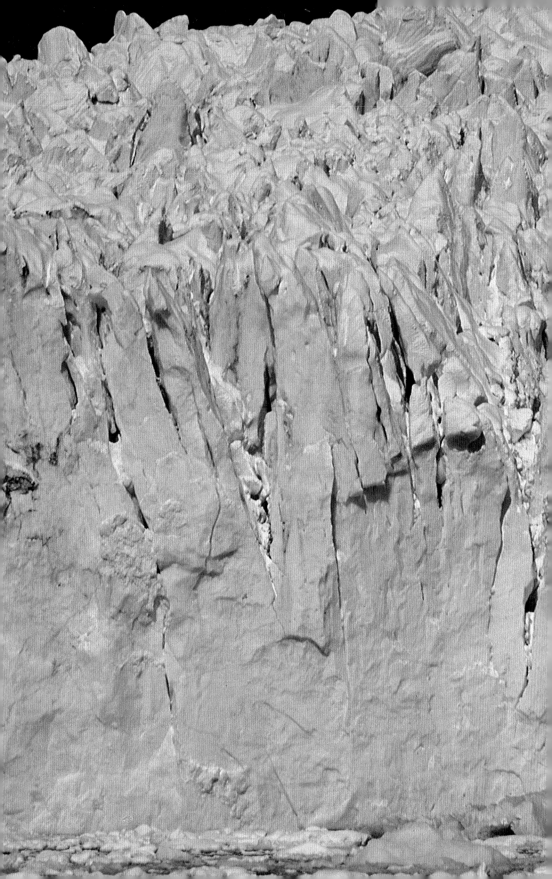

75 Cape Crozier, Ross Island from seaward – destination of Wilson's 1911 winter journey in search of the Emperor penguin eggs.

76 The *Greenpeace* Expedition at the Bay of Whales, Ross ice shelf, marking Antarctica Day, 1 February 1986 (courtesy Doug Allan).

feet up a vertical cliff face where engineers constructed an elaborate cable car system to transport both men and materials.

De Wit uses these examples to illustrate how similar mining operations could be carried out in the Dufek Massif. He details the project from the initial exploration drilling programme costing perhaps ten million dollars in order to establish the reserve—in this case platinum, already known to exist in the Dufek Massif but only in small quantities at this time—through the construction phase including the building of both hard rock and ice runways for transport aircraft and an ice road to the coast, where the Soviet base Druzhnaya and the Argentine's Belgrano could be utilized as ice-port facilities. The ore would be shipped out to smelters in Argentina, Brazil and Australia and further afield to the United States and Japan. De Wit stresses that such an operation either here or in any other area of the Antarctic would have to be commercially viable but, given that condition, the technology is available. Platinum, he points out, is essential to anti-pollution processes and as such is bound to be in increasing demand. This perhaps is a metaphor for resources in general. They are finite, they will be scarce, but demand will not slacken. In time the Antarctic proposition will be irresistible, if not essential.

Dr de Wit places his Antarctic mining scenario in a political context. With eighty-five percent of the world's present platinum production coming from South Africa (a founder member of the Antarctic Treaty), a large new external source could be used as an economic lever on South Africa to bring about political change with regard to human rights. Furthermore he believes that a form of scientific colonialism is being practised in the Antarctic by the rich industrialized nations, who constitute the overwhelming majority of the consultative parties, reaching agreements under the Treaty that safeguard their own long-term interests. Old-fashioned Imperialism has been replaced by this new and more subtle version which seeks the same ends but does so whilst making attractive and misleading overtures to an unsuspecting public audience.

De Wit's analysis contains an echo of Olaf Stapleton's words, but his ideas are rooted in practical propositions and they are the product of an informed and serious scientist. He understands that the Antarctic Treaty remains intact only as long as there is nothing of commercial value to be gained from Antarctica and he expects the breakdown of the status quo as soon as science and technology, politics and economics converge at the same point.

The *Glomar Challenger* discovery acted as a signal to the other Treaty nations, and to those who had never before seriously considered Antarctica, that the Continent's mineral potential and future exploitation was an opportunity that must be grasped. The Americans, Russians and West Germans were quick to respond. So too were the Japanese, whose economic 'miracle' and advanced industrial society relies entirely on imported oil. The increasing instability of the Middle East during the 1970s and successive oil crises made the Japanese feel particularly vulnerable. In September 1979 they launched a major geophysical survey programme using their research ship the *Hakurei Maru*. The survey covered the Ross, Weddell and Bellingshausen Seas and was conducted under the watchful eye of the Japan National Oil Corporation. With the agreement of the Japanese Ministry of International Trade and Industry the programme received an initial budget of more than twelve million dollars.

The necessity of finding a solution politically acceptable to everyone involved has already found its precedent in the Falklands War. Uncomfortably close to the Antarctic, the conflict involved two nations signatory to the Antarctic Treaty, who dispute not only the sovereignty of the Falkland Islands but also the same slice of Antarctic territory. With both fishery and oil resources potential around the Falklands, some analysts believe that Argentina's decision to invade was at least partly motivated by a desire to secure her options on future development of these resources. Although thwarted, the invasion may well have been viewed by Argentina as a first move towards securing her Antarctic options. It is not without significance either that, while the war was being fought, Argentine and British scientists continued their usual friendly dialogue within the Antarctic consultative meetings. This demonstrates the success of the Treaty in building up a mutual trust between scientists but it also indicates that their respective political masters may well have ideas quite contrary to the agreements being reached. It appears that governments support Antarctic science because they believe it can further their own national policies towards the area quite irrespective of whether these accord with the existing Treaty. What this amounts to is a clear divergence of purpose between the scientists on the one hand and the politicians on the other.

As things are, Argentina continues to press its claim and even

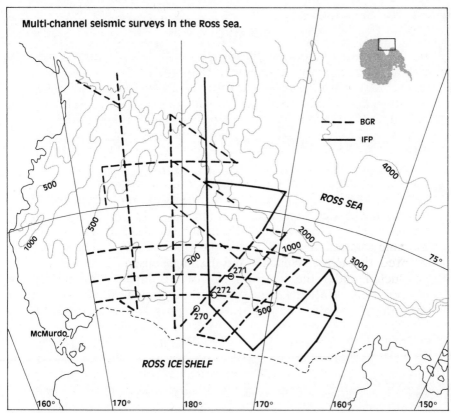

Multi-channel seismic surveys in the Ross Sea.

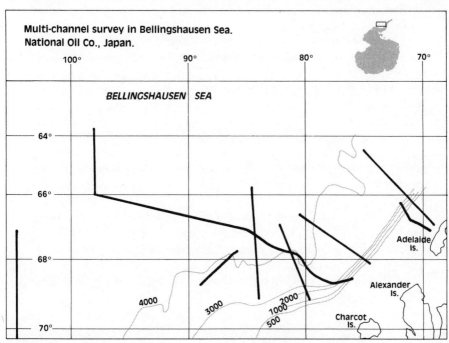

Multi-channel survey in Bellingshausen Sea.
National Oil Co., Japan.

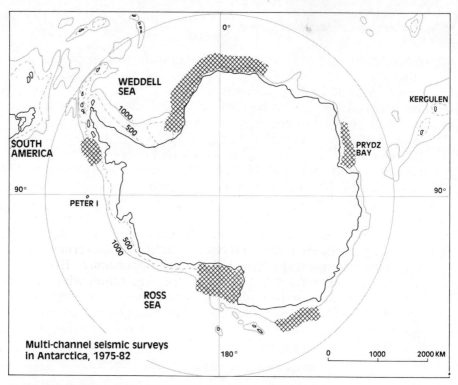

Multi-channel seismic surveys
in Antarctica, 1975-82

0   1000   2000 KM

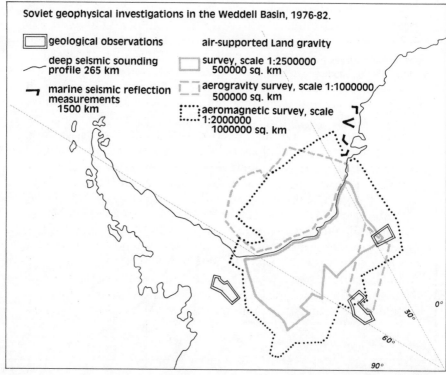

Soviet geophysical investigations in the Weddell Basin, 1976-82.

☐ geological observations   air-supported Land gravity

  deep seismic sounding   ☐ survey, scale 1:2500000
  profile 265 km   500000 sq. km

┐ marine seismic reflection   ☐ aerogravity survey, scale 1:1000000
  measurements   500000 sq. km
  1500 km   ☐ aeromagnetic survey, scale
                                       1:2000000
                                       1000000 sq. km

under a moderate democratic government maintains an unarmed military presence on her Antarctic bases on the Peninsula and insists on stamping the passport of anyone who wishes to go ashore. With marriages, the birth of babies, schooling facilities and families generally encouraged to live on the bases, Argentine Antarctic science seems to have taken a back seat in preference to a form of colonial occupation. In International Law however, this sort of action carries weight in substantiating territorial claims. An interesting sidelight on the British/Argentine dispute concerns the little known Scottish National Antarctic Expedition of 1902–04. This expedition led by W. S. Bruce established its base on Laurie Island in the South Orkneys. At the end of the expedition Bruce offered his base to the British Government, who quite unexpectedly turned down the opportunity. Bruce, offended by this refusal, offered it to the Argentines who had been helpful to his expedition. The Argentines have occupied the Laurie Island base ever since and it is the longest continuously-manned scientific station in Antarctica. Hardly surprisingly, the Argentines use this occupancy as very effective ammunition in their dispute with Britain over the Antarctic territorial claim.

One result of the Falklands conflict was that within six months of the end of hostilities the British Government doubled the British Antarctic Survey's budget to £9.5 million annually. The ice patrol vessel HMS *Endurance* under threat of withdrawal in 1981, at a saving on running costs of £3 million a year, was reprieved. Britain's 'Fortress Falklands' policy, an airbase with missile silos costing over £900 million, her continued military presence on South Georgia, her declaration of a 200 mile fishing zone around the islands, all are indicators of a drastic turn-around in her attitude to the whole area. The politicians might want it to be believed the war was fought for good old-fashioned patriotic motives but someone in Whitehall woke up and realized there was a lot more at stake than 1800 islanders and two million sheep.

Other South American countries, Brazil, Uruguay and Peru, are showing an increasing interest in Antarctica. Brazil has a rapidly expanding Polar Institute and now spends more money on biological research than the United States. And so South Atlantic military strategy has taken on an importance few would have foreseen a decade ago. Britain entrenched on 'Fortress Falklands', guarding her traditional gateway to the Antarctic, now faces the South American continent, whose nations are similarly determined to have their share of Antarctica's resources.

Against this increasingly unpredictable background, the continuance of the Antarctic Treaty beyond 1991, incorporating a minerals agreement to all nations involved, looms as the critical factor in maintaining co-operation in the Antarctic and as the agent for diffusing possible military confrontation within the Treaty area as well as outside it. The possibility of military conflict in the nuclear age is so fraught with hazard that, however remote the possibility, it is enough to persuade governments to look for alternatives. Is it possible that the price of continued peace in Antarctica and in the world beyond is to be paid for by preparing the way for the exploitation of the last continent? Faced with that alternative there are few who would consider the price of war worth paying. Such a fate for Antarctica is not hard to imagine for it accords entirely with the brutalizing philosophy of industrial power and military might, the deadly alliance that has engulfed the world, destroying its beauty, poisoning its natural systems and imprisoning its citizens.

And so what of the future and where is the relationship of the present to the visions of Stapleton, the conclusion of Maarten de Wit and the responsibilities which face the members of the Antarctic Treaty? What of Stapleton's 'new supply of oil' and his 'unexpectedly rich coalfields'?

We do know that Antarctica contains the world's largest coalfield. Coal was the first mineral discovered on the continent by Shackleton's *Nimrod* expedition of 1907. Although widespread throughout Antarctica, particularly in the Transantarctic mountains and near the Amery Ice-shelf, the quality of the coal is fairly low-grade and it has a high ash content. This resource is definitely not worth exploiting at present, but then again the world might regard these reserves very differently in the future. For instance, for all but those with a vested interest or still blinkered by the propaganda, nuclear power is not the safe, cheap means of future energy we have been led to believe. It is the headstone being erected over humanity's grave. With a combination of huge financial uncertainties, worsening accidents and the unsolved waste-disposal problem (the Antarctic ice sheet has been seriously proposed as a nuclear waste dump—mercifully rejected by Antarctic scientists) it may only be a matter of time before the dream of cheap nuclear energy becomes the nightmare of the past. Already in the United States, no reactor has been built since the Three Mile Island accident in 1978. With the development of a new generation of coal burning power stations it is now possible to produce energy cheaply, efficiently and, most importantly, free of the pollution which in the past has been coal's greatest drawback. The new stations developed in Canada can also operate efficiently on low-grade coals. The world has huge reserves of this resource and, given the only sane course of action is to phase out nuclear energy, then, until adequate funding is given to alternative technologies, coal is the most attractive option, and Antarctic coal could well help to meet the energy requirements of the future. Not for another two or three hundred years perhaps, but that is no time at all, and it is in this perspective that mankind needs to think of its future if it is to have one at all.

As far as we can tell no one yet knows Antarctica's true oil potential. Whether oil has been found secretly is open to question. It would not be surprising. But no one is really going to declare what they know, the discoveries they have made, or the plans they have laid until the political climate is right and the Antarctic Treaty nations have succeeded in formulating the agreement that gives the oil companies, the industrialists and the multi-national corporations the incentives and the legal framework with which they can proceed with the exploitation of Antarctica.

Meanwhile the consultative parties continue the debate in a continuing series of special meetings that have now been going on for over a decade. All parties are keenly aware that agreement must be reached soon if they are to have a Minerals Convention ratified by the time the Treaty comes up for review in 1991. Time is not on their side. Pressures are mounting for a settlement but each grouping involved has its own ideas regarding the form such a settlement should take. Third World governments, the United Nations, the international industrial community, the conservationists—each regards itself as the representative of Antarctica's future. Apart from some conservationists, all accept that exploitation is inevitable, indeed some would argue that it must be actively promoted. Faced with this, the consultative parties say that all they can hope for is to limit the damage as much as possible when the exploitation starts. No one disputes the grave environmental risks that would be created and the appalling consequences resulting from oil spills and toxic contamination on the fragile Antarctic ecosystem.

Alone among these voices, the more radical conservationists argue that no exploitation should ever take place in Antarctica and that the entire Antarctic Treaty area should be declared a World Park. In 1972, the Second World Conference on National Parks recommended unanimously that the Antarctic Continent and the surrounding seas should become the first World Park under the auspices of the United Nations. This proposal was subsequently taken to the 1975 Antarctic Treaty meeting but nothing more has happened and, given the secrecy of the Treaty meetings, it seems likely that the idea was rejected as impossibly altruistic, despite its obvious attractions and advantages to pure science. It was in a sense too late even then, for the compromise that would accommodate exploitation had already been made.

I am reminded of a conversation I had some years ago. It took place on the bridge of a ship bucking its way through an Antarctic gale halfway between South Georgia and the South Orkney Islands. The man with whom I was enjoying this experience had been one of the principal architects of the Antarctic Treaty, an eminent polar historian, a pioneering Antarctic ornothologist and a diplomat of remarkable skill as the success of his endeavours amply demonstrates. As the bows plunged and the ship shuddered and huge seas crashed over the bridge he reminisced about his early days in Antarctica in the 1930s—about being under sail in seas like this in a much smaller ship, the difficulties and the fun of the life and the research, the excitement, the romance and the challenge of it all—it was all so very different then. After a while we got around to the Treaty, but he seemed not to want to say very much about it and I felt it was certainly not my place to push the talk where he didn't want it to go. So he didn't say much except in a roundabout way.

'Don't worry about what you can't achieve,' he said in reference to some modest ambition or other of mine, 'just concentrate on what's possible. Forget about the impossible—that's how we did the Antarctic Treaty.' Of course I did not believe him; at least I knew it wasn't that simple and he could see I didn't believe him. So he smiled, slightly, like the old fox he was and turned to watch the seas again and said not another word for a very long time.

By virtue of its integrity, Antarctic science has been an inspiration to mankind; the ideals of the Antarctic Treaty have given men hope in a beleagured world. These achievements required great courage as well as a vision of the future unclouded by such temporary expedients that the present often appears to demand. Those people with whom responsibility for the fate of this vision now rests should not falter, neither should they compromise these things through the fear that they cannot be upheld. Once lost they can never be regained. In the words of a leading conservationist, 'There can be no justification for the exploitation of Antarctica except in terms of human greed. For we do not need Antarctica's supposed resources but merely desire them to give longevity to a way of life which must, ultimately, come to terms with its own bankruptcy. We have to stop somewhere in our quest for more resources, because resources are finite. Should we not stop this rape before we destroy the last remaining great wilderness, rather than afterward?'

Antarctica is the last link in the chain which has held man securely under the protection of the natural world since he first emerged into the global wilderness. If he destroys that link he himself will be endangered as never before. Scientists were shocked that the snows falling over Antarctica were so soon contaminated with the radioactive fallout from the nuclear accident at Chernobyl. Through her last remaining wilderness nature signals her warnings.

PART IV
THE FOURTH WAVE

10

THE BAY OF WHALES

Little more than 200 years have passed since Captain Cook went in search of Antarctica. Sailing around a pre-industrial planet he was in no doubt that nature held sway beyond the immediate scope of European civilization. Indeed Cook's voyages are a graphic reminder that wilderness prevailed throughout the world at that time and that the peoples and cultures he encountered were essentially nature-centred in their relationship with the surrounding environment. The history of the last 200 years has been the history of the destruction of that global wilderness by the predatory expansion of European man. The principal agent of that destruction has been the irreversible momentum of his man-centred science and technology inspired by the belief that it was his God-given duty to achieve total domination over the natural world. With such powerful means at his disposal that mission has been overwhelmingly successful. We are left now with only shrinking enclaves of natural habitat which, lacking anything more substantial, we are proud to call wilderness in memory of something that has gone for ever.

Before its colonization the North American continent was entirely wilderness. It was however a wilderness inhabited by people who understood, valued and respected it. The North American Indian was at home in this wilderness; his love and comprehension of it we began to appreciate only when we had all but destroyed both of them. In just 350 years over three and a half million square miles of natural forest, plain, marsh and mountain have been recreated in man's image. Today less than two percent of that original wilderness remains. A similar story can be told for much of the rest of the planet and the destruction continues unchecked. In whatever perspective one chooses to view it, human beings are clearly overwhelming the earth.

At the time of Cook's voyages in the second half of the eighteenth century, world population numbered around 750 million people, the result of a gentle increase which had been taking place since the time of the Agricultural Revolution some 10,000 years ago. Then came the Industrial Revolution and with it man's numbers increased dramatically. Initially the pressure of people was felt in Europe where frantic industrialization caused massive social upheaval. But there was the convenient safety valve in the empty, waiting spaces of the New World. Europeans in their millions emigrated overseas taking their technology with them. Thus, without realizing it, the eventual destruction of the wilderness was assured. By 1850, eighty years after Cook, world population had almost doubled to 1200 million, by 1900 to 1600 million and by 1950 to 2500 million. By 1986 almost five billion people were living on earth. Mankind has already filled the most accessible areas of the world. To accommodate the needs of humanity's rising tide only the less suitable, more intractable places remain and it is here that human beings are engaged in a desperate battle with nature, the poor simply in order to survive, the rich to expand already dangerously misshapen economies based upon their materialist philisophy.

In the Himalayas I have seen the extent to which the natural forest has been stripped from the mountainsides by an expanding population in search of firewood, building materials and the bare necessities of life. They can only go upwards and they will stop only when they reach the snowline and have nowhere left to go. I was shocked, but not so much as my companion, a Nepalese plant-hunter who returned to find only eroded mountain slopes where ten years before he had walked among the Rhododendron forests in all their glory. To see such destruction with one's own eyes is to know the truth of man's impact upon the natural world.

Flying over the Amazon basin I have witnessed one of contemporary man's most shameful deeds as he lays waste the largest tropical rainforest on earth. At the present rate of felling, burning and blasting it will have all but gone in the next twenty years, to say nothing of the indigenous Indian tribes, the animals and birds, the insects and plants as yet unknown to us along with a third of the world's oxygenating capacity. At present, tropical rainforests cover six percent of the world's land surface and they contain almost fifty percent of the earth's known animal and insect species. They are being cleared at the rate of a hundred acres a minute by multinational companies supplying the escalating material demands for our urban-industrial societies. Again, seeing is believing.

In Africa, which once overwhelmed me with the beauty of her music and her culture, the loss of natural habitat together with its disappearing wildlife have become symptomatic of that unhappy continent's desperate plight. People must compete with animals for the dwindling resource of land where not so long ago nature seemed irrepressible in her capacity to provide more than enough for all. The dark continent was never so dark until Europeans named and made it so.

And I do not have to hold these far-flung examples of destruction in my mind's eye to know the truth. Within a few miles of my home I can observe the same processes at work in the Scottish Highlands where the pressures of tourism, leisure pursuits, unregulated forestry, unsuitable agricultural practices, inappropriate industries and the insidious spread of the military combine in an onslaught upon the landscape which leaves one seriously doubting that a single acre will remain free to receive the ebb and flow of the seasons beyond this guttering century of ours. The evidence is before our eyes and should alone convince us that we are killing the earth. But most often we choose not to see, for what we know in our hearts we can so easily deny in our heads. And we will never face the truth so long as we continue to argue over statistics and computer models, holding blindly to our faith in the 'technological fix' and the philosophy of 'progress', meaning unlimited growth.

Should man survive the chaos and destruction he is inflicting upon himself and his surroundings, then the ultimate danger lies in the perishable quality of his higher aspirations. The search for happiness and love, the cleansing breath of individual freedom and spiritual enlightenment; these things will cease to exist as surely as the natural world from which they arose perishes around him. The loss of wild places is not only a physical deprivation, it represents the abandonment of the fundamental influence on man's psychological development which has both inspired and sustained him throughout his evolution. 'When man obliterates wilderness he repudiates the evolutionary force that put him on this planet,' wrote the physicist J. A. Rush and, he continued, 'in a deeply terrifying sense, man is on his own.'

Virtually half the world's population, over 2000 million people, live in urban surroundings and their number is growing faster by a quarter than the increase in total population. Almost 91 percent of the British people live in cities, constituting the most urban community in the world. Suburbia is so extensive in England that it is now called 'the country', which indeed it is but no longer a green and pleasant land. In the latter part of the twentieth century, the city-dweller is already the characteristic human type. Urbanized thinking increasingly dominates every aspect of our lives. The politicians, planners, bureaucrats, scientists and technologists of every description inhabit a world bordered by concrete, steel and glass, totally cut off from anything that remotely resembles nature, and in this hermetically sealed environment they dream up the future of the world—it is easy to understand why nature is treated so contemptuously.

Formerly it was the radical thinkers who urged that man could only benefit from science applied as technology, and gain in the process total mastery over his environment. In other words nature was there to be exploited and fit only to serve the purposes of man. Those who recoiled in horror—the poets for instance—were dismissed as cranks, while others who recommended restraint and caution were brushed aside. Today the radical approach is undoubtedly associated with those who are attempting to turn this tide of thought before it carries us to a disaster from which recovery will be impossible. Their concerted efforts have been in evidence for little more than a decade or two at most. It is too early to pronounce the success or otherwise of their challenge to the orthodoxy which proclaims as a central article of faith the belief that technology will provide the answer to all man's problems.

The consciousness of people all over the world has been aroused to the danger and there is an increased awareness of the total dimensions and inter-relationship of the problems confronting us. Slowly the Environment Revolution gathers momentum responding to the most serious challenge to its survival the human species has ever faced. From a sense of impending tragedy resistance grows.

Antarctica, the last true wilderness, has emerged as the symbol of our age, the evocation of the natural world in its time of greatest crisis. It represents the last chance man has of a change of heart so necessary in preceding the reconciliation with nature that will determine the future of our planet. For this reason alone, Antarctica is moving steadily towards the centre of the stage in world affairs. What happens there will be of paramount import-

77 *Opposite page* Fast-ice breaking out of Marguerite Bay, Antarctic Peninsula.

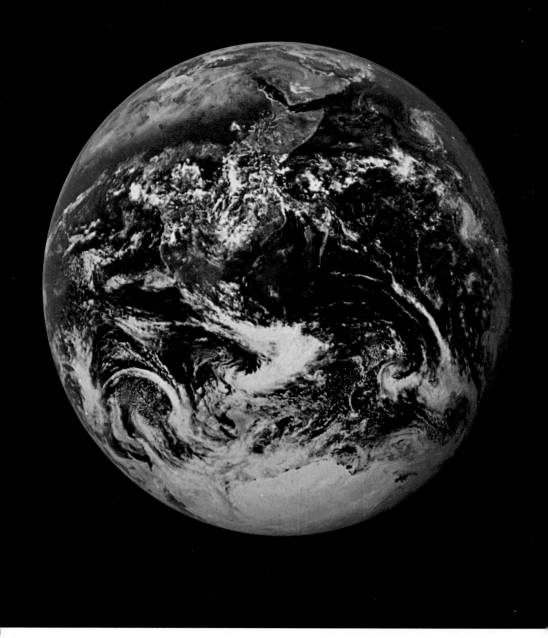

79 Planet of Contrasts: Viewed from space, the continent of Antarctica shines clearly through the surrounding cloud masses circling the Southern Ocean. To the north the burnt colours of Africa's deserts glow either side of the equatorial belt with its speckled clouds of tropical storms.

78 *Previous page* Weathered bergs locked in the winter sea ice – South Orkney Islands.

ance for us all. As such, mankind is faced with an unprecedented challenge to its fundamental values—its basic humanity. It is a challenge that has been recognized by conservationists throughout the world. Organizations such as the Antarctic & Southern Ocean Coalition (ASOC), the Fund for Animals in Australia, Friends of the Earth, the World Wildlife Fund, the International Union for the Conservation of Nature (IUCN), Greenpeace and many, many others are united in their opposition to the exploitation and inevitable destruction of Antarctica. Their wish is to see this unique continent declared a World Park, protected for ever for the benefit and inspiration of future generations. It would be the greatest monument that twentieth-century man could leave to the future, a redeeming act of courage, wisdom and sanity prevailing above the common chaos of our darkened world.

The Bay of Whales lies 400 miles east of Ross Island, a natural harbour, a sheltered indentation in the otherwise unbroken face of the ice cliff. It was first described by Ross in 1843 but he had no reason to name what he believed was a temporary feature of the constantly changing ice 'barrier'. Scott called it 'Balloon Bight' in 1902 because he was able to get ashore there and rise in a hot air balloon and look for the first time across the formidable immensity of the ice shelf beyond. It was Shackleton who renamed it the Bay of Whales in 1908 because there were indeed so many whales surrounding their ship. He thought he might establish his base there for his attempt on the Pole, but fearing the ice might break away he returned to the safer shores of Ross Island. In 1911 Amundsen, realizing the position of the Bay of Whales had barely altered since first reported, took his chance with nature and established 'Framheim' from where he launched his journey to the Pole. And in the 1930s and 40s Admiral Byrd constructed a number of bases here from which he made his pioneering flights over the Continent. The Bay of Whales is then a place imbued with the history of man's endeavours in Antarctica and the scene of his changing attitudes and techniques towards it. And although there is no trace of him, nature has somehow held the soul of man within the atmosphere—one senses the impression of past events in the surrounding desolation so that one shivers not only from the cold. Here on 2 January 1986 another expedition landed, a party of thirty-six men and women, citizens of ten nations ashore on the continent of Antarctica. The day was cold and grey, drift blowing from the surrounding ice cliffs, the rough sea beyond the

bay black between passing snow squalls. On the confined area of
bay ice stood little groups of penguins. Adelies, some still moulting, huddled together against the drift while nearby two Emperor
penguins stood imperiously immobile watching these unexpected
visitors who then unfurled a flag of rainbow colours and posed for
a photograph beside their ship. Within twelve hours the visitors
had gone, leaving behind only their vanishing footprints. Their
coming and their going had conveyed no outward sign of drama.
The significance of their landing was for them overshadowed by
their failure to establish a base on Ross Island. For the international conservation group Greenpeace this short landing was a
diversion following weeks of waiting off Ross Island for the fast-ice
to break out of McMurdo Sound. Until this happened they could
not approach Cape Evans on the south-west coast of the island
where, close to the historic huts of both Scott and Shackleton, they
planned to set up the first non-governmental base in Antarctica, a
practical demonstration of the seriousness with which the conservation movement intends to pursue its call for a World Park in
Antarctica. In the event, time ran out and Greenpeace had to call
off their expedition. But it was only a temporary defeat for they
intended to return in a fresh attempt the following season. They
were not the first to have their hopes dashed by the Antarctic ice.

Standing together with that group in the Bay of Whales, I
realized that almost twenty years had passed since I had first come
to the Antarctic. I had been then a young man filled with the
exuberance of youth in the happy and simple anticipation of a
forthcoming adventure. I was not entirely prepared for the impact
Antarctica was to make on me and could not have foreseen how
the experience was to transform my life. Antarctica opened my
eyes. It made me vividly aware of the dramatic difference between
the world that is inhabited by man and that which is subject only
to the hand of nature.

The last twenty years has been a period of profound and rapid
change throughout the world. Antarctica has not been spared
from that change and the remorseless dynamics of technology and
man's ascendency over nature are as much in evidence there as
anywhere. Antarctica is no longer a place apart and I do not see
it as I once did. Its embattled wilderness, whether in the mind's
eye or in reality, no longer brings to me that peace of mind that
I once associated with its timeless inviolability.

Antarctica has left a restless longing in my heart, trembling like a mirage on a far horizon, beckoning towards an incomprehensible perfection for ever beyond the reach of mortal man. Its overwhelming beauty touches one so deeply that it is like a wound, remaining for ever as tender to the touch of the inquisitorial world as on the day when those extraordinary vistas of ice first cut their way into the deeper levels of consciousness.

If you go into the wilderness you may find peace, but, because that wilderness itself is no longer inviolate, your peace will be disturbed by the vision it affords you of the world from which you have come and the destructive forces it contains. All life now hangs upon the slender thread which the creature man has created and which he alone now holds from moment to moment to moment.

200 years ago Coleridge, through the figure of the Ancient Mariner, warned of the consequences following upon European man's decisive break with nature.

> He went like one that hath been stunned,
> And is of sense forlorn:
> A sadder and a wiser man,
> He rose the morrow morn.

POSTSCRIPT

On 16 January 1987 the expedition ship *Greenpeace* arrived once again at the entrance to McMurdo Sound. After waiting for nine days the ice began breaking out of the Sound and on 25 January the ship was able to anchor offshore at Cape Evans, Ross Island. Here, within sight of the huts of the Scott and Shackleton expeditions, Greenpeace established the first non-governmental base in Antarctica since the International Geophysical Year and the signing of the Antarctic Treaty in 1959. It marks a small but courageous step among many that must be taken in the attempt to secure World Park status for Antarctica and to save the last true wilderness from the irreversible consequences of impending exploitation. It is a step too that seems to accord more purposefully with Antarctica's history and place in the world and may yet create a bridge to the future, to new visions of Antarctica which we have not seen and which we have yet to understand.

APPENDIX 1

The Antarctic Treaty

[Signed by the original twelve nations in Washington, December 1959; came into effect 23 June 1961]

The Governments of Argentina, Australia, Belgium, Chile, the French Republic, Japan, New Zealand, Norway, the Union of South Africa, the Union of Soviet Socialist Republics, the United Kingdom of Great Britain and Northern Ireland, and the United States of America:

Recognizing that it is in the interest of all mankind that Antarctica shall continue forever to be used exclusively for peaceful purposes and shall not become the scene or object of international discord:

Acknowledging the substantial contributions to scientific knowledge resulting from international co-operation in scientific investigation in Antarctica:

Convinced that the establishment of a firm foundation for the continuation and development of such co-operation on the basis of freedom of scientific investigation in Antarctica as applied during the International Geophysical Year accords with the interests of science and the progress of all mankind:

Convinced also that a treaty ensuring the use of Antarctica for peaceful purposes only and the continuance of international harmony in Antarctica will further the purposes and principles embodied in the Charter of the United Nations:

Have agreed as follows:

Article I

1. Antarctica shall be used for peaceful purposes only. There shall be prohibited, *inter alia,* any measures of a military nature, such as the establishment of military bases and fortifications, the carrying out of military manoeuvers, as well as the testing of any type of weapons.

2. The present Treaty shall not prevent the use of military personnel or equipment for scientific research or for any other peaceful purpose.

Article II
Freedom of scientific investigation in Antarctica and co-operation toward that end, as applied during the International Geophysical Year, shall continue, subject to the provisions of the present Treaty.

Article III
1. In order to promote international co-operation in scientific investigation in Antarctica, as provided for in Article II of the present Treaty, the Contracting Parties agree that, to the greatest extent feasible and practicable:
   a. information regarding plans for scientific programs in Antarctica shall be exchanged to permit maximum economy and efficiency of operations:
   b. scientific personnel shall be exchanged in Antarctica between expeditions and stations:
   c. scientific observations and results from Antarctica shall be exchanged and made freely available.
2. In implementing this Article, every encouragement shall be given to the establishment of co-operative working relations with those Specialized Agencies of the United Nations and other international organizations having a scientific or technical interest in Antarctica.

Article IV
1. Nothing contained in the present Treaty shall be interpreted as:
   a. renunciation by any Contracting Party of previously asserted rights of or claims to territorial sovereignty in Antarctica:
   b. a renunciation or diminution by any Contracting Party of any basis of claim to territorial sovereignty in Antarctica which it may have whether as a result of its activities or those of its nationals in Antarctica, or otherwise:
   c. prejudicing the position of any Contracting Party as regards its recognition or non-recognition of any other State's right of or claim or basis of claim to territorial sovereignty in Antarctica.
2. No acts or activities taking place while the present Treaty is in force shall constitute a basis for asserting, supporting or denying a claim to territorial sovereignty in Antarctica or create any rights of sovereignty in Antarctica. No new claim, or enlargement of an existing claim, to terroritorial sovereignty in Antarctica shall be asserted while the present Treaty is in force.

Article V
1. Any nuclear explosions in Antarctica and the disposal there of radioactive waste material shall be prohibited.
2. In the event of the conclusion of international agreements concerning the use of nuclear energy, including nuclear explosions and the disposal

of radioactive waste material, to which all of the Contracting Parties whose representatives are entitled to participate in the meetings provided for under Article IX are parties, the rules established under such agreements shall apply in Antarctica.

Article VI

The provisions of the present Treaty shall apply to the area south of 60° South Latitude, including all ice shelves, but nothing in the present Treaty shall prejudice or in any way affect the rights, or the exercise of the rights, of any State under international law with regard to the high seas within that area.

Article VII

1. In order to promote the objectives and ensure the observance of the provisions of the present Treaty, each Contracting Party whose representatives are entitled to participate in the meetings referred to in Article IX of the Treaty shall have the right to designate observers to carry out any inspection provided for by the present Article. Observers shall be nationals of the Contracting Parties which designate them. The names of observers shall be communicated to every other Contracting Party having the right to designate observers, and like notice shall be given of the termination of their appointment.

2. Each observer designated in accordance with the provisions of paragraph 1 of this Article shall have complete freedom of access at any time to any or all areas of Antarctica.

3. All areas of Antarctica, including all stations, installations and equipment within those areas, and all ships and aircraft at points of discharging or embarking cargoes or personnel in Antarctica, shall be open at all time to inspection by any observers designated in accordance with paragraph 1 of this Article.

4. Aerial observation may be carried out at any time over any or all areas of Antarctica by any of the Contracting Parties having the right to designate observers.

5. Each Contracting Party shall, at the time when the present Treaty enters into force for it, inform the other Contracting Parties, and thereafter shall give them notice in advance, of

   a. all expeditions to and within Antarctica, on the part of its ships or nationals, and all expeditions to Antarctica organized in or proceeding from its territory:

   b. all stations in Antarctica occupied by its nationals: and

   c. any military personnel or equipment intended to be introduced by it into Antarctica subject to the conditions prescribed in paragraph 2 of Article 1 of the present Treaty.

Article VIII

1. In order to facilitate the exercise of their functions under the present Treaty, and without prejudice to the respective positions of the Contracting Parties relating to jurisdiction over all other persons in Antarctica, observers designated under paragraph 1 of Article VII and scientific personnel exchanged under subparagraph 1 (b) of Article III of the Treaty, and members of the staffs accompanying any such persons, shall be subject only to the jurisdiction of the Contracting Party of which they are nationals in respect of all acts or omissions occurring while they are in Antarctica for the purpose of exercising their functions.

2. Without prejudice to the provisions of paragraph 1 of this Article, and pending the adoption of measures in pursuance of subparagraph 1 (e) of Article IX, the Contracting Parties concerned in any case of dispute with regard to the exercise of jurisdiction in Antarctica shall immediately consult together with a view to reaching a mutually acceptable solution.

Article IX

1. Representatives of the Contracting Parties named in the preamble to the present Treaty shall meet at the City of Canberra within two months after the date of entry into force of the Treaty, and thereafter at suitable intervals and places, for the purpose of exchanging information, consulting together on matters of common interest pertaining to Antarctica, and formulating and considering, and recommending to their Governments, measures in furtherance of the principles and objectives of the Treaty, including measures regarding:

    a. use of Antarctica for peaceful purposes only:

    b. facilitation of scientific research in Antarctica:

    c. facilitation of international scientific co-operation in Antarctica:

    d. facilitation of the exercise of the rights of inspection provided for in Article VII of the Treaty:

    e. questions relating to the exercise of jurisdiction in Antarctica:

    f. preservation and conservation of living resources in Antarctica.

2. Each Contracting Party which has become a party to the present Treaty by accession under Article XIII shall be entitled to appoint representatives to participate in the meetings referred to in paragraph 1 of the present Article, during such time as that Contracting Party demonstrates its interest in Antarctica by conducting substantial scientific research activity there, such as the establishment of a scientific station or the despatch of a scientific expedition.

3. Reports from the observers referred to in Article VII of the present Treaty shall be transmitted to the representatives of the Contracting Parties participating in the meetings referred to in paragraph 1 of the present Article.

4. The measures referred to in paragraph 1 of this Article shall become effective when approved by all the Contracting Parties whose representatives were entitled to participate in the meetings held to consider those measures.

5. Any or all of the rights established in the present Treaty may be exercised as from the date of entry into force of the Treaty whether or not any measures facilitating the exercise of such rights have been proposed, considered or approved as provided in this Article.

Article X

Each of the Contracting Parties undertakes to exert appropriate efforts, consistent with the Charter of the United Nations, to the end that no one engages in any activity in Antarctica contrary to the principles or purposes of the present Treaty.

Article XI

1. If any dispute arises between two or more of the Contracting Parties concerning the interpretation or application of the present Treaty, those Contracting Parties shall consult among themselves with a view to having the dispute resolved by negotiation, inquiry, mediation, conciliation, arbitration, judicial settlement or other peaceful means of their own choice.

2. Any dispute of this character not so resolved shall, with the consent, in each case, of all parties to the dispute, be referred to the International Court of Justice for settlement; but failure to reach agreement on reference to the International Court shall not absolve parties to the dispute from the responsibility of continuing to seek to resolve it by any of the various peaceful means referred to in paragraph 1 of this Article.

Article XII

1a. The present Treaty may be modified or amended at any time by unanimous agreement of the Contracting Parties whose representatives are entitled to participate in the meetings provided for under Article IX. Any such modification or amendment shall enter into force when the depositary Government has received notice from all such Contracting Parties that they have ratified it.

b. Such modification or amendment shall thereafter enter into force as to any other Contracting Party when notice of ratification by it has been received by the depositary Government. Any such Contracting Party from which no notice of ratification is received within a period of two years from the date of entry into force of the modification or amendment in accordance with the provisions of subparagraph 1 (a) of this Article shall be deemed to have withdrawn from the present Treaty on the date of the expiration of such period.

2a. If after the expiration of thirty years from the date of entry into

force of the present Treaty, any of the Contracting Parties whose representatives are entitled to participate in the meetings provided for under Article IX so requests by a communication addressed to the depositary Government, a Conference of all the Contracting Parties shall be held as soon as practicable to review the operation of the Treaty.
b. Any modification or amendment to the present Treaty which is approved at such a Conference by a majority of the Contracting Parties there represented, including a majority of those whose representatives are entitled to participate in the meetings provided for under Article IX, shall be communicated by the depositary Government to all the Contracting Parties immediately after the termination of the Conference and shall enter into force in accordance with the provisions of paragraph I of the present Article.
c. If any such modification or amendment has not entered into force in accordance with the provisions of subparagraph 1 (a) of this Article within a period of two years after the date of its communication to all the Contracting Parties, any Contracting Party may at any time after the expiration of that period give notice to the depositary Government of its withdrawal from the present Treaty; and such withdrawal shall take effect two years after the receipt of the notice by the depositary Government.

Article XIII
1. The present Treaty shall be subject to ratification by the signatory States. It shall be open for accession by any State which is a Member of the United Nations, or by any other State which may be invited to accede to the Treaty with the consent of all the Contracting Parties whose representatives are entitled to participate in the meetings provided for under Article IX of the Treaty.
2. Ratification of or accession to the present Treaty shall be effected by each State in accordance with its constitutional processes.
3. Instruments of ratification and instruments of accession shall be deposited with the Government of the United States of America, hereby designated as the depositary Government.
4. The depositary Government shall inform all signatory and acceding States of the date of each deposit of an instrument of ratification or accession, and the date of entry into force of the Treaty and of any modification or amendment thereto.
5. Upon the deposit of instruments of ratification by all the signatory States, the present Treaty shall enter into force for those States and for States which have deposited instruments of accession. Thereafter the Treaty shall enter into force for any acceding State upon the deposit of its instrument of accession.
6. The present Treaty shall be registered by the depositary Government pursuant to Article 102 of the Charter of the United Nations.

Article XIV

The present Treaty, done in the English, French, Russian, and Spanish languages, each version being equally authentic, shall be deposited in the archives of the Government of the United States of America, which shall transmit duly certified copies thereof to the Governments of the signatory and acceding States.

IN WITNESS WHEREOF, the undersigned Plenipotentiaries, duly authorized, have signed the present Treaty.

DONE at Washington this first day of December one thousand nine hundred and fifty-nine.

[*Here follow the signatures of the Plenipotentiaries.*]

APPENDIX 2

Recommendation III–VIII

Agreed Measures for the Conservation of Antarctic Fauna and Flora
1964

The Representatives, taking into consideration Article IX of the Antarctic Treaty, and recalling Recommendation I–VIII of the First Consultative Meeting and Recommendation II–II of the Second Consultative Meeting, recommend to their Governments that they approve as soon as possible and implement without delay the annexed 'Agreed Measures for the Conservation of Antarctic Fauna and Flora.'

PREAMBLE
The Governments participating in the Third Consultative Meeting under Article IX of the Antarctic Treaty.
Desiring to implement the principles and purposes of the Antarctic Treaty;
Recognizing the scientific importance of the study of Antarctic fauna and flora, their adaptation to their rigorous environment, and their interrelationship with that environment;
Considering the unique nature of these fauna and flora, their circumpolar range, and particularly their defencelessness and susceptibility to extermination;
Desiring by further international collaboration within the framework of the Antarctic Treaty to promote and achieve the objectives of protection, scientific study, and rational use of these fauna and flora; and
Having particular regard to the conservation principles developed by the Scientific Committee on Antarctic Research (SCAR) of the International Council of Scientific Unions;
Hereby consider the Treaty Area as a Special Conservation Area and have agreed on the following measures:

ARTICLE I: Area of Application
1. These Agreed Measures shall apply to the same area to which the

Antarctic Treaty is applicable (hereinafter referred to as the Treaty Area) namely the area south of 60° South Latitude, including all ice shelves.

2. However, nothing in these Agreed Measures shall prejudice or in any way affect the rights, or the exercise of the rights, of any State under international law with regard to the high seas within the Treaty Area, or restrict the implementation of the provisions of the Antarctic Treaty with respect to inspection.

3. The Annexes to these Agreed Measures shall form an integral part thereof, and all references to the Agreed Measures shall be considered to include the Annexes.

ARTICLE II: Definitions

For the purposes of these Agreed Measures:

a. 'Native mammal' means any member, at any stage of its life cycle, or any species belonging to the Class Mammalia indigenous to the Antarctic or occurring there through natural agencies of dispersal, except whales.

b. 'Native bird' means any member, at any stage of its life cycle (including eggs), of any species of the Class Aves indigenous to the Antarctic or occurring there through natural agencies of dispersal.

c. 'Native plant' means any kind of vegetation at any stage of its life cycle (including seeds), indigenous to the Antarctic or occurring there through natural agencies of dispersal.

d. 'Appropriate authority' means any person authorized by a Participating Government to issue permits under these Agreed Measures.

   'The functions of an authorized person will be carried out within the framework of the Antarctic Treaty. They will be carried out exclusively in accordance with scientific principles and will have as their sole purpose the effective protection of Antarctic fauna and flora in accordance with these Agreed Measures.'

e. 'Permit' means a formal permission in writing issues by an appropriate authority as defined at paragraph d. above.

f. 'Participating Government' means any government for which these Agreed Measures have become effective in accordance with Article XIII of these Agreed Measures

ARTICLE III: Implementation

Each Participating Government shall take appropriate action to carry out these Agreed Measures.

ARTICLE IV: Publicity

The Participating Governments shall prepare and circulate to members of expeditions and stations information to ensure understanding and observance of the provisions of these Agreed Measures, setting forth in particular prohibited activities, and providing lists of specially protected species and specially protected areas.

ARTICLE V: Cases of Extreme Emergency

The provisions of these Agreed Measures shall not apply in cases of extreme emergency involving possible loss of human life or involving the safety of ships or aircraft.

ARTICLE VI: Protection of Native Fauna

1. Each Participating Government shall prohibit within the Treaty Area the killing, wounding, capturing or molesting of any native mammal or native bird, or any attempt at any such act, except in accordance with a permit.

2. Such permits shall be drawn in terms as specific as possible and issued only for the following purposes:

   a. to provide indispensable food for men or dogs in the Treaty Area in limited quantities, and in conformity with the purposes and principles of these Agreed Measures;

   b. to provide specimens to scientific study or scientific information;

   c. to provide specimens for museums, zoological gardens, or other educational or cultural institutions or uses.

3. Permits for Specially Protected Areas shall be issued only in accordance with the provisions of Article VIII.

4. Participating Governments shall limit the issue of such permits so as to ensure as far as possible that:

   a. no more native mammals or birds are killed or taken in any year than can normally be replaced by natural reproduction in the following breeding season;

   b. the variety of species and the balance of the natural ecological systems existing within the Treaty Area are maintained.

5. The species of native mammals and birds listed in Annex A of these Measures shall be designated 'Specially Protected Species,' and shall be accorded special protection by Participating Governments.

6. A Participating Government shall not authorize an appropriate authority to issue a permit with respect to a Specially Protected Species except in accordance with paragraph 7 of this Article.

7. A permit may be issued under this Article with respect to a Specially Protected Species, provided that:

   a. it is issued for a compelling scientific purpose, and

   b. the actions permitted thereunder will not jeopardize the existing natural ecological system or the survival of that species.

ARTICLE VII: Harmful Interference

1. Each Participating Government shall take appropriate measures to minimize harmful interference within the Treaty Area with the normal living conditions of any native mammal or bird, or any attempt at such harmful interference, except as permitted under Article VI.

2. The following acts and activities shall be considered as harmful interference:

    a. allowing dogs to run free,

    b. flying helicopters or other aircraft in a manner which would unnecessarily disturb bird and seal concentrations, or landing close to such concentrations (*e.g.*, within 200 m),

    c. driving vehicles unnecessarily close to concentrations of birds and seals (*e.g.*, within 200 m),

    d. use of explosives close to concentrations of birds and seals,

    e. discharge of firearms close to bird and seal concentrations (*e.g.*, within 300 m),

    f. any disturbance of bird and seal colonies during the breeding period by persistent attention from persons on foot.

However, the above activities, with the exception of those mentioned in a. and e. may be permitted to the minimum extent necessary for the establishment, supply and operation of stations.

3. Each Participating Government shall take all reasonable steps towards the alleviation of pollution of the waters adjacent to the coast and ice shelves.

ARTICLE VIII: Specially Protected Areas

1. The areas of outstanding scientific interest listed in Annex B shall be designated 'Specially Protected Areas' and shall be accorded special protection by the Participating Governments in order to preserve their unique natural ecological system.

2. In addition to the prohibitions and measures of protection dealt with in other Articles of these Agreed Measures, the Participating Governments shall in Specially Protected Areas further prohibit:

    a. the collection of any native plant, except in accordance with a permit;

    b. the driving of any vehicle;

    c. entry by their nationals, except in accordance with a permit issued under Article VI or under paragraph 2a. of the present Article or in accordance with a permit issued for some other compelling scientific purpose.

3. A permit issued under Article VI shall not have effect within a Specially Protected Area except in accordance with paragraph 4 of the present Article.

4. A permit shall have effect within a Specially Protected Area provided that:

a. it was issued for a compelling scientific purpose which cannot be served elsewhere; and

b. the actions permitted thereunder will not jeopardize the natural ecological system existing in the Area.

ARTICLE IX: Introduction of Non-Indigenous Species, Parasites and Diseases

1. Each Participating Government shall prohibit the bringing into the Treaty Area of any species of animal or plant not indigenous to that Area, except in accordance with a permit.

2. Permits under paragraph 1 of this Article shall be drawn in terms as specific as possible and shall be issued to allow the importation only of the animals and plants listed in Annex C. When any such animal or plant might cause harmful interference with the natural system if left unsupervised within the Treaty Area, such permits shall require that it be kept under controlled conditions and, after it has served its purpose, it shall be removed from the Treaty Area or destroyed.

3. Nothing in paragraphs 1 and 2 of this Article shall apply to the importation of food into the Treaty Area so long as animals and plants used for this purpose are kept under controlled conditions.

4. Each Participating Government undertakes to ensure that all reasonable precautions shall be taken to prevent the accidental introduction of parasites and diseases into the Treaty Area. In particular, the precautions listed in Annex D shall be taken.

ARTICLE X: Activities Contrary to the Principles and Purposes of These Measures

Each Participating Government undertakes to exert appropriate efforts, consistent with the Charter of the United Nations, to the end that no one engages in any activity in the Treaty Area contrary to the principles or purposes of these Agreed Measures.

ARTICLE XI: Ships' Crews

Each Participating Government whose expeditions use ships sailing under flags of nationalities other than its own shall, as far as feasible, arrange with the owners of such ships that the crews of these ships observe these Agreed Measures.

ARTICLE XII: Exchange of Information

1. The Participating Governments may make such arrangements as may be necessary for the discussion of such matters as:

a. the collection and exchange of records (including records of permits) and statistics concerning the number of each species of native mammal and bird killed or captured annually in the Treaty Area;

b. the obtaining and exchange of information as to the status of native mammals and birds in the Treaty Area, and the extent to which any species needs protection;

c. the number of native mammals or birds which should be permitted to be harvested for food, scientific study, or other uses in the various regions;

d. the establishment of a common form in which this information shall be submitted by Participating Governments in accordance with paragraph 2 of this Article.

2. Each Participating Government shall inform the other Governments in writing before the end of November of each year of the steps taken and information collected in the preceding period of 1st July to 30th June relating to the implementation of these Agreed Measures. Governments exchanging information under paragraph 5 of Article VII of the Antarctic Treaty may at the same time transmit the information relating to the implementation of these Agreed Measures.

ARTICLE XIII: Formal Provisions

1. After the receipt by the Government designated in Recommendation I–XIV (5) of notification of approval by all Governments whose representatives are entitled to participate in meetings provided for under Article IX of the Antarctic Treaty, these Agreed Measures shall become effective for those Governments.

2. Thereafter any other Contracting Party to the Antarctic Treaty may, in consonance with the purposes of Recommendation II–VII, accept these agreed Measures by notifying the designated Government of its intention to apply the Agreed Measures and to be bound by them. The Agreed Measures shall become effective with regard to such Governments on the date of receipt of such notification.

3. The designated Government shall inform the Governments referred to in paragraph 1 of this Article of each notification of approval, the effective date of these Agreed Measures and of each notification of acceptance. The designated Government shall also inform any Government which has accepted these Agreed Measures of each subsequent notification of acceptance.

ARTICLE XIV: Amendment

1. These Agreed Measures may be amended at any time by unanimous agreement of the Governments whose Representatives are entitled to participate in meetings under Article IX of the Antarctic Treaty.

2. The Annexes, in particular, may be amended as necessary through diplomatic channels.

3. An amendment proposed through diplomatic channels shall be submitted in writing to the designated Government which shall communicate it to the Governments referred to in paragraph 1 of the present Article

for approval; at the same time, it shall be communicated to the other Participating Governments.

4. Any amendment shall become effective on the date on which notifications of approval have been received by the designated Government and from all of the Governments referred to in paragraph 1 of this Article.

5. The designated Government shall notify those same Governments of the date of receipt of each approval communicated to it and the date on which the amendment will become effective for them.

6. Such amendment shall become effective on that same date for all other Participating Governments, except those which before the expiry of two months after that date notify the designated Government that they do not accept it.

APPENDIX 3

Recommendations of Second World Conference on National Parks 1972

The Group recommended to governments that 'high priority be given to the conservation of representative biomes and ecosystems on land and sea that are still virtually undisturbed', and 'in particular . . . that special attention be given to . . . polar regions . . .'

Recommendation 5 called on governments to establish Antarctica as a World Park under the auspices of the United Nations:

'Recognizing the great scientific and aesthetic value of the unaltered natural ecosystems of the Antarctic Continent and the seas surrounding it;

Recognizing that the Antarctic Treaty provides, to an unprecendented degree, protection to these ecosystems;

Believing that, in this second century of the national park movement, the concept of world parks should be promoted;

Considering that Antarctica offers special opportunities for the implementation of this concept;

The Second World Conference on National Parks, meeting at Grand Teton National Park, USA, in September 1972:

Recommends that the nations party to the Antarctic Treaty should negotiate to establish the Antarctic Continent and the surrounding seas as the first world park, under the auspices of the United Nations.'

APPENDIX 4

World National Parks Congress

Congrès Mondial des Parcs Nationaux

RECOMMENDATIONS OF THE WORLD NATIONAL PARKS CONGRESS
Under Part V of the Rules of Procedure of the Congress, the Congress is called upon to issue Recommendations which provide guidance for the furtherance of its objectives. To this end, a Recommendations Committee has been constituted. It has received draft recommendations from participants, and, in accordance with the Rules of Procedure, has sought to amalgamate similar drafts, and to keep the total number of recommendations submitted for the consideration of the Congress to no more than 20. The Committee's set of Recommendations for Congress' consideration is attached.

PREAMBLE TO RECOMMENDATIONS
The Recommendations of the World National Parks Congress, meeting in Bali, Indonesia, October 1982, relate to protected areas which are the subject of the Congress. It is in this field that the participants are expert and can offer advice.

However, the participants recognize that, while protected areas have a central and essential role to play in achieving conservation of living resources, which is a vital ingredient of sustainable development, the selection, establishment and management of protected areas alone are not sufficient to secure the integration of conservation and development. The other measures are outlined in the World Conservation Strategy.

Moreover, the successful pursuit of the full range of conservation efforts at the national and international levels depends upon progress in related fields. These include raising the living standards of many people in the developing world who are forced by their poverty to over-exploit natural resources, reducing the trend towards over-consumption and waste of resources by the more affluent, controlling pollution, securing a much more rapid and sustained reduction in the rate of population increase, and achieving disarmament.

Nonetheless, protected areas have a vital role to play in the social, economic, cultural and spiritual progress of humanity. Their importance has too often been neglected in the past. The Declaration of Bali seeks to redress this by securing wider and fuller understanding of the significance of protected areas in the quest for a better way of life. The following Recommendations provide the basis for implementing the intent of the Declaration.

4: ANTARCTICA

RECOGNIZING the great scientific and aesthetic value of the natural ecosystems of the Antarctic Continent and the seas surrounding it and their importance in maintaining the stability of the global marine environment and atmosphere, and AWARE that the Antarctic provides one of the best places to measure global pollution;

ACKNOWLEDGING the achievements of the Consultative Parties in their stewardship under the Antarctic Treaty in protecting the Antarctic environment from harmful interference;

RECOGNIZING that a mineral regime is now being developed which may lead to the exploration and exploitation of the mineral resources of the region;

CONCERNED that the environmental effects of mineral exploration and exploitation in the Antarctic have been inadequately studied and that mineral resource exploration and exploitation are likely to affect adversely the unique environment of the Antarctic and other ecosystems dependent on the Antarctic environment;

RECALLING that the Second World Conference on National Parks in 1972 recommended that nations party to the Antarctic Treaty should establish the Antarctic Continent and surrounding seas as the first World Park under the auspices of the United Nations, and that other protective designations are being proposed to reflect the unique status of the area;

BELIEVING that, in this second century of the national park movement, the concepts of international parks, reserves and protected areas should be promoted and that the concept of a world park and other appropriate designations should be developed more urgently;

CONSIDERING that Antarctica offers special opportunities for the implementation of these concepts and noting that the 15th General

Assembly of IUCN instructed the Council, Commissions and the Director General of IUCN to initiate the preparation of a Conservation Strategy for the Antarctic environment and the Southern Ocean and in particular to seek appropriate forms of designation for the Antarctic environment as a whole and the specific sites within it which merit special attention;

NOTING also that there are appropriate forms of designation which do not imply any change of jurisdiction and that management could be by means of a zoning system providing for a range of uses, but with some uses prohibited in all zones, for example, nuclear testing (which already is prohibited under the Antarctic Treaty);

The World National Parks Congress, meeting in Bali, Indonesia, October 1982:

CONGRATULATES IUCN for its 1981 General Assembly Resolution (15/20) on Antarctica and urges all nations and organizations to work towards its implementation;

RECOMMENDS that the Antarctic Treaty Parties in cooperation with all nations should further enhance the conservation status of the Antarctic environment and foster measures which would:

a. maintain for all time the intrinsic values of the Antarctic environment for mankind and the global ecosystem;

b. ensure that all human activities are compatible with the maintenance of these values;

c. ascribe to the Antarctic environment as a whole an internationally protected area designation which connotes worldwide its unique character and values and the special measures accorded to its planning, management and conversation;

URGES that no minerals regime be brought into operation until such time as full consideration has been given to protecting the Antarctic environment completely from minerals activities and the environmental risks have been fully ascertained and safeguards developed to avoid adverse environmental effects, and thus to maintain the voluntary restriction on mineral development;

URGES FURTHER that the Antarctic Treaty Parties and other interested governments and organizations initiate a comprehensive evaluation of the Antarctic environment and its dependent ecosystems to identify and designate both continental and marine areas to be protected in perpetuity;

URGES the Antarctic Treaty Parties to include advisers from non-governmental organizations interested in the Antarctic environment on national delegations and to pursue policies of open information;

RECOMMENDS that IUCN seek to establish close working relation-ships with the scientific organizations which advise the Antarctic Treaty Parties.

APPENDIX 5

International Union for Conservation of Nature and Natural Resources— 1981 General Assembly Resolution

ANTARCTICA ENVIRONMENT AND THE SOUTHERN OCEAN

Preamble

1. *Recognizing* the importance of Antarctica and its Continental shelf ('the Antarctic environment') and the Southern Ocean for the world as a whole, particularly in maintaining the stability of the global marine environment and atmosphere, and the paramount importance to mankind of its great wilderness qualities (for science, education and inspiration);

2. *Recalling* the continued and long established interest that IUCN has in the conservation of the ecosystems of the Antarctica environment as well as in the conservation of the species and habitats that it supports;

3. *Mindful* that the World Conservation Strategy (prepared by IUCN with the advice, cooperation and financial assistance of UNEP and WWF and in collaboration with FAO and UNESCO) identifies Antarctica and the Southern Ocean as a priority for international action;

4. *Noting* that eleven Antarctic Treaty Consultative Parties are represented in IUCN and that they have already espoused the aims of the World Conservation Strategy;

5. *Aware* of the achievements of the Consultative Parties in their stewardship under the Antarctic Treaty in protecting the Antarctica environment from harmful interference, and the provision of measures for the conservation of flora and fauna, guidelines to minimize harmful effects of human activities, and measures specifically related to tourism activities;

6. *Also Cognizant* of the fact that the Consultative Parties are presently considering the establishment of a regime to govern both commercial exploration and exploitation of any mineral resources should this ever

prove acceptable and that any exploitation of minerals would adversely affect the values of the Antarctica environment;

7. *Further Aware* of the additional efforts of the same nations to enhance the conservation and sustainable use of the living resources of the region, in particular by the initiative taken to negotiate and adopt the Convention for the Conservation of Antarctic Seals (1972) and the Convention on the Conservation of Antarctic Marine Living Resources (1980);

8. *Taking Note* of the action taken by the International Whaling Commission with regard to whaling in the Southern Ocean and the relevance to that ocean of other activities affecting conservation of the marine environment generally;

9. *Recalling* that the Second World Conference on National Parks in 1972 recommended that nations party to the Antarctic Treaty should establish the Antarctic Continent and surrounding seas as the first World Park and that other protective designations are being proposed to reflect the unique status of the area;

10. *Concerned* further that the effective planning, management and conservation of the Antarctica environment can only be achieved by thorough consideration of feasible alternatives and if all actions are based on restraint and scientific knowledge, as well as through cooperation and coordination;

The General Assembly of IUCN, at its 15th Session in Christchurch, New Zealand, 11–23 October 1981:

THE ANTARCTICA ENVIRONMENT

General

11. *Strongly Recommends* that the Antarctic Treaty Consultative Parties should further enhance the status of the Antarctica environment and foster measures which would:

    a. maintain for all time the intrinsic values of the Antarctica environment for mankind and the global ecosystem;

    b. ensure that all human activities are compatible with the maintenance of these values;

    c. ascribe to the Antarctica environment as a whole a designation which connotes worldwide its unique character and values and the special measures accorded to its planning, management and conservation:

12. *Urges* the Parties to ensure the protection of the Antarctica environment from harmful interference, as expressed in Recommendation 5 of the Ninth Meeting of the Consultative Parties;

MINERALS

13. *Urges* that no mineral regime be brought into operation until such time as full consideration has been given to protecting the Antarctica

environment completely from minerals activities and the environmental risks have been fully ascertained and safeguards developed to avoid adverse environmental effects;

Communication and Consultation

14. *Urges* the Consultative Parties to recognize the increased interest in the Antarctica environment of the world community, and therefore that they:

   a. mobilize and draw upon the goodwill and expertise freely available to support their work by effective communication and consultation with interested parties;

   b. foster public interest and awareness by well-informed educative measures based on accurate reporting and dissemination of their policies and actions in relation to the Antarctica environment: and

   c. invite representatives from appropriate non-governmental organizations (including IUCN and ASOC) to participate in meetings according to normal international practice;

15. *Further Urges* national delegations to the Antarctic Treaty to keep fully in touch and consult with NGOs in their countries concerned with the Antarctica environment and to include advisers from these bodies in their delegations;

Membership

16. *Urges* all nations concerned with the future of the Antarctica environment to accede to the Antarctic Treaty;

Research and Conservation—General

17. *Considers* that the Antarctic Treaty Consultative Parties should ensure that research and conservation action is coordinated and that, as a priority, the research programmes needed to protect the Antarctic ecosystem and allow informed decision-making are ascertained, together with the institutions best suited to undertake them;

18. *Urges* full support to on-going scientific efforts and the undertaking of long term, large scale cooperative research programmes focused on the ecological structure and processes of the Antarctica environment and on their role with regard to globally relevant phenomena, such as weather and climate;

19. *Stresses* the necessity to possess sufficient results of such research before management decisions are taken with regard to both living and non-living resources and the need to maintain this research effort so that such decisions may be related to a continuously evolving situation;

20. *Calls Upon* the Consultative Parties to take the lead in such research and conservation programmes;

21. *Urges* all organizations whose activities and expertise are of relevance to these research and conservation tasks to contribute as appropriate;

22. *Pledges* the support and expertise of IUCN in the establishment and carrying out of such programmes;

23. **And Particularly Recommends that:**
  a. the Consultative Parties expand the network of sites meriting special protection within the overall framework of measures for the Antarctica environment;
  b. continued attention to be given to coordination of research and other activities now being carried out in Antarctica to prevent or minimize harmful environmental consequences such as air pollution and wastes;
  c. continuous monitoring be made of the consequences of tourism activities, applying strict controls as necessary;
  d. the possible ecological impact of the utilization of icebergs be studied and ascertained well in advance of any such utilization;
  e. vigilance be exercised on the implementation of the measures prohibiting the introduction of alien species.

The Convention on the Conservation of Antarctic Marine Living Resources 1980

25. *Expresses* its satisfaction that the Marine Living Resources Convention provides the elements necessary to realize an ecosystem approach to the conservation and management of the natural resources of the area;

26. *Pledges* to make IUCN expertise available to the Commission and the Scientific Committee created under the Convention and urges the development of cooperative relationships with the Commission and Scientific Committee, as foreseen by Article XXIII of the Convention;

27. *Recalls* that the dynamics of the Southern Ocean are still poorly known, and urges the Parties to the Convention to exercise caution in its implementation by:
  a. developing all fisheries only in conjunction with scientific advice designed to provide the best understanding of the functioning of the ecosystem, and, as a consequence;
  b. establishing all such fisheries on an experimental basis for an adequate length of time, with an initial conservative quota by area and appropriate enforcement of such quotas.

28. *Urges* further that:
  a. as a high priority feeding grounds of threatened and endangered whales be identified and closed to krill fishing;
  b. some areas be closed to fishing *ab initio*, and at least one large sanctuary be established where krill harvesting would be prohibited or permitted only for scientific purposes in order to provide for adequate baseline areas;
  c. an evaluation be made of the role and status of finfish and squid before substantial exploitation takes place;

d. all data be provided, on an agreed standardized scientific basis, including that from fishing operations carried out over a reasonable past period of time, to facilitate the establishment of a central data bank which can utilize data from all relevant sources;

e. appropriate coordination of objectives and activities under the International Whaling Commission be established, in particular over the implementation of measures aiming at the recovery of those whales whose populations have been depleted;

f. the development of dynamic models of the Southern Ocean ecosystem be initiated, bearing in mind the depletion of many whale species;

g. in the process of developing the fishery on a scientific basis, the development of cooperative relationships with appropriate organizations be effectively carried out.

29. *Recommends* further that the Parties to the Convention better inform the scientific and conservation communities of the action they take to protect the Southern Ocean, including reporting on discussions and actions pertaining to environmental conservation issues, and inviting representatives from appropriate NGOs (such as IUCN and ASOC) to participate in appropriate meetings;

30. *Urges* that IUCN be given accredited status as an adviser to the Scientific Committee of the Convention Commission;

31. *Urges* all nations concerned with the future of the Antarctica environment and the Southern Ocean to support the operation of the Convention and to accede to it as soon as possible;

32. *Recommends* that, notwithstanding current worldwide economic difficulties, the significance of the Southern Ocean demands that it be accorded high priority in the allocation of resources adequate to ensure the effective operation of the Commission and its Scientific Committee.

The Minerals of Antarctica

33. *Commends* the Consultative Parties for their decision to refrain from exploration of Antarctic mineral resources for the time being;

34. *Urges* that the Treaty Parties keep IUCN and the scientific and conservation communities well informed of any proposed activities in the Antarctica environment and *urges* further that they seek the views of IUCN on any which would affect the conservation of the Antarctica environment;

35. *Pledges* to make IUCN expertise available to the Treaty Parties and other bodies and organizations as appropriate to conduct or cooperate in conducting studies necessary to ensure that activities carried on in Antarctica have minimum effects on the ecosystem considered.

This 15th General Assembly, in Consequence, Instructs
Council, the Commissions, and the Director General of IUCN
A. to take all steps necessary in the implementation of the pledges which

it has made in relation to the Antarctica environment and the Southern Ocean and, in particular, to ensure that, wherever possible, IUCN representation at relevant meetings related thereto is by persons with appropriate expertness;

B. so soon as financial resources permit. to ensure that IUCN's Programme during the coming triennium has regard to the necessity of monitoring developments pertinent to the conservation of species and habitats of Antarctica and the Southern Ocean, and of the ecosystems of which they are a part, with a view to making appropriate recommendations to governments during the coming triennium;

C. to initiate the preparation of a Conservation Strategy for the Antarctica environment and the Southern Ocean in cooperation with the world scientific and conservation communities and to foster appropriate scientific and educational programmes, collaborating on these, where relevant, with the scientific Committee of the Commission on Marine Living Resources;

D. in particular in this Strategy, to seek appropriate forms of designation for the Antarctica environment as a whole and the specific sites within it which merit special attention;

E. to see the necessary additional resources for this ANTARCTICA PROJECT.

APPENDIX 6

Convention on the Conservation of Antarctic Marine Living Resources 1982

The Contracting Parties,

Recognizing the importance of safeguarding the environment and protecting the integrity of the ecosystem of the seas surrounding Antarctica;
Noting the concentration of marine living resources found in Antarctic waters and the increased interest in the possibilities offered by the utilization of these resources as a source of protein;
Conscious of the urgency of ensuring the conservation of Antarctic marine living resources;
Considering that it is essential to increase knowledge of the Antarctic marine ecosystem and its components so as to be able to base decisions on harvesting on sound scientific information;
Believing that the conservation of Antarctic marine living resources calls for international co-operation with due regard for the provisions of the Antarctic Treaty and with the active involvement of all States engaged in research or harvesting activities in Antarctic waters;
Recognizing the prime responsibilities of the Antarctic Treaty Consultative Parties for the protection and preservation of the Antarctic environment and, in particular, their responsibilities under Article IX, paragraph 1 (f) of the Antarctic Treaty in respect of the preservation and conservation of living resources in Antarctica;
Recalling the action already taken by the Antarctic Treaty Consultative Parties including in particular the Agreed Measures for the Conservation of Antarctic Fauna and Flora, as well as the provisions of the Convention for the Conservation of Antarctic Seals;
Bearing in mind the concern regarding the conservation of Antarctic marine living resources expressed by the Consultative Parties at the Ninth Consultative Meeting of the Antarctic Treaty and the importance of the provisions of Recommendation IX-2 which led to the establishment of the present Convention;

Believing that it is in the interest of all mankind to preserve the waters surrounding the Antarctic continent for peaceful purposes only and to prevent their becoming the scene or object of international discord;

Recognizing, in the light of the foregoing, that it is desirable to establish suitable machinery for recommending, promoting, deciding upon and co-ordinating the measures and scientific studies needed to ensure the conservation of Antarctic marine living organisms;

Have agreed as follows:

Article I

1. This Convention applies to the Antarctic marine living resources of the area south of 60° South latitude and to the Antarctic marine living resources of the area between that latitude and the Antarctic Convergence which form part of the Antarctic marine ecosystem.

2. Antarctic marine living resources means the populations of fin fish, molluscs, crustaceans and all other species of living organisms, including birds, found south of the Antarctic Convergence.

3. The Antarctic marine ecosystem means the complex of relationships of Antarctic marine living resources with each other and with their physical environment.

4. The Antarctic Convergence shall be deemed to be a line joining the following points along parallels of latitude and meridians of longitude: 50°S, 0°; 50°S, 30°E; 45°S, 30°E; 45°S, 80°E; 55°S, 80°E; 55°S, 150°E; 60°S, 150°E; 60°S, 50°W; 50°S, 50°W; 50°S, 0°.

Article II

1. The objective of this Convention is the conservation of Antarctic marine living resources.

2. For the purposes of this Convention, the term 'conservation' includes rational use.

3. Any harvesting and associated activities in the area to which this Convention applies shall be conducted in accordance with the provisions of this Convention and with the following principles of conservation:

a. prevention of decrease in the size of any harvested population to levels below those which ensure its stable recruitment. For this purpose its size should not be allowed to fall below a level close to that which ensures the greatest net annual increment;

b. maintenance of the ecological relationships between harvested, dependent and related populations of Antarctic marine living resources and the restoration of depleted populations to the levels defined in sub-paragraph (a) above; and

c. prevention of changes or minimization of the risk of changes in the marine ecosystem which are not potentially reversible over two or three decades, taking into account the state of available knowledge of the direct and indirect impact of harvesting, the effect of the introduction of alien species, the effects of associated activities on the marine ecosystem and of the effects of environmental changes, with the aim of making possible the sustained conservation of Antarctic marine living resources.

Article III

The Contracting Parties, whether or not they are Parties to the Antarctic Treaty, agree that they will not engage in any activities in the Antarctic Treaty area contrary to the principles and purposes of that Treaty and that, in their relations with each other, they are bound by the obligations contained in Articles I and V of the Antarctic Treaty.

Article IV

1. With respect to the Antarctic Treaty area, all Contracting Parties, whether or not they are Parties to the Antarctic Treaty, are bound by Articles IV and VI of the Antarctic Treaty in their relations with each other.

2. Nothing in this Convention and no acts or activities taking place while the present Convention is in force shall:

   a. constitute a basis for asserting, supporting or denying a claim to territorial sovereignty in the Antarctic Treaty area or create any rights of sovereignty in the Antarctic Treaty area;

   b. be interpreted as a renunciation or diminution by any Contracting Party of, or as prejudicing, any right of claim or basis of claim to exercise coastal state jurisdiction under international law within the area to which this Convention applies;

   c. be interpreted as prejudicing the position of any Contracting Party as regards its recognition or non-recognition of any such right, claim or basis of claim;

   d. affect the provision of Article IV, paragraph 2, of the Antarctic Treaty that no new claim, or enlargement of an existing claim, to territorial sovereignty in Antarctica shall be asserted while the Antarctic Treaty is in force.

Article V

1. The Contracting Parties which are not Parties to the Antarctic Treaty acknowledge the special obligations and responsibilities of the Antarctic Treaty Consultative Parties for the protection and preservation of the environment of the Antarctic Treaty area.

2. The Contracting Parties which are not Parties to the Antarctic Treaty agree that, in their activities in the Antarctic Treaty area, they will observe as and when appropriate the Agreed Measures for the Conservation of Antarctic Fauna and Flora and such other measures as have been recommended by the Antarctic Treaty Consultative Parties in

fulfilment of their responsibility for the protection of the Antarctic environment from all forms of harmful human interference.

3. For the purposes of this Convention, 'Antarctic Treaty Consultative Parties' means the Contracting Parties to the Antarctic Treaty whose Representatives participate in meetings under Article IX of the Antarctic Treaty.

Article VI

Nothing in this Convention shall derogate from the rights and obligations of Contracting Parties under the International Convention for the Regulation of Whaling and the Convention for the Conservation of Antarctic Seals.

Article VII

1. The Contracting Parties hereby establish and agree to maintain the Commission for the Conservation of Antarctic Marine Living Resources (hereinafter referred to as 'the Commission').

2. Membership in the Commission shall be as follows:

a. each Contracting Party which participated in the meeting at which this Convention was adopted shall be a Member of the Commission;

b. each State Party which has acceded to this Convention pursuant to Article XXIX shall be entitled to be a Member of the Commission during such time as that acceding Party is engaged in research or harvesting activities in relation to the marine living resources to which this Convention applies;

c. each regional economic integration organization which has acceded to this Convention pursuant to Article XXIX shall be entitled to be a Member of the Commission during such time as its States members are so entitled;

d. a Contracting Party seeking to participate in the work of the Commission pursuant to sub-paragraphs (b) and (c) above shall notify the Depositary of the basis upon which it seeks to become a Member of the Commission and of its willingness to accept conservation measures in force. The Depositary shall communicate to each Member of the Commission such notification and accompanying information. Within two months of receipt of such communication from the Depositary, any Member of the Commission may request that a special meeting of the Commission be held to consider the matter. Upon receipt of such request, the Depositary shall call such a meeting. If there is no request for a meeting, the Contracting Party submitting the notification shall be deemed to have satisfied the requirements for Commission Membership.

3. Each Member of the Commission shall be represented by one representative who may be accompanied by alternate representatives and advisers.

Article VIII

The Commission shall have legal personality and shall enjoy in the territory of each of the States Parties such legal capacity as may be necessary to perform its function and achieve the purposes of this Convention. The privileges and immunities to be enjoyed by the Commission and its staff in the territory of a State Party shall be determined by agreement between the Commission and the State Party concerned.

Article IX

1. The function of the Commission shall be to give effect to the objective and principles set out in Article II of this Convention. To this end, it shall:

    a. facilitate research into and comprehensive studies of Antarctic marine living resources and of the Antarctic marine ecosystem;

    b. compile data on the status of and changes in population of Antarctic marine living resources and on factors affecting the distribution, abundance and productivity of harvested species and dependent or related species or populations;

    c. ensure the acquisition of catch and effort statistics on harvested populations;

    d. analyse, disseminate and publish the information referred to in sub-paragraphs (b) and (c) above and the reports of the Scientific Committee;

    e. identify conservation needs and analyse the effectiveness of conservation measures;

    f. formulate, adopt and revise conservation measures on the basis of the best scientific evidence available, subject to the provisions of paragraph 5 of this Article;

    g. implement the system of observation and inspection established under Article XXIV of this Convention;

    h. carry out such other activities as are necessary to fulfil the objective of this Convention.

2. The conservation measures referred to in paragraph 1 (f) above include the following:

    a. the designation of the quantity of any species which may be harvested in the area to which this Convention applies;

    b. the designation of regions and sub-regions based on the distribution of populations of Antarctic marine living resources;

    c. the designation of the quantity which may be harvested from the populations of regions and sub-regions;

    d. the designation of protected species;

    e. the designation of size, age and, as appropriate, sex of species which may be harvested;

    f. the designation of open and closed seasons for harvesting;

g. the designation of the opening and closing of areas, regions or sub-regions for purposes of scientific study or conservation, including special areas for protection and scientific study;

h. regulation of the effort employed and methods of harvesting, including fishing gear, with a view, inter alia, to avoiding undue concentration of harvesting in any region or sub-region;

i. the taking of such other conservation measures as the Commission considers necessary for the fulfilment of the objective of this Convention, including measures concerning the effects of harvesting and associated activities on components of the marine ecosystem other than the harvested populations.

3. The Commission shall publish and maintain a record of all conservation measures in force.

4. In exercising its functions under paragraph 1 above, the Commission shall take full account of the recommendations and advice of the Scientific Committee.

5. The Commission shall take full account of any relevant measures or regulations established or recommended by the Consultative Meetings pursuant to Article IX of the Antarctic Treaty or by existing fisheries commissions responsible for species which may enter the area to which this Convention applies, in order that there shall be no inconsistency between the rights and obligations of a Contracting Party under such regulations or measures and conservation measures which may be adopted by the Commission.

6. Conservation measures adopted by the Commission in accordance with this Convention shall be implemented by Members of the Commission in the following manner:

a. the Commission shall notify conservation measures to all Members of the Commission:

b. conservation measures shall become binding upon all Members of the Commission 180 days after such notification except as provided in sub-paragraphs (c) and (d) below;

c. If a Member of the Commission, within ninety days following the notification specified in sub-paragraph (a), notifies the Commission that it is unable to accept the conservation measure, in whole or in part, the measure shall not, to the extent stated, be binding upon that Member of the Commission;

d. in the event that any Member of the Commission invokes the procedure set forth in sub-paragraph (c) above, the Commission shall meet at the request of any Member of the Commission to review the conservation measure. At the time of such meeting and within thirty days following the meeting, any Member of the Commission shall have the right to declare that it is no longer able to accept the conservation measure, in which case the Member shall no longer be bound by such measure.

Article X

1. The Commission shall draw the attention of any State which is not a Party to this Convention to any activity undertaken by its nationals or vessels which, in the opinion of the Commission, affects the implementation of the objective of this Convention.

2. The Commission shall draw the attention of all Contracting Parties to any activity which, in the opinion of the Commission, affects the implementation by a Contracting Party of the objective of this Convention or the compliance by that Contracting Party with its obligations under this Convention.

Article XI

The Commission shall seek to co-operate with Contracting Parties which may exercise jurisdiction in marine areas adjacent to the area to which this Convention applies in respect of the conservation of any stock or stocks of associated species which occur both within those areas and the area to which this Convention applies, with a view to harmonizing the conservation measures adopted in respect of such stocks.

Article XII

1. Decisions of the Commission on matters of substance shall be taken by consensus. The question of whether a matter is one of substance shall be treated as a matter of substance.

2. Decisions on matters other than those referred to in paragraph 1 above shall be taken by a simple majority of the Members of the Commission present and voting.

3. In Commission consideration of any item requiring a decision, it shall be made clear whether a regional economic integration organization will participate in the taking of the decision and, if so, whether any of its member States will also participate. The number of Contracting Parties so participating shall not exceed the number of member States of the regional economic integration organization which are Members of the Commission.

4. In the taking of decisions pursuant to this Article, a regional economic integration organization shall have only one vote.

Article XIII

1. The headquarters of the Commission shall be established at Hobart, Tasmania, Australia.

2. The Commission shall hold a regular annual meeting. Other meetings shall also be held at the request of one-third of its members and as otherwise provided in this Convention. The first meeting of the Commission shall be held within three months of the entry into force of this Convention, provided that among the Contracting Parties there are at least two States conducting harvesting activities within the area to which

this Convention applies. The first meeting shall, in any event, be held within one year of the entry into force of this Convention. The Depositary shall consult with the signatory States regarding the first Commission meeting, taking into account that a broad representation of such States is necessary for the effective operation of the Commission.

3. The Depositary shall convene the first meeting of the Commission at the headquarters of the Commission. Thereafter, meetings of the Commission shall be held at its headquarters, unless it decides otherwise.

4. The Commission shall elect from among its members a Chairman and Vice-Chairman, each of whom shall serve for a term of two years and shall be eligible for re-election for one additional term. The first Chairman shall, however, be elected for an initial term of three years. The Chairman and Vice-Chairman shall not be representatives of the same Contracting Party.

5. The Commission shall adopt and amend as necessary the rules of procedure for the conduct of its meetings, except with respect to the matters dealt with in Article XII of this Convention.

6. The Commission may establish such subsidiary bodies as are necessary for the performance of its functions.

Article XIV

1. The Contracting Parties hereby establish the Scientific Committee for the Conservation of Antarctic Marine Living Resources (hereinafter referred to as 'the Scientific Committee') which shall be a consultative body to the Commission. The Scientific Committee shall normally meet at the headquarters of the Commission unless the Scientific Committee decides otherwise.

2. Each Member of the Commission shall be a member of the Scientific Committee and shall appoint a representative with suitable scientific qualifications who may be accompanied by other experts and advisers.

3. The Scientific Committee may seek the advice of other scientists and experts as may be required on an ad hoc basis.

Article XV

1. The Scientific Committee shall provide a forum for consultation and co-operation concerning the collection, study and exchange of information with respect to the marine living resources to which this Convention applies. It shall encourage and promote co-operation in the field of scientific research in order to extend knowledge of the marine living resources of the Antarctic marine ecosystem.

2. The Scientific Committee shall conduct such activities as the Commission may direct in pursuance of the objective of this Convention and shall:

   a. establish criteria and methods to be used for determinations concerning the conservation measures referred to in Article IX of this Convention;

b. regularly assess the status and trends of the populations of Antarctic marine living resources;

c. analyse data concerning the direct and indirect effects of harvesting on the populations of Antarctic marine living resources;

d. assess the effects of proposed changes in the methods or levels of harvesting and proposed conservation measures;

e. transmit assessments, analyses, reports and recommendations to the Commission as requested or on its own initiative regarding measures and research to implement the objective of this Convention;

f. formulate proposals for the conduct of international and national programs of research into Antarctic marine living resources.

3. In carrying out its functions, the Scientific Committee shall have regard to the work of other relevant technical and scientific organizations and to the scientific activities conducted within the framework of the Antarctic Treaty.

Article XVI

1. The first meeting of the Scientific Committee shall be held within three months of the first meeting of the Commission. The Scientific Committee shall meet thereafter as often as may be necessary to fulfil its functions.

2. The Scientific Committee shall adopt and amend as necessary its rules of procedure. The rules and any amendments thereto shall be approved by the Commission. The rules shall include procedures for the presentation of minority reports.

3. The Scientific Committee may establish, with the approval of the Commission, such subsidiary bodies as are necessary for the performance of its functions.

Article XVII

1. The Commission shall appoint an Executive Secretary to serve the Commission and Scientific Committee according to such procedures and on such terms and conditions as the Commission may determine. His term of office shall be for four years and he shall be eligible for re-appointment.

2. The Commission shall authorize such staff establishment for the Secretariat as may be necessary and the Executive Secretary shall appoint, direct and supervise such staff according to such rules, and procedures and on such terms and conditions as the Commission may determine.

3. The Executive Secretary and Secretariat shall perform the functions entrusted to them by the Commission.

Article XVIII
The official languages of the Commission and the Scientific Committee shall be English, French, Russian and Spanish.

Article XIX
1. At each annual meeting, the Commission shall adopt by consensus its budget and the budget of the Scientific Committee.
2. A draft budget for the Commission and the Scientific Committee and any subsidiary bodies shall be prepared by the Executive Secretary and submitted to the Members of the Commission at least sixty days before the annual meeting of the Commission.
3. Each Member of the Commission shall contribute to the Budget. Until the expiration of five years after the entry into force of this Convention, the contribution of each Member of the Commission shall be equal. Thereafter the contribution shall be determined in accordance with two criteria: the amount harvested and an equal sharing among all Members of the Commission. The Commission shall determine by consensus and proportion in which these two criteria shall apply.
4. The financial activities of the Commission and Scientific Committee shall be conducted in accordance with financial regulations adopted by the Commission and shall be subject to an annual audit by external auditors selected by the Commission.
5. Each Member of the Commission shall meet its own expenses arising from attendance at meetings of the Commission and of the Scientific Committee.
6. A Member of the Commission that fails to pay its contributions for two consecutive years shall not, during the period of its default, have the right to participate in the taking of decisions in the Commission.

Article XX
1. The Members of the Commission shall, to the greatest extent possible, provide annually to the Commission and to the Scientific Committee such statistical, biological and other data and information as the Commission and Scientific Committee may require in the exercise of their functions.
2. The Members of the Commission shall provide, in the manner and at such intervals as may be prescribed, information about their harvesting activities, including fishing areas and vessels, so as to enable reliable catch and effort statistics to be compiled.
3. The Members of the Commission shall provide to the Commission at such intervals as may be prescribed information on steps taken to implement the conservation measures adopted by the Commission.
4. The Members of the Commission agree that in any of their harvesting activities, advantage shall be taken of opportunities to collect data needed to assess the impact of harvesting.

Article XXI

1. Each Contracting Party shall take appropriate measures within its competence to ensure compliance with the provisions of this Convention and with conservation measures adopted by the Commission to which the Party is bound in accordance with Article IX of this Convention.

2. Each Contracting Party shall transmit to the Commission information on measures taken pursuant to paragraph 1 above, including the imposition of sanctions for any violation.

Article XXII

1. Each Contracting Party undertakes to exert appropriate efforts, consistent with the Charter of the United Nations, to the end that no one engages in any activity contrary to the objective of this Convention.

2. Each Contracting Party shall notify the Commission of any such activity which comes to its attention.

Article XXIII

1. The Commission and the Scientific Committee shall co-operate with the Antarctic Treaty Consultative Parties on matters falling within the competence of the latter.

2. The Commission and the Scientific Committee shall co-operate, as appropriate, with the Food and Agriculture Organization of the United Nations and with other Specialized Agencies.

3. The Commission and the Scientific Committee shall seek to develop co-operative working relationships, as appropriate, with inter-governmental and non-governmental organizations which could contribute to their work, including the Scientific Committee on Antarctic Research, the Scientific Committee on Oceanic Research and the International Whaling Commission.

4. The Commission may enter into agreements with the organizations referred to in this Article and with other organizations as may be appropriate. The Commission and the Scientific Committee may invite such organizations to send observers to their meetings and to meetings of their subsidiary bodies.

Article XXIV

1. In order to promote the objective and ensure observance of the provisions of this Convention, the Contracting Parties agree that a system of observation and inspection shall be established.

2. The system of observation and inspection shall be elaborated by the Commission on the basis of the following principles:

    a. contracting Parties shall co-operate with each other to ensure the effective implementation of the system of observation and inspection, taking account of the existing international practice. This system shall include, inter alia, procedures for boarding and inspection by observers and inspectors designated by the Members of the Commission and procedures for flag state prosecution and sanctions on the basis of evidence resulting from such boarding and inspections. A report of such prosecutions and sanctions imposed shall be included in the information referred to in Article XXI of this Convention;

b. in order to verify compliance with measures adopted under this Convention, observation and inspection shall be carried out on board vessels engaged in scientific research or harvesting of marine living resources in the area to which this Convention applies, through observers and inspectors designated by the Members of the Commission and operating under terms and conditions to be established by the Commission;

c. designated observers and inspectors shall remain subject to the jurisdiction of the Contracting Party of which they are nationals. They shall report to the Member of the Commission by which they have been designated which in turn shall report to the Commission.

3. Pending the establishment of the system of observation and inspection, the Members of the Commission shall seek to establish interim arrangements to designate observers and inspectors and such designated observers and inspectors shall be entitled to carry out inspections in accordance with the principles set out in paragraph 2 above.

Article XXV

1. If any dispute arises between two or more of the Contracting Parties concerning the interpretation or application of this Convention, those Contracting Parties shall consult among themselves with a view to having the dispute resolved by negotiation, inquiry, mediation, conciliation, arbitration, judicial settlement or other peaceful means of their own choice.

2. Any dispute of this character not so resolved shall, with the consent in each case of all Parties to the dispute, be referred for settlement to the International Court of Justice or to arbitration; but failure to reach agreement on reference to the International Court or to arbitration shall not absolve Parties to the dispute from the responsibility of continuing to seek to resolve it by any of the various peaceful means referred to in paragraph 1 above.

3. In cases where the dispute is referred to arbitration, the arbitral tribunal shall be constituted as provided in the Annex to this Convention.

Article XXVI

1. This Convention shall be open for signature at Canberra from 1 August to 31 December 1980 by the States participating in the Conference on the Conservation of Antarctic Marine Living Resources held at Canberra from 7 to 20 May 1980.

2. The States which so sign will be the original signatory States of the Convention.

Article XXVII
1. This Convention is subject to ratification, acceptance or approval by signatory States.
2. Instruments of ratification, acceptance or approval shall be deposited with the Government of Australia, hereby designated as the Depositary.

Article XXVIII
1. This Convention shall enter into force on the thirtieth day following the date of deposit of the eighth instrument of ratification, acceptance or approval by States referred to in paragraph 1 of Article XXVI of this Convention.
2. With respect to each State or regional economic integration organization which subsequent to the date of entry into force of this Convention deposits an instrument of ratification, acceptance, approval or accession, the Convention shall enter into force on the thirtieth day following such deposit.

Article XXIX
1. This Convention shall be open for accession by any State interested in research or harvesting activities in relation to the marine living resources to which this Convention applies.
2. This Convention shall be open for accession by regional economic integration organizations constituted by sovereign States which include among their members one or more States Members of the Commission and to which the States members of the organization have transferred, in whole or in part, competences with regard to the matter covered by this Convention. The accession of such regional economic integration organizations shall be the subject of consultations among Members of the Commission.

Article XXX
1. This Convention may be amended at any time.
2. If one-third of the Members of the Commission request a meeting to discuss a proposed amendment the Depositary shall call such a meeting.
3. An amendment shall enter into force when the Depositary has received instruments of ratification, acceptance or approval thereof from all the Members of the Commission.
4. Such amendment shall thereafter enter into force as to any other Contracting Party when notice of ratification, acceptance or approval by it has been received by the Depositary. Any such Contracting Party from which no such notice has been received within a period of one year from the date of entry into force of the amendment in accordance with

paragraph 3 above shall be deemed to have withdrawn from this Convention.

Article XXXI
1. Any Contracting Party may withdraw from this Convention on 30 June of any year, by giving written notice not later than 1 January of the same year to the Depositary, which, upon receipt of such a notice, shall communicate it forthwith to the other Contracting Parties.
2. Any other Contracting Party may, within sixty days of the receipt of a copy of such a notice from the Depositary, give written notice of withdrawal to the Depositary in which case the Convention shall cease to be in force on 30 June of the same year with respect to the Contracting Party giving such notice.
3. Withdrawal from this Convention by any Member of the Commission shall not affect its financial obligations under this Convention.

Article XXXII
The Depositary shall notify all Contracting Parties of the following:
    a. signatures of this Convention and the deposit of instruments of ratification, acceptance, approval or accession;
    b. the date of entry into force of this Convention and of any amendment thereto.

Article XXXIII
1. This Convention, of which the English, French, Russian and Spanish texts are equally authentic, shall be deposited with the Government of Australia which shall transmit duly certified copies thereof to all signatory and acceding Parties.
2. This Convention shall be registered by the Depositary pursuant to Article 102 of the Charter of the United Nations. Drawn up at Canberra this twentieth day of May 1980.
In Witness Whereof the undersigned, being duly authorized, have signed this Convention.

[*Here follow the signatures on behalf of the parties to the Agreement, including Australia.*]

Annex for an Arbitral Tribunal
1. The arbitral tribunal referred to in paragraph 3 of Article XXV shall be composed of three arbitrators who shall be appointed as follows:
    a. The Party commencing proceedings shall communicate the name of an arbitrator to the other Party which, in turn, within a period of forty days following such notification, shall communicate the name of the second arbitrator. The Parties shall, within a period of sixty days following appointment of the second arbitrator, appoint the third

arbitrator, who shall not be a national of either Party and shall not be of the same nationality as either of the first two arbitrators. The third arbitrator shall preside over the tribunal.

b. If the second arbitrator has not been appointed within the prescribed period, or if the Parties have not reached agreement within the prescribed period on the appointment of the third arbitrator, that arbitrator shall be appointed, at the request of either Party, by the Secretary-General of the Permanent Court of Arbitration, from among persons of international standing not having the nationality of a State which is a Party to this Convention.

2. The arbitral tribunal shall decide where its headquarters will be located and shall adopt its own rules of procedure.

3. The award of the arbitral tribunal shall be made by a majority of its members, who may not abstain from voting.

4. Any Contracting Party which is not a Party to the dispute may intervene in the proceedings with the consent of the arbitral tribunal.

5. The award of the arbitral tribunal shall be final and binding on all Parties to the dispute and on any Party which intervenes in the proceedings and shall be complied with without delay. The arbitral tribunal shall interpret the award at the request of one of the Parties to the dispute or of any intervening Party.

6. Unless the arbitral tribunal determines otherwise because of the particular circumstances of the case, the expenses of the tribunal, including the remuneration of its members, shall be borne by the Parties to the dispute in equal shares.

APPENDIX 7

The Antarctic Declaration

The Antarctic Declaration

Drawn up by Greenpeace International during 1984 in advance of their campaign to protect Antarctica from all forms of exploitation and to promote the concept of the World Park. It bears similarity to the Antarctic Treaty on a number of important points but differs fundamentally on the issue of exploitation.

The undersigned;

Recognizing that it is in the interests of all humankind that Antarctica shall continue forever to be used exclusively for peaceful purposes and shall not become the scene or object of international discord;

Acknowledging the substantial contributions to scientific knowledge resulting from international co-operation in scientific investigation in Antarctica;

Convinced that the establishment of a firm foundation for the continuation and development of such co-operation on the basis of freedom of scientific investigation in Antarctica as applied during the International Geophysical Year accords with the interests of science and the progress of all humankind;

Convinced also that a declaration ensuring the use of Antarctica for peaceful and environmentally benign purposes only and the continuance of international harmony in Antarctica will further the purposes and principles embodied in the Charter of the United Nations;

Have agreed as follows:

Article I	The provisions of this Declaration shall apply to the area south of 60 degrees South Latitude, including all oceans and ice shelves.
Article II	Antarctica shall be used for peaceful purposes only. Any measures of a military nature, such as the establishment of military bases and fortifications, the carrying out of military manoeuvres or research, or the testing of storage of any type of weapons shall be prohibited.
Article III	Freedom of scientific investigation in Antarctica and

co-operation toward that end, as initiated during the International Geophysical Year and implemented since, shall continue. This shall include the full and free exchange of scientific data.

Article IV   Any nuclear explosions in Antarctica, or the operation of any nuclear power plant, or the disposal there of radioactive waste material shall be prohibited.

Article V   There shall be logistical co-operation among all those who undertake operations in Antarctica.

Article VI   All human activity in the Antarctic shall be subject to the following code of conduct:

1. No activity may be undertaken which would endanger the wilderness values of Antarctica;

2. No activity may be undertaken which will damage the habitat of any native mammal or bird in Antarctica.

Compliance with the above rules shall be monitored by the Antarctic Environmental Protection Agency, which shall provide impartial and professional advice.

Article VII   Exploration for or exploitation of mineral resources in Antarctica shall not be permitted.

Article VIII   The taking of marine resources (excluding mammals and birds) within the area covered by this Declaration shall be permitted only where there is clear evidence that the level of catch will not have any long term effect on the distribution, viability, or population dynamics of either that stock or other, non-target, species.

Article IX   The taking of native mammal or bird species within the area covered by this Declaration shall not be permitted.

Article X   Each of the Contracting Parties undertakes to exert appropriate efforts, consistent with the Charter of the United Nations, to the end that no one engages in any activity in Antarctica contrary to the principles and purposes of this Declaration.

Article XI   This Declaration shall be open for signature by any citizen or organization. Signed copies shall be deposited with any office of Stichting Greenpeace Council or those holding a licence to use the name 'Greenpeace'.

Article XII   This Declaration, done in English, Danish, Dutch, French, German, Spanish and Swedish, all versions being equally authentic, shall be deposited in the archives of Stichting Greenpeace Council. Authentic versions in other languages may from time to time be made available.

In witness thereof, the undersigned have signed this Declaration:

SOURCES

CHAPTER ONE
The Rime of the Ancient Mariner. Samuel Taylor Coleridge. J.M.Dent, London. 1974 Everyman Library edition.
The Journals of Captain James Cook on his voyage of Discovery. Ed. J.C.Beaglehole (1955) Hakluyt Soc & Cambridge University Press.
The Voyages of the Resolution & Adventure (1772–75). James Cook. Ed. J.C.Beaglehole Hakluyt Soc.London 1961.
The White Road. L.P.Kirwan. Hollis & Carter London 1959.
South Georgia: The British Empire's sub-Antarctic Outpost. L.Harrison Matthews. Simpkin Marshal Ltd London 1931.
A Voyage towards the South Pole performed in the years 1822–24; containing an examination of the Antarctic Sea. James Weddell reprint from second ed. published 1827 Longman, London by David & Charles 1970.
Voyages round the World. E.Fanning New York 1833.
World Atlas of Exploration. E. Newby. Mitchell Beazley London 1975.
The Island of South Georgia. R.K.Headland. CUP 1984.
Courtauld Institute Journal Vol XIX Nos 1–2, 1956.

CHAPTER TWO
The Voyage of Captain Bellingshausen to the Antarctic Seas 1819–1821. Trans. from the Russian: Hakluyt Soc 1945. Ed. F. Debenham.
Polar Record. No 40 July 1950. (SPRI)
Geographical Review No 20 Oct 1940. American Geo Soc of New York.
Voyages around the World. E.Fanning.New York 1833.
A Voyage towards the South Pole. J.Weddell. David & Charles 1970.

The Antarctic Circumpolar Ocean. George Deacon. CUP 1984.
The Rime of the Ancient Mariner. J.M.Dent London 1974.

CHAPTER THREE
A Voyage of Discovery & Research in the Southern & Antarctic Regions during the years 1839–43. Captain Sir James Clark Ross. David & Charles reprints 1969. Originally published John Murray 1847.
The Diaries of Captain Robert Scott. A Record of the Second Antarctic Expedition 1910–1912. Vol VI. Sledging Diaries Nov 1911–March 1912. (B.M. ADD. MSS 51033–35) University Microfilms Ltd 1968. Facsimile of original.
Our Wandering Continents. A. Du Toit. London 1937.
The World of Ice. James L. Dyson. London 1963.
Antarctica. T.Hatherton. Methuen London 1965.
Antarctic Research. Ed. Sir Raymond Priestly, R.J.Adie,G. de Q. Robin. Butterworths, London 1964.
The Antarctic. H.G.R.King. London 1969.

PART II THE SECOND WAVE
First on the Antarctic Continent. C.Borchgrevink. Newnes London 1900.
To the South Polar Regions. L.C.Bernacchi.

CHAPTER FOUR
Diary of the Discovery Expedition to the Antarctic Regions 1901–04. Edward Wilson. Ed. from original mss by Ann Savours. Blandford Press London 1966.
The Worst Journey in the World. Apsley Cherry-Garrard. Vol I & II. Constable London 1922.
Scott's Last Expedition Vol I. Smith Elder & Co London 1913.
Diary of the Terra Nova *Expedition to the Antarctic.* Facsimile London Blandford 1972.

CHAPTER FIVE
The North-West Passage. R.Amundsen. London 1921.
Scott of the Antarctic. R.Pound. Cassell London 1966.
The South Pole. An Account of the Norwegian Antarctic Expedition in the Fram *1910–1912.* Roald Amundsen. Reprint C.Hurst & Co London 1976.
Scott & Amundsen. Roland Huntford. Hodder & Stoughton 1979.

South to the Pole—The Early History of the Ross Sea Sector of Antarctica. L.B.Quartermain. OUP 1967.
The Diaries of Captain Robert Scott Vol VI. Facsimile 1968.
A World of Men. Wally Herbert. Eyre & Spottiswood 1968.
The Worst Journey in the World Vol II. Cherry-Garrard. Constable 1922.
South with Scott. Admiral Sir Edward R.G.R.Evans. Collins London.
Scott's Last Expedition Vol I. Smith Elder & Co London 1913.
Scott's Men. David Thomson. Allen Lane London 1977.

CHAPTER SIX
South—The Story of the 1914–17 Expedition. E. Shackleton. Heinemann 1919.
The Life of Sir Ernest Shackleton. Hugh Robert Mill. Heinemann 1923.
The Great Antarctic Rescue. F.A.Worsley. Times Books 1977.
South to the Pole. L.B.Quartermain. OUP 1967.
The Heart of the Antarctic. E.Shackleton. Vol I. Heinemann 1909.
Shackleton. Margery & James Fisher. James Barrie London 1957.
Shackleton. R. Huntford. Hodder & Stoughton 1985.
Shackleton's Last Voyage. The Story of the Quest. F.Wild. Cassell 1923.

CHAPTER SEVEN
Moby-Dick or *The Whale.* Herman Melville. Penguin ed. 1980.
A Voyage towards the South Pole etc. J. Weddell. David & Charles 1970.
A Voyage of Discovery & Research in the Southern & Antarctic Regions. Captain James Ross. Vol I. David & Charles reprints.
The Rime of the Ancient Mariner. J.M.Dent London 1974.
The Story of Whaling. Bill Spence. Conway 1980.
The Whale. Ed.L. Harrison Matthews. Allen & Unwin 1968.
The Natural History of the Whale. L. Harrison Matthews. Weidenfeld & Nicolson 1978.
Whales. W.N.Bonner. Blandford 1980.
Polar Record. Reports on IWC Meetings.
The Times.
Antarctica. Ed. W.N. Bonner & D.W.H.Walton. Pergamon 1985.
The Southern Ocean. FAO United Nations 1977.

CHAPTER EIGHT
Little America. R.Byrd. Putnam 1930.
Discovery. R.Byrd. Putnam 1935.
Challenge to the Poles—Highlights of Arctic & Antarctic Aviation. John Grierson. G.T.Foulis & Co 1964.
Alone. R.Byrd. London 1939.
The White Road. L.P.Kirwan. London 1959.
The Crossing of Antarctica. V.Fuchs & E.Hillary. Cassell 1958.
The Antarctic. H.G.R.King. 1969.
Antarctic Research. Butterworths London 1964.

CHAPTER NINE
Last & First Men. Olaf Stapleton. Penguin 1959.
Antarctic Law & Politics. F.M.Auburn. C.Hurst & Co London 1982.
Antarctic Resources Policy: Scientific, Legal & Political issues;. Ed. F.O.Vicuna. CUP 1983.
Antarctica & its resources. Barbara Mitchell & Jon Tinker. Earthscan publication.
Possible Environmental Effects of Mineral Exploration & Exploitation in Antarctica. Ed. J.H.Zumberge.
Minerals & Mining in Antarctica. Maarten de Wit. OUP 1984.
Antarctica—A Continent in Transition. IIED 1980.
Arctic & Antarctic. A modern geographical synthesis. D. Sugden. Blackwell Oxford 1982.
Antarctic Mineral Resources. IIED. Barbara Mitchell. 1982.
Antarctica—Key Environments. Pergamon 1985.
Oil & other Minerals in the Antarctic. Rockefeller Foundation & Scientific Committee on Antarctic Research. M.W.Holdgate & Jon Tinker. 1979.
Polar Record Vol 22 No137: Vol 23 No143: Vol 22 No141
Central Intelligence Agency. Polar Regions Atlas. Washington 1978.
Antarctica: World Law and the Last Wilderness. K. Suter. FOE Sydney 1980.

CHAPTER TEN
Population Resources Environment: Issues in Human Ecology. Paul R. & Anne H.Ehrlich. W.H.Freeman & Co San Francisco 1970.

The Environmental Revolution: A guide for the New Masters of the Earth. Max Nicholson. Hodder & Stoughton 1970.

The Limits to Growth: A Report for the Club of Rome's project on the predicament of mankind. Earth Ilsnad London 1972.

The Seventh Enemy: The Human Factor in the Global Crisis. Ronald Higgins. Pan Books 1980.

Notes for the Future. Robin Clarke. Thames & Hudson 1975.

Wilderness. Anthony Smith. Allen & Unwin 1978.

The New State of the World Atlas. M.Kidron & R.Segal. Pan Books 1984.

The Rime of the Ancient Mariner. J.M.Dent London 1974.

FURTHER READING

Animals of the Antarctic: Ecology of the Far South, B. Stonehouse, Peter Lowe, 1972

Another World, H. J. P. Arnold, Sidgwick & Jackson, 1975

Antarctic Ecology, Martin Holdgate, 1970 (2 vols)

The Antarctic Problem : An historical & political study, E. W. H. Christie, 1951

Antarctica, John Bechervaise, Cassell (Sydney), 1979

Antarctica, Readers Digest, 1985

Antarctica : A Treatise on the Southern Continent, J. Gordon Hayes, Butterworth, 1928

Antarctica : The Last Continent, Ian Cameron, Cassell, 1974

Antarctica : Two Years Amongst the Ice of the South Pole, Otto Nordenskjöld, 1905

Antarctica—Wilderness at Risk, Barney Brewster, FOE/Reed, 1982

Birds of the Antarctic, Edward Wilson, ed. Brian Roberts, Blandford, 1967

Captain Cook, the Seaman's Seaman, A. Villiers, 1967

Coleridge, E. K. Chambers, 1938

Coleridge : Poet and Revolutionary 1772–1804, John Cornwell, 1973

A Continent for Science : The Antarctic Adventure, R. S. Lewis, Secker & Warburg, 1965

The Conquest of the South Pole, J. Gordon Hayes, Butterworth, 1932

The Fatal Impact : The Invasion of the South Pacific 1767–1840, Alan Moorehead, Hamish Hamilton, 1966

A History of Polar Exploration, David Mountfield, Hamlyn, 1974

Life of Captain Cook, H. Carrinton, 1967

Lost Leviathan, F. D. Ommanney, John Murray Ltd, 1971

My Life as an Explorer, Roald Amundsen, 1927

Photographer of the World—A biography of Herbert Ponting, H. J. P. Arnold, Sidgwick & Jackson, 1969

Quest for a Continent, W. Sullivan, 1957

The Ross Sea Shore Party 1914–17, R. W. Richard, Cambridge, 1965

Scott's Last Voyage, ed. Ann Savours, Sidgwick & Jackson, 1974

Scott of the Antarctic, Elizabeth Huxley, Weidenfeld & Nicolson, 1977

The Seventh Continent : Antarctica in a Resource Age, D. Shapley, Washington, 1983

The Siege of the South Pole : The Story of Antarctic Exploration, H. H. Mill, 1905

The Voyage of the 'Discovery', R. F. Scott, 1905

The Whale & his Captors, H. T. Cheever, 1852

Whalers & Whaling, E. Chatterton, 1925

INDEX

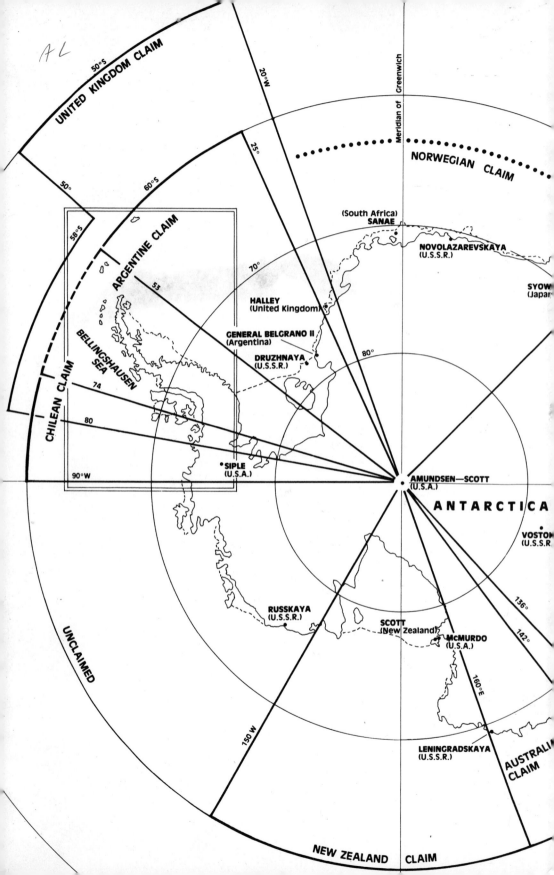